THE LUCKY AND THE LOST

THE LIVES OF TITANIC'S CHILDREN

JOHN BOILEAU
with PATRICIA BOILEAU THERIAULT

NIMBUS
PUBLISHING
— NIMBUS.CA —

Nimbus Publishing Limited
3660 Strawberry Hill St
Halifax, NS B3K 5A9
(902) 455-4286
nimbus.ca

Nimbus Publishing is based in Kjipuktuk, Mi'kma'ki, the traditional territory of the Mi'kmaq People.

Printed and bound in Canada
NB 1652

Editor: Raya P. Morrison
Editor for the press: Angela Mombourquette
Design: Heather Bryan
Cover images: Library of Congress, Serial and Government Publications Division; Public domain via Wikimedia Commons

Library and Archives Canada Cataloguing in Publication

Title: The lucky and the lost : the lives of Titanic's children / John Boileau with Patricia Boileau Theriault.
Names: Boileau, John, author.
Description: Includes bibliographical references and index.
Identifiers: Canadiana (print) 20240283872 | Canadiana (ebook) 20240283899 | ISBN 9781774712689 (softcover) | ISBN 9781774712870 (EPUB)
Subjects: LCSH: Titanic (Steamship) | LCSH: Ocean liner passengers—North Atlantic Ocean—Biography. | LCSH: Shipwreck victims—North Atlantic Ocean—Biography. | LCSH: Shipwrecks—North Atlantic Ocean—History. | LCSH: Shipwreck survival—North Atlantic Ocean—History. | LCSH: Children—Biography. | LCGFT: Biographies.
Classification: LCC G530.T6 B65 2024 | DDC 910.9163/4—dc23

Canada NOVA SCOTIA   Canada Council   Conseil des arts
                      for the Arts   du Canada

Nimbus Publishing acknowledges the financial support for its publishing activities from the Government of Canada, the Canada Council for the Arts, and from the Province of Nova Scotia. We are pleased to work in partnership with the Province of Nova Scotia to develop and promote our creative industries for the benefit of all Nova Scotians.

To emigrant children all over the world who are making perilous journeys today in search of a better tomorrow.

And to Wayne, who would have been so proud.

CONTENTS

INTRODUCTION

The story of the Royal Mail Ship (RMS) *Titanic* and its passengers and crew is one that has always fascinated me. My interest in it led to the publication of *Halifax and Titanic* by Nimbus Publishing in 2012, on the centennial of what is likely the most famous civilian marine disaster of all time. During various book signings for *Halifax and Titanic*, some of my most ardent—and knowledgeable—readers were kids. I soon became aware *Titanic's* story held a special fascination for young people. They knew the tale and were eager to learn more. At the time, I mentally filed this bit of information and carried on with other writing tasks.

But *Titanic's* story was always there, surfacing now and then with thoughts about another book on the subject. Part of the problem with writing about *Titanic*, however, is that so much information exists about the ship in books, articles, films, documentaries, discussion groups, websites, museums, theme parks, and exhibits that it is difficult to write something new.

Then I had my "Aha!" moment, confirmed by a review of the existing literature: not that much has been written about children on *Titanic*— although many books about the liner have been written *for* children. And in the works that do exist, none of the authors treat the children and their experiences in a macro sense. I ran my idea past the editorial staff at Nimbus and received a same-day go-ahead to proceed.

Most *Titanic* books, if they mention children at all, tend to concentrate on a chosen few and do not include children in the subsequent operations to recover the dead, the unborn children among the passengers, the hundreds of instant orphans created by the sinking, or the later lives of child survivors. Some groups are excluded entirely, such as the many Lebanese families aboard, who, by the way, were considered Syrian at the time.

This book tries to make up for such shortcomings by looking at the experiences of all 160 children aged sixteen and under who were aboard *Titanic*: 151 passengers, 5 crew members, and 4 children who had disembarked in Cherbourg or Queenstown (now Cobh), known variously as cross-channel passengers or day trippers. It not only includes their backstories, but also their "forwardstories" to round out their lives—and deaths. Their stories span more than one hundred years.

This is much more difficult to do, of course, for many of the children who died in the sinking and especially true for those in third class. What is known of some of their short lives is in relation to their parents. In this book, all the children on *Titanic* are mentioned by name, no matter how little is known about them. We've done this to honour them, for in the words of George Eliot, "Our dead are never dead to us until we have forgotten them." This book follows in more detail the stories and experiences of these children—both the lucky who survived and the lost who perished. We tell their stories with sadness.

I have been greatly assisted in this task by my sister, Patricia Theriault, as a researcher, fact checker, and writer. Pat last helped me with my 2005 book, *Half-Hearted Enemies: Nova Scotia, New England and the War of 1812.* At the time, I used her considerable research abilities, but now took advantage of her significant editing and writing skills as well. Together we visited the three *Titanic* graveyards and the Maritime Museum of the Atlantic in Halifax, while Pat visited the summer colony in her state of Maine where a young *Titanic* survivor had died, the headquarters of the Titanic Historical Society in Indian Orchard, Massachusetts, the Titanic Centennial Memorial in Springfield, Massachusetts, and the Women's Titanic Memorial in Washington, DC.

Others who assisted in the research and writing of this book include Pat's daughter, Caroline Theriault, whose input in the early writing stages was invaluable, Roger Marsters (curator of marine history at the Maritime Museum of the Atlantic), Professor Julie Hedgepeth Williams (author of *A Rare Titanic Family: The Caldwells' Story of Survival* and Albert Caldwell's great-niece), and Blair Beed (author of *Titanic Victims in Halifax Graveyards* and a local *Titanic* expert). In the end, however, I take responsibility for any errors of fact or interpretation.

The staff at Nimbus with whom I worked were, as usual, knowledgeable and cooperative. Thanks to managing editor Whitney Moran, nonfiction editor Angela Mombourquette, editor Raya P. Morrison, and designer Heather Bryan.

A final note for the modern reader on monetary values: Some values (at the time of the sinking or later) have the equivalent current Canadian dollar value in the parentheses next to them for clarity. Also, in 1912 British currency was not yet decimalized (that only happened in 1971). The pound was divided into twenty shillings, while a shilling consisted of twelve pence. Thirteen shillings and eight pence in 1912 would be roughly equal today to £100, US$127, or C$170. Put another way, £1 then equals about £146 now.

John Boileau
Halifax, Nova Scotia
March 31, 2024
115th anniversary of the start of the construction of Titanic

PRELUDE – FIRST TO DIE

Early on the morning of Wednesday, April 20, 1910, fifteen-year-old Samuel Scott left his lodgings at 70 Templemore Street in the Ballymacarret area of Belfast, heading to work at the nearby massive Harland and Wolff shipyard. Two gigantic new passenger liners were under construction there. On the way, he stopped briefly at his mother's a few doors down on the same side of the street at number 104.

Sam had recently moved out of his mother's modest four-room rented house, possibly to alleviate overcrowding. Two families—three adults and nine children—lived there. Sam's job at the shipyard, where he worked as a "catch boy" in a riveting gang, paid him £2 (C$500) a week. This employment brought him a new level of independence, which allowed him to take up his new lodgings and help with the crowding situation in his mother's house.

At the time, Belfast was a booming industrial centre, based on two labour-intensive industries: linen production and shipbuilding, as well as the many offshoot businesses they created. Hopefuls flooded in from the countryside in anticipation of getting work. Women, known as "Millies," dominated linen manufacturing, while only men worked in "The Yard."

The mills and the shipyards were difficult and dangerous places of employment. Work was hard, stretching from 6:00 A.M. to 5:30 P.M. daily, except for Saturday, when it stopped at 1:00 P.M. This left only Sunday as a full day of rest (although in the Protestant-dominated city, all shops and pubs, and even city parks and playgrounds, were closed on the Lord's Day). The health and safety regulations of today were unknown. Electricity and hydraulic machinery were hazardous, relatively new, and their dangers not fully appreciated. Machinery was noisy. Accidents were frequent and often fatal.

After calling at his Ma's (and perhaps picking up something for lunch), young Sam joined the flood of thousands of cloth-capped, hobnail-booted men heading toward "The Yard" through an early-morning mist. Arriving at Harland and Wolff on Queen's Island, he stood in line to pick up a small wooden rectangle with his worker's number on it, his "bourd,"

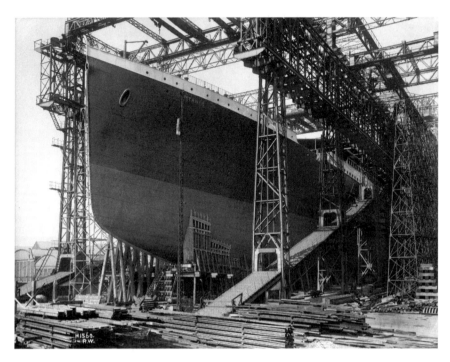

Titanic *in its construction gantry, 1911.*

from the timekeeper's hatch. Sam then moved to SS 401—the future *Titanic*—the ship he was working on at the time.

Sam's job as a catch boy was one of a five-person riveting gang. First, a bellow boy heated a rivet in a small bucket of burning coals until it was white hot. He then picked the rivet out of the fire with a pair of long-handled tongs and threw it into the air, where the rest of the gang stood on scaffolding. The catch boy—Sam in this case—caught the rivet in a tin and, with a pair of short-handled tongs, put it into a pre-drilled hole in one of the steel plates that made up the ship's hull.

A holder-on drove the rivet home with a sledgehammer and then held his hammer against it. On the other side of the plate, two riveters with a different type of hammer took turns beating the rivet to shape it against the plate. The noise from hundreds of riveters was deafening. As the rivet cooled, it contracted and pulled the plates tightly together. Gangs were paid by the rivet, so they had to work well together. A bellow boy who did not heat the rivets to the right temperature or a catch boy who failed to snag most of the rivets tossed to him was quickly out of a job. Workers used more than three million rivets to build *Titanic*.

Sometime that afternoon, Sam missed his footing, slipped off a ladder, and fell seven metres (twenty-three feet) to his death. No one had seen him fall; he was discovered lying on the ground, motionless and bleeding. At the inquest, the coroner stated the cause of death was "shock following fracture of the skull."

Sam was the first of eight workers to die building *Titanic*. He was also the first child whose death was related to *Titanic*. Two years later, another eighty-three children would follow him.

Harland and Wolff gave Sam's mother sixteen shillings (two hundred dollars) in compensation for his death. It was enough to bury him, but not enough to buy a headstone as well. As a result, Sam was buried in an unmarked grave in Belfast City Cemetery.

In August 2011, eight months before the centennial of the sinking, a headstone was erected over his grave through the efforts of various individuals and organizations. It contains the words "NEARER MY GOD TO THEE" from the hymn that many believe to be the last piece of music played on *Titanic* as it sank to its watery grave.

PART 1 – VISION TO VOYAGE

If you look in your dictionary you will find: Titans—a race of people vainly striving to overcome the forces of nature. Could anything be more unfortunate than such a name, anything more significant?

—Sir Arthur H. Rostron, captain of the rescue ship *Carpathia*

CHAPTER 1

A NEW HOME PORT

We went on the day on the boat train...I was 7, I had never seen a ship before...it looked very big...everybody was very excited, we went down to the cabin and that's when my mother said to my father that she had made up her mind quite firmly that she would not go to bed in that ship, she would sit up at night.

—Eva Hart, 7 on *Titanic*

The *Titanic* story began with after-dinner cigars and port on a pleasant mid-summer evening in Downshire House, an elegant residence on London's elite Belgrave Square, in 1907.

It ended less than five years later with the needless deaths of more than fifteen hundred men, women, and children on the cold, moonless night of April 15, 1912, in the middle of the Atlantic.

The most famous ship in history became its most famous marine disaster, a mere five days into its maiden voyage.

How could this have happened?

An Idea is Realized

The after-dinner conversation between the chair of the massive Harland and Wolff shipyard in Belfast, Lord Pirrie, and the chair of the White Star Line of Liverpool, J. Bruce Ismay, centred on how best to respond to the latest challenge from White Star's main rival, the Cunard Line. Pirrie and Ismay decided the best way to combat them was with luxury, rather than speed. The *Olympic* class of vessels was born.

For the new class, Pirrie and Ismay envisaged three giant liners of unrivalled size and opulence, which would appeal not only to wealthy upper-class passengers but also to an expanding and flourishing middle class, as well as the vast and lucrative immigrant trade. The White Star Line had already established a market in transporting immigrants and constructed its ships to carry more third-class passengers than other lines. It was also one of the first companies to have more expensive first- and second-class accommodation along with less expensive third-class quarters in the same ship. And even then, its third-class facilities rivalled higher classes in the ships of other lines. Pirrie and Ismay went so far as to choose the names for the new ships to emphasize their enormity: *Olympic*, *Titanic*, and *Gigantic*.

Construction of *Titanic* started on March 31, 1909, three and a half months after *Olympic*'s keel was laid down. It took more than three thousand men and boys (20 percent of Harland and Wolff's workforce) labouring for three more years to complete *Titanic*.

Titanic's lavishness has never been equalled. There were ten decks, seven of them for passengers—from A at the top (also known as the promenade deck) to G at the bottom. Every cabin had running water, a luxury that many immigrants would not have had even in their homes. The most iconic part of *Titanic*'s interior was undoubtedly the grand staircase for the use of first-class passengers. It was lit by natural light through an overhead glass dome during the day and by crystal lights at night.

Titanic lived up to its name. When it was finished, it was the largest man-made moveable object in history.

Just before 6:00 A.M. on Monday, April 2, 1912, five tugboats towed *Titanic* from its Harland and Wolff jetty, down the River Lagan, past banks crowded with hundreds of cheering, waving spectators, and into Belfast Lough to begin its sea trials. An hour after their successful completion at 7:00 P.M. that night, the ship turned and headed toward Southampton, almost 1,100 kilometres (685 miles) away.

Home Port

After an uneventful twenty-eight-hour voyage from Belfast, five tugs of the Red Funnel Line met *Titanic* at Southampton just before midnight on April 3. Working together, they manoeuvred the 47,071-tonne (46,328-ton) behemoth into its place at Pier 44. *Titanic*'s parent company, the White Star Line, had been founded in Liverpool, which remained its home port for many years. In the spring of 1907, however, the line made two experimental crossings from Southampton to New York via Cherbourg, France, and Queenstown (Cobh), Ireland. This route proved to be successful, and a new weekly express service was started from Southampton. As this port was much closer to London than Liverpool was, it offered a clear advantage in travelling time. Additionally, Cherbourg provided a continental port that allowed more passengers to be taken aboard.

To accommodate the larger *Olympic* class at Southampton, a new and much larger dock had to be built and dredged to more than twelve metres (thirty-nine feet). There were three sailings to New York each week from the White Star dock. Captain Edward John (known as "E. J." by his crew) Smith, who would go on to command *Titanic,* had been in charge of *Olympic* when it made its maiden voyage from the new berth. A busy time awaited *Titanic* in Southampton, as the liner had to take on additional crew, plus provisions and coal, before it could accept any passengers for its maiden voyage, a mere week away.

Olympic and *Titanic* were not the first ships of note to leave Southampton. For over two thousand years, geography had favoured this English Channel port on the mid-coast of southern England. Not only was the entrance to the harbour protected by the Isle of Wight, but the two rivers into the port, Itchen and Test, were notable for a double tide. This gave ships seventeen hours of rising and high water. From Roman times, the fortunes of Southampton had always risen and fallen like the tides in its harbour. In the thirteenth century, a wine trade flourished with nearby France and more distant ports in Spain. In 1415, Henry V sailed from Southampton for the Battle of Agincourt.

After a period of decline, the town saw renewed industry in the sixteenth century, when fleeing Huguenots brought their skills as artisans in serge cloth. In 1620, *Mayflower* sailed from Southampton with Pilgrims bound for the New World, where they could experience their particular form of religious freedom. In the seventeenth century, the port fell on hard times again due to the plague, frequent wars, and the decline of the wool industry. In the eighteenth century, however, Southampton became a destination for an entirely different kind of relationship with the sea as people journeyed there to enjoy its spa waters and the new recreational activity of sea bathing.

The nineteenth century brought steamships to Southampton and a rail link directly to London. Significant improvements were made to the docks, and the port became the new terminus for both passengers (including the flood of immigrants to North America) and transatlantic mail. When the White Star Line made Southampton the port of departure for its large ocean liners in 1907, the city became England's main passenger port. By 1912, Southampton's population (called Sotonians) had swelled to 120,000, most of whom were dependent in one way or another on shipping. In addition to the crew who served aboard the ships, there were dockworkers, employees of the various companies that provisioned the ships with everything from beer to flowers to fruit, workers at the maintenance facilities for the ships, uniform makers, laundry hands, hotel workers, and numerous others whose livelihood depended on the port.

Children as Crew

Titanic had arrived in Southampton with only a skeleton crew on board; the remainder would join the ship in its new home port. The crew was divided into three departments: Deck (77 officers, surgeons, quartermasters, masters-at-arms, boatswains, lookouts, officers' stewards, certain tradesmen, and several able-bodied seamen); Engineering (325 engineers, boiler men, firemen/stokers, trimmers, greasers, and electricians); and Victualling (417 stewards, of whom 20 were female, plus galley staff). Some groups aboard *Titanic* were neither passengers nor crew but fell somewhere in between: à la carte restaurant staff (68 waiters and supervisors employed by contracted restaurant manager Luigi Gatti, who drew them from his two London restaurants); guarantee group (9 representatives of Harland and Wolff); musicians (8 bandsmen); postal clerks (2 British and 3 American); and wireless operators (2 Marconi employees). In total, there were 908 crew members aboard *Titanic*; 724—some 80 percent—were from Southampton.

Among the crewmembers who boarded in Southampton, five were between the ages of fourteen and sixteen—still children by today's standards. Like many born in Southampton, Arthur Barratt had followed in his father's footsteps and gone to sea, contributing in this way to the family finances. He was hired as a bellboy and, although only fifteen, had

Titanic *in Southampton, April 1912.*

previously served on the SS *St. Louis*. Similarly, sixteen-year-old Clifford Harris grew up in Southampton with a seafaring dad. One of ten children, he had already served aboard the RMS *Asturias* before he signed on to *Titanic* as a bellboy. Also on the ship was his nineteen-year-old brother, Charles, a saloon steward in second class.

Titanic *in Southampton before departure.*

Fourteen-year-old Frederick Hopkins was likewise serving on his second ship, though he gave his age upon signing on *Titanic* as sixteen. His father had served in the British Army, and although Fred was born in England, the family had lived in India for a time. After retirement, his dad worked as a caretaker for the White Star Line offices, and perhaps it was he who helped young Fred secure his position as a plate steward. Another fourteen-year-old, William Watson, had been born in London, where his father was a sanitary inspector. In the 1911 census, he was listed as a schoolboy, but by 1912 he had already served as a bellboy on *Titanic*'s sister ship *Olympic*. Sixteen-year-old Paolo Crovella, who had been born in Italy, followed his siblings to London, where he worked as a waiter. Italian restaurateur Luigi Gatti hired him for the à la carte restaurant aboard *Olympic* and then as an assistant waiter aboard *Titanic*.

These teenagers were employed to look after the needs of the transatlantic passengers, but was any thought given to ensuring their safe passage?

TITANIC PROVISIONS

Titanic required a huge amount of provisions for its passengers and crew. Among the food and drink loaded at Southampton were:

MEAT & FISH	VEGETABLES & GRAINS
Fresh meat–34,019 kg (75,000 lb)	Potatoes–41 tonnes (40 long tons)
Fresh fish–4,990 kg (11,000 lb)	Asparagus–800 bundles
Salt and dried fish–1,814 kg (4,000 lb)	Onions–1,588 kg (3,500 lb)
Bacon and ham–3,402 kg (7,500 lb)	Tomatoes–1,588 kg (3,500 lb)
Poultry and game–11,340 kg (25,000 lb)	Green peas–1,021 kg (2,250 lb)
Sausages–1,134 kg (2,500 lb)	Lettuce–7,000 heads
Sweetbreads–1,000	Rice and dried beans–4,536 kg (10,000 lb)

BAKERY & BREAKFAST	EGGS & DAIRY
Flour–250 barrels	Fresh eggs–40,000
Cereals–4,536 kg (10,000 lb)	Fresh milk–6,819 L (1,500 gal)
Bread–1,000 loaves	Condensed milk–2,728 L (600 gal)
Coffee–998 kg (2,200 lb)	Ice cream–1,989 L (437.5 gal)
Tea–363 kg (800 lb)	Fresh butter–2,722 kg (6,000 lb)
Sugar–4,536 kg (10,000 lb)	Fresh cream–1,364 L (300 gal)
Jams and preserves–508 kg (1,120 lb)	

FRUITS	BEVERAGES
Apples–36,000	Beer–20,000 bottles
Oranges–36,000	Wines–1,500 bottles
Lemons–16,000	Spirits–850 bottles
Grapefruit–13,000	Mineral water–15,000 bottles
Grapes–454 kg (1,000 lb)	And to accompany an after-dinner drink: Cigars–8,000

Preparing and serving these vast quantities of food and drink required 57,600 pieces of crockery, pots, and pans; 44,000 pieces of cutlery; and 29,000 pieces of glassware. Among the more esoteric items were 100 grape scissors, 300 celery glasses, 400 toast racks, 400 asparagus tongs, 1,000 finger bowls, 1,000 oyster forks, 1,500 mustard spoons, 2,000 egg spoons, and 3,000 beef tea cups and saucers.

Coal

Besides the provisions for passengers and crew outlined on page 8, *Titanic* required another vital commodity before it could sail: coal. In April 1912, however, there was a problem with its availability. Earlier in the year, British miners had gone on strike in an attempt to change their convoluted wage structure to a different one, which recommended a minimum wage for everyone who worked in the mines. The strike's impact was wide-ranging as Britain depended heavily on coal. Factories, trains, ships, and even ordinary households needed it to provide heat and power.

When *Titanic* arrived in Southampton, several White Star Line ships, as well as those of other lines, were stranded in port due to the coal shortage. The company decided *Titanic's* heavily promoted maiden voyage had to take place as advertised. It transferred coal from some of its other ships so the liner could make it to New York. This resulted in some passengers being switched from their original bookings to *Titanic*. Although a few were initially upset with this, most were delighted to be able to sail on the maiden voyage of the large and luxurious liner.

Titanic should have carried 8,128 tonnes (8,000 long tons) of coal, enough for a return voyage, but this amount was reduced as the ship would have been able to take on more coal in New York. In another coal-conserving measure, *Titanic* would steam at an average speed of twenty-two knots, below its top speed, which would consume less coal.

Classes Aboard *Titanic*

Most passengers intending to sail on *Titanic* arrived on two boat trains from London. The first, which carried second- and third-class passengers, left Waterloo Station at 7:30 A.M. to arrive at 10:04:30 A.M., while the second, carrying first-class passengers, left at 9:45 A.M. and arrived at 11:30 A.M. It was particularly important to allow time for the fumigation of non-British immigrants before first-class travellers arrived. Not all passengers arrived by boat train on the day of the sailing, however. Some—especially those in first class—arrived the day before and stayed at hotels, such as the South Western Hotel.

Aboard the giant ship, accommodation was perhaps the greatest indicator of the difference between the three classes, second only to dining arrangements. While those in first and second class, whether singles, couples, or families with children, had private cabins, the same was not true for third class. Single men and women in steerage on lower decks were segregated, with males accommodated forward and females aft. Married women travelling alone or with their children also occupied cabins in the stern. Third-class family accommodation was amidships, separating the single passengers. Those in steerage also had access to their own small outdoor space on D Deck (its size directly proportional to their class).

But for some passengers, simply being in first class was not enough; they wanted more. The White Star Line answered their demand for extra service with a method pioneered by the Hamburg-American Line. First-class passengers were offered the opportunity to dine in an à la carte restaurant, which required booking in advance, and in an accompanying café known as the Café Parisien.

TITANIC TICKET COSTS

Class of Accommodation	Cost in 1912 (£)	Cost in 2023 (£)	Cost in 1912 (CAD/ USD)	Cost in 2023 (CAD)	Cost in 2023 (USD)
First-class suite	£870	£127,139	$4,350	$216,616	$161,142
First-class berth	£30	£4,384	$150	$7,469	$5,556
Second-class berth	£12	£1,754	$60	$2,989	$2,223
Third-class berth	£3–£8	£438– £1,169	$15–$40	$746– $2,706	$555– $1,482

Even though eleven-year-old William Carter II came from a wealthy Philadelphia family and was travelling first class, he was astonished by the opulence he saw aboard *Titanic*:

> When I saw the inside of the ship I thought I was in a dream because I have never seen something so elegant. As I headed to my room, I walked up the 1st class staircase. I thought in no way they could have this on a boat. When I walked into our 1st class rooms I thought I was the richest person in the world because of how beautiful of a room I was staying in... When I walked out onto the deck space I was amazed by how big it was.

CHAPTER 2

DEPARTING SOUTHAMPTON

British Empire Child Passengers

Among the children of the many nationalities who boarded *Titanic* in Southampton, the greatest number was from the British Empire: thirty-nine British, two Canadian, and one South African. One British child was going for a short visit, and the Canadians were returning home after a holiday. The rest were emigrants, including two who were returning to the United States after a trip to England. Twenty-five British children were travelling with families, thirteen were accompanied by a single parent only, and one was completely on his own. None of the British children were in first class, sixteen were in second class, and the remainder were in third. All of them were destined for the United States, except for one family who was travelling to Canada.

Bessie Allison with Loraine and Trevor.

First Class

The only passengers with children who boarded at Southampton in first class were members of the wealthy Allison family of Montreal—father, Hudson, American-born mother, Bessie, daughter, Loraine (34 months), and son, Trevor (11 months). (The ages of all children under three years, i.e., 35 months or less, are shown in months). Hud (short for Hudson) Allison was a self-made millionaire and junior partner in a Montreal brokerage firm. The Allison party also included four servants hired in England: nanny, maid, cook, and chauffeur. The family, their nanny, and the maid were in first-class cabins, while the cook and chauffeur were in second-class. Hud had even changed the family's original travel plans so they could sail on *Titanic* with some old friends. The Allison family's fate would be one of the most tragic of a voyage earmarked by tragedy.

Second Class

The mother of thirteen-year-old Madeline Mellenger had not had an easy life. Mrs. Mellenger's husband had deserted her after a financial scandal, leaving her to raise five children. Almost penniless and having lost the family home, Mrs. Mellenger divided her children among relatives while she worked as a maid for rich families. Somehow, she found enough money to send Madeline to a boarding school outside of London. The Mellengers (usually misspelled as "Mellinger") were on their way to Bennington in the southwest corner of Vermont. Mrs. Mellenger had secured employment there as a housekeeper on the summer estate of the Colgate family, founders of the well-known toothpaste brand.

George Sweet (14) of Somerset was headed for New Jersey, travelling with the Herman family. George was employed by Mr. Samuel Herman, a farmer and hotel owner, and soon became a part of the family, which included Mr. Herman's wife and their twin daughters. The Hermans had fallen on relatively difficult times (but not so difficult as to preclude travelling second class) and decided to immigrate to Bernardsville, a few kilometres west of Newark. Mr. Herman's brother-in-law worked there as a steward at a country club. George never made it into a lifeboat—likely because of his age—and died in the sinking along with Mr. Herman. He was a day short of his fifteenth birthday.

Thomas Mudd (16) came from a large Suffolk family, with ten of thirteen children surviving past infancy. Two older brothers had immigrated earlier to Radnor, Pennsylvania, a few kilometres west of Philadelphia. Thomas, a bookkeeper, decided to join them and bought a ticket. After he boarded the ship in Southampton, he sent his mom a postcard, noting, "The *Titanic* is a splendid boat, and you hardly know you are moving. Will write more fully later." Thomas never got to write later, as he died in the sinking. In 1998, his postcard sold at auction for £3,600 (C$13,810). Thomas Mudd and George Sweet were the only children in second class to die.

The West family—father, pregnant mother, and daughters, Constance (4) and Barbara (10 months)—was travelling from their home in Bournemouth, near Southampton, where Mr. West worked as a floorwalker in a department store. They were travelling to Gainesville, Florida, where Mr. West hoped to start a fruit-growing enterprise.

William (3) and Sibley (10 months) Richards were part of a large party that included their mother, grandmother, aunt, uncle, and great-aunt (who was in third class). All were on their way from Cornwall to join Mrs. Richards's husband, who had secured employment in Akron, Ohio, earlier.

Mrs. Wells was also on her way from Cornwall to Akron to join her husband and her brother, who had emigrated there two years earlier and found employment. Travelling with Mrs. Wells were her children, Joan (4) and Ralph (28 months). The family had been booked on *Oceanic* but, like several others, had been transferred because of the coal strike.

Jane Quick and her daughters, Winnifred (Winnie, 8) and Phyllis (32 months), were returning to Detroit after a visit with relatives in Plymouth. Mr. Quick and his family had settled in Detroit two years earlier, where he worked as a plasterer.

Scottish-born Baptist minister John Harper was travelling to Chicago, where he had been booked to preach for three months at a series of revival meetings. Mr. Harper was a widower who had established a church in London. He brought his six-year-old daughter, Annie (known variously as Nana or Nina), along for the trip, as well as his cousin, who was his daughter's nanny.

Twice-widowed Agnes Davies, her son from her most recent marriage, John Jr. (8), and a son from a previous marriage, Joseph Nicholls (19), were travelling from Cornwall to Houghton, on Michigan's Upper Peninsula. Her intention was to join her eldest son (Joseph's brother) and his wife there. To raise the £37 (C$9,200) for their tickets, Mrs. Davies sold all the family's belongings. Aboard *Titanic*, mother and younger son shared a cabin with two other women, one of whom was a family friend.

Harvey Collyer, his wife, and eight-year-old Marjorie were on their way from Hampshire to Payette, Idaho. Mr. Collyer ran a grocery store, and the couple was very active in their church, where he was a sexton. Family friends had gone to Payette several years earlier and established a successful fruit farm, urging the Collyers to follow them. When Mrs. Collyer developed tuberculosis, the appeal of the Idaho climate became the deciding factor in their move. The day before they left, neighbours and friends called on the family to say farewell, and that afternoon members of the family's church rang the bells for more than an hour in Mr. Collyer's honour.

In his last letter from *Titanic*, Mr. Collyer noted, "So far we are having a delightful trip; the weather is beautiful and the ship magnificent...it's like a floating town....You would not imagine you were on a ship...we will post again at new [*sic*] York then when we get to Payette...don't worry about us." Mr. Harvey never got to post those letters.

Elizabeth Watt and her daughter, Robertha (Bertha, 12), were travelling the farthest, to Portland, Oregon. Mrs. Watt's husband had gone ahead and departed Glasgow the previous October. Aboard *Titanic*, Mrs. Watt and Bertha shared their cabin with two other women. Mrs. Watt was not as appreciative of *Titanic*'s opulence as Mr. Collyer was, however. In her last letter, she wrote, "Oh dear. The style is awful. It seems it is not a fast boat, it is built for comfort, not speed...." Ironically, it was *Titanic*'s speed that was a major contributing factor to the disaster that was about to unfold.

There was also a family from South Africa aboard *Titanic*: Thomas and Elizabeth Brown, along with their daughter, Edith (15). Business had not been good for Mr. Brown, a usually prosperous Cape Town hotel and property owner, so he decided to move to Seattle, where his sister-in-law lived. Initially, Mrs. Brown was appalled at being in second class, as the family usually cruised first class, but was somewhat mollified when she saw *Titanic*'s standards for second class.

The lone immigrant family headed to Canada was the Harts from Essex. Benjamin, Esther, and Eva (7) were travelling to Winnipeg, where Mr. Hart intended to open a drugstore. According to Eva, from the time

Mrs. Hart boarded *Titanic*, she "had a premonition and she never went to bed in that ship at night at all. She sat up for three nights so she slept during the day and I was with my father." It was an eerie foreboding of the fate that awaited them.

Third Class

Youngsters William (Willie, 9) and Neville (3) Coutts were travelling with their mom from London to New York to join their dad, who had gone ahead and secured employment. Mr. Coutts, a gold and silver engraver, had sent his family enough money to buy second-class tickets, but Mrs. Coutts purchased third-class ones instead, hoping to use the difference to help set up their new home on Fourth Avenue in Brooklyn.

Like Mrs. Mellenger's, Margaret Ford's husband had deserted her, which forced her into a hardscrabble existence raising chickens in Sussex. In 1911, one of Mrs. Ford's daughters had immigrated to the United States and was employed as a servant for a rich Long Island family. Her stories convinced her mother to emigrate as well. Mrs. Ford was travelling with William (14), who was already working as a post office messenger, and Robina (7), plus two older children, Dollina (20) and Edward (18), and a family friend.

Mrs. Ford's daughter's experience also convinced her mother's older sister and her master plumber husband to emigrate with their two children, William (8) and Catherine (7) Johnston. The Surrey-based family had originally planned to sail the previous October but decided to wait and travel with the Fords. Although both families were booked on the SS *Philadelphia*, they had to switch to *Titanic* due to the coal strike. The destination of the group of ten was New London, Connecticut, where Mrs. Ford's brother lived. Sadly, the final destination for the entire Ford-Johnston party would end up being somewhere in the mid-Atlantic.

Boarding *Titanic* was easy for Southampton resident Edith Peacock and her children. Mr. Peacock had preceded his wife to the United States. He lived in Newark, New Jersey, where he worked at the powerhouse of the Public Service Corporation. Mrs. Peacock was travelling with her four-year-old daughter, Treasteall, and seven-month-old son, Albert, whom Mr. Peacock had never seen. In anticipation of the family's

The Goodwin family died in the sinking, including baby Sidney (not in picture).

reunion, Mr. Peacock had purchased toys for Treasteall and a baby carriage for Albert. Unfortunately, that reunion never took place.

The Goodwin family was one of the largest aboard *Titanic*. Mr. and Mrs. Goodwin, along with Lillian (16), Charles (14), William (13), Jessie (12), Harold (10), and baby Sidney (19 months) were on their way from Peterborough, Cambridgeshire, to Niagara Falls, New York. Although Mr. Goodwin had been a printer, at the time he was a labourer in a foundry. His brother and two sisters had immigrated to the United States, and all had settled in Niagara Falls. His brother had told Mr. Goodwin about job opportunities at a new power station, so the family decided to move. One sister and her husband loaned him the money for the family's group ticket, and the other sister gave him money. They also found a house for the Goodwins and furnished it. As with so many others, their original liner's sailing was cancelled due to the coal strike, and the family ended up on *Titanic*. The whole family was lost in the disaster, although baby Sidney later figured prominently in one of *Titanic*'s greatest mysteries.

Leah Aks and her ten-month-old son, Philip (known as Frank), were on their way to Norfolk, Virginia. Mrs. Aks and her husband were Polish

Jews who had settled in London, where Mr. Aks was a tailor. He had gone ahead to Norfolk in January and saved enough money to have his wife and baby son join him.

John Sage operated a small bakery and confectioner's shop in Peterborough, Cambridgeshire, where he lived with his wife and family that had grown to five boys and four girls by 1911. The family was on their way to Jacksonville, Florida, where Mr. Sage had earlier purchased a fruit farm. Mr. Sage and his eldest son, George (19), had travelled to Canada in April 1911 to investigate the family immigrating abroad. They ended up in Winnipeg, where they worked as waiters on dining cars of the Canadian Pacific Railway. Once the two saved enough money, Mr. Sage put a deposit on an orchard in Jacksonville, where he intended to grow pecans. In a postcard to his wife, he noted, "Jacksonville is quite the most wonderful of places."

Mr. Sage returned to England in September, while son George followed later. Local lore in Peterborough notes none of the rest of the family were as enthusiastic about the move as Mr. Sage. He originally intended for the family to travel on the passenger ship *Philadelphia* from Liverpool, but had to change plans due to the coal strike. Instead, they boarded *Titanic* at Southampton on a ticket that cost almost £70 (C$17,435). The children were Stella (20), George (19), Douglas (18), Frederick (16), Dorothy (14), William (Will, 12), Ada (10), Constance (7), and Thomas (5). The entire family was lost in the sinking, but Will's body was recovered.

Frank (Frankie) Goldsmith (9) and his parents were headed to Detroit from their home in Kent. Around 1910, Mrs. Goldsmith's parents and several of her siblings had immigrated to Detroit, and the Goldsmiths decided to join them. Their decision was partly driven by the desire to make a clean break after the loss of their six-year-old son Bertie to diphtheria in late 1911. The family was travelling with two acquaintances, Alfred Rush (17) and Thomas Theobald, in his thirties.

Bertram Dean and his wife had decided to immigrate to Wichita, Kansas, where Mr. Dean had family and friends. A house was available for them there, and Mr. Dean hoped to open a tobacco shop, having previously run a pub in London. Accompanying them were twenty-three-month-old Bert and two-month-old Millvina, the youngest person on

Titanic. In a postcard mailed to her parents, Mrs. Dean noted, "We are enjoying ourselves fine up to now. Little baby was very restless." The "restless" baby would go on to become the most famous of all *Titanic* survivors.

American Child Passengers

The other group of English-speakers who boarded *Titanic* at Southampton consisted of nine American families with fourteen children, travelling in all three classes. Two families were in first class, with three children. The wealthy Carter family of Philadelphia was returning home after a year abroad. Their party con-

Mr. and Mrs. Goldsmith with Frankie (left) and Bertie, 1907.

sisted of William and Lucile and their children, Lucile (14) and William Thornton II (11). Travelling with the Carters were maid, manservant, chauffeur, and two dogs. *Titanic*'s forward hold also carried car enthusiast Mr. Carter's new 25-horsepower 1912 Renault CB Coupe de Ville (the setting for the steamy love scene between Jack and Rose in James Cameron's *Titanic*).

Sixteen-year-old Georgette Madill was travelling with her mom, her cousin, and her mom's maid. The residents of St. Louis, Missouri, had been vacationing in Europe after the death of Georgette's stepfather the previous December, which made her mother a widow for the second time.

Second Class

Five American children from three families were in second class. Nellie Becker and her three children, Ruth (12), Marion (4), and Richard (21 months), were travelling from India to Benton Harbor, Michigan, to seek treatment for Richard's illness. Lutheran missionary Rev. Becker had run an orphanage in Guntur, a city near India's east coast, for several years. In fact, all three children had been born there. Baby Richard was ill, and doctors believed he would have a better chance of survival in the US than in India. As a fourth child had died of diphtheria in 1907 (in the same month that Marion was born), the parents did not want to risk the loss of another child. Mrs. Becker left her husband behind when they travelled to his hometown, but he intended to join his family later.

Americans who had journeyed even farther than the Beckers were Albert and Sylvia Caldwell, along with their ten-month-old son, Alden. For two years, the couple had been teaching at the Bangkok Christian College for Boys in Siam (modern Thailand), which operated under the auspices of the Presbyterian Board of Foreign Missions. Although Mrs. Caldwell was contracted to teach for seven years, when her health began to fail—compounded by her pregnancy with Alden—her doctor ordered her to return to the US. The

Albert, Alden, and Sylvia Caldwell aboard Titanic *in Southampton.*

head of the school and other missionaries disagreed with this decision, so much so that the head asked the board to have Mrs. Caldwell examined by its doctors on arrival in New York to ensure she was definitely ill. If she were not, the young couple would have to pay for their return trip—a daunting prospect. The Caldwells' destination was the village of Biggsville, Illinois, close to the state's western border with Iowa. Their lengthy trip to Britain was marked by Mrs. Caldwell's seasickness in the Indian Ocean and a cholera scare in Italy. In London, they managed to get tickets for *Titanic* due to a cancellation and were delighted, as they thought the large ship would help alleviate Mrs. Caldwell's nausea.

Marshall Drew (8), whose mom had died within two weeks of giving birth to him in 1904, was being raised by his father's childless brother and his wife, whom Marshall called "Mother." Uncle James (who operated a marble monument business with his older brother) and Aunt Lulu had taken Marshall to England aboard *Olympic* in the fall of 1911 and gone to Cornwall to visit relatives of the Drews. The three were returning to Southold, on the northeastern end of New York's Long Island. After they boarded *Titanic*, Mr. Drew and Marshall were able to tour some of the ship's first-class facilities, including the gymnasium and barbershop.

Third Class

Four American families were in third class and had six children among them. Virginia Emanuel (6) and her mother, an actress and aspiring singer who performed under the stage name of Elise Martin, had arrived in England on January 31. Mrs. Martin had travelled first-class aboard *Olympic*, while Virginia and her American nursemaid were relegated to second class. When Mrs. Martin signed a six-month contract, she remained in London and soon sent Virginia and the nursemaid to Virginia's grandparents in Manhattan aboard *Titanic*. This time they were in steerage and shared a cabin with a young Englishwoman.

John Cribb, who was originally from Australia, and his daughter, Laura (16), a shop assistant, were travelling from Dorset, England, to Newark, New Jersey. His wife and the rest of the family remained in Dorset, intending to join Mr. Cribb and Laura later. The peripatetic couple had two children born in Newark, including Laura, and two in Dorset. Mr. Cribb had been a butler or steward for several prominent New York families and was intending to resume such a position. He had made twenty-three trips across the Atlantic. The twenty-fourth would be his last.

The story of Rhoda Abbott and her two boys exemplifies the many different versions that exist of the lives of some of *Titanic*'s passengers. Depending on the source, she met and married Stanton Abbott either in England or after she immigrated to Providence, Rhode Island. Stanton was a professional boxer, who was either a British or an American—lightweight or middleweight—champion. History records her name incorrectly as Rosa (even famed *Titanic* author Walter Lord got it wrong), as that is the name mistakenly listed in *Titanic*'s passenger manifest. Every other source, such as birth, marriage, and death certificates, census records, and passport details, shows her name as Rhoda. In Providence, the Abbotts had two children: Rossmore (16) and Eugene (13). By 1911, the couple had separated, and Rhoda and her boys returned to England aboard *Olympic* to live with her widowed mother in St. Albans, Hertfordshire. Rhoda worked as a seamstress, while Rossmore was a bootmaker and Eugene a student.

The boys were unhappy in England and yearned to return to their friends and way of life in Providence. Their mother's business had not gone well either, and when she realized her sons would likely do better in the US, she decided to return for their sake. She initially booked passage on an old, small liner and was delighted when it was changed to *Titanic* due to the coal strike. The family took the train to Southampton and boarded the ship early on April 10. Once they found their cabin near the stern of the ship with other family accommodation, Mrs. Abbott unpacked while the boys explored their new surroundings. She met some of the ladies from nearby cabins and spent much of her time during the voyage conversing with them.

Austin van Billiard was originally from North Wales, Pennsylvania, but had travelled to France to find work as an electrician at the 1900 Paris Exposition. There, he met and married an Englishwoman, whose father happened to be in Paris on business. James and Walter were born within two and a half years of the marriage, and in 1906 the family moved to southern Africa so Mr. van Billiard could try his luck at diamond mining. After six years of harsh conditions (and two more children), he decided to return to the United States and try his hand as a diamond merchant. The van Billiards first went to London, where his wife's parents lived, so she could recover her health after their years in Africa. Mr. van Billiard took his two eldest children, James (10) and Walter (9) aboard *Titanic*, leaving his wife and the rest of the family to join them later.

Just Passing Through

In the days before *Titanic's* departure and up to the morning of its sailing, passengers poured into Southampton from across Europe. Over three hundred of them were classified as transmigrants; that is, they arrived on tickets purchased in their home country for passage not just *to* England, but *through* England. After legislations enacted in 1905 and 1906, the British Board of Trade departure lists required the nationality of passengers who fell into the category of transmigrants—"Alien (non-British) passengers (other than 1st-class passengers) who arrive in the United Kingdom having in their possession Prepaid Through Tickets and in respect of whom security has been given that they will proceed to places outside the United Kingdom"—to be recorded.

Of course, arriving just a few hours before departure, such as those coming down on the London trains, was not feasible for those who had been travelling many days to various English ports. Not only had the coal strike thrown ship departure dates into a state of havoc, it also meant these transmigrants needed longer accommodation in Southampton. On Albert Road, not far from the docks and the White Star Line offices, was the Atlantic Hotel, which catered to this traffic. Originally called the Emigrants' Home, it had been taken over by John and Ada Doling. Indeed, Mrs. Doling, accompanied by her sister-in-law Elsie Doling, also intended to sail on *Titanic*. Leaving her two sons with their dad, Mrs. Doling was planning not only to visit her mom in New York, but also to further develop the transmigrant trade. She may also have been newly pregnant. According to a childhood friend of the Doling brothers, "the Dolings were the agents...between the Americans and the European faction." It is quite possible that some of the travellers found accommodation here.

Whether from Britain, Scandinavia, other parts of Europe, or Lebanon/Syria, third-class passengers followed the same pattern of chain migration. Historically, when a population migrates from one country to another, the first to arrive in the new location establish themselves and then assist their friends and relatives in making the same journey. Steerage was largely populated by these emigrants who were joining family in North America and might even have employment waiting for them. Moreover, this pattern often led to communities of immigrants settling in the same location, such as the Irish in New York City and the Lebanese in Pennsylvania. In addition to those emigrating for the first time, many third-class passengers were returning from trips abroad to visit family they had left behind.

Scandinavians

By far the largest group of transmigrants arriving in Southampton hailed from Sweden, Norway, Denmark, and Finland, with Sweden being the point of origin for the majority of them. In fact, Swedish was the second-most spoken language aboard *Titanic.* Among the 123 Swedes who arrived in Southampton were 29 children from 13 different families. More often than not, these Swedes were not the first in their extended families to emigrate, nor had all their children been born in Sweden. Although Sweden was a relatively small country of only five and a half million people, by 1912 over a million Swedes were living in the US, as a result of two previous waves of immigration driven largely by economic factors. The population of Sweden was growing, but opportunities for employment were not, since industrialization had not yet reached a country largely dependent on farming, forestry, and mining. Moreover, at the turn of the century, mandatory military service for males was expanded to 240 days, causing many young men to emigrate. Finally, at birth every Swede automatically became a member of the Swedish Lutheran church. The United States was seen as a beacon of freedom—both financial and religious.

Correspondence and visits from those who had previously emigrated encouraged family members and neighbours to seek new opportunities abroad. The White Star Line, dependent upon the emigrant trade to fill its large liners, hired people like Ernst Danbom as recruiters. Ernst, who was born in Iowa, and his Swedish wife (who had immigrated in 1905) were on an extended honeymoon in Sweden where their son Gilbert (5 months) was born. They convinced Mrs. Danbom's sister and her farmer husband to immigrate with their five children: Sigrid (11), Ingeborg (9), Ebba (6), Sigvard (4), and Ellis (27 months) Andersson. While the Danboms were returning to Iowa, the Anderssons were headed for Winnipeg, Manitoba, where another sister of the two women had previously immigrated.

Many other families with ties to the United States were also on *Titanic*, such as the Swedish-American Asplunds, with their five children: Filip (13), Clarence (9), twins Carl and Lillian (5), and Felix (3). The parents had previously immigrated to Worcester, Massachusetts, where their four oldest children were born, but had returned to Sweden in 1907 so Mr. Asplund could help his recently widowed mother. Felix was born there in 1909. By 1912, however, they decided to sell their farm and return to Worcester, where Mr. Asplund hoped to get his old job back and where other members of their extended family lived. With proceeds from the sale of the farm, they signed a contract with the White Star Line for 795 kronor (C$5,671) which would provide them one third-class cabin and passage from Gothenburg, the largest port in western Sweden, to Worcester. Gothenburg was the same port from which most of the *Titanic*-bound passengers departed aboard the SS *Calypso,* sailing to Hull, East Yorkshire, and from there by train to Southampton.

Also aboard *Calypso* was the Skoog family with their four American-born children: Karl (11), Mabel (9), Harald (5), and Margit (24 months). The parents had immigrated to Iron Mountain, Michigan, in 1900, where Mr. Skoog worked for a mining company but, in the fall of 1911, they moved back to Sweden. After having lived for several years in the US, perhaps the Skoogs found their homeland not as they remembered, because they decided to return to Michigan in the spring of 1912. In addition to their own family, they were travelling with two young female relatives, who were immigrating to the same area. The entire group lost their lives in the disaster. It is possible that their escape from steerage was slowed because young Karl used crutches, having lost his left leg and the toes on his right foot in a railroad accident when he was seven.

Also departing from Gothenburg, the Sandström family, mother Agnes and her American-born daughters, Marguerite (4) and Beatrice (20 months), was returning to San Francisco after a visit to relatives in Sweden. Similarly, Elna Ström and her American-born daughter, Telma

(28 months), were returning to their home in Indiana Harbor, Indiana, after a three-month visit with Mrs. Ström's parents. But for a small accident, they would not have been travelling aboard *Titanic*. Telma had scalded her hand with hot water, which delayed their departure while the injury healed. As it was, once on board, Mrs. Ström had to take Telma to a nurse every day to have her dressing changed. Mrs. Ström's younger brother was travelling with them, leaving behind his wife and two children. On board *Titanic* the Ströms and Sandströms shared a third-class cabin. Each family would experience a different fate.

Three young Swedish men, each travelling alone, also began their journeys to the US aboard *Calypso*. Hans Eklund (16) was headed to Prescott, Arizona, where his uncle lived. Olaf Osén, also sixteen, borrowed money from his dad to travel to South Dakota with a promise to support his parents back in Sweden after he secured employment. The youngest solo traveller was Johan Svensson, just fourteen, who was also on his way to South Dakota where his father and a sister had previously immigrated. Before he left home, Johan's mother had sewn 15 kronor (C$108) into his jacket lining. Surprisingly, among the three solo Swedes, only young Johan survived.

The Johnson family of Illinois, who left Sweden from the port of Malmö, is an example of the mixed heritage of many Scandinavians. Mrs. Johnson had been born in Finland and immigrated to Chicago, where she married a Swedish immigrant. Their two children, Harold (4) and Eleanor (20 months), were born in St. Charles, Illinois, a town just west of Chicago that was home to a large Swedish-American community. Mrs. Johnson had gone to Finland with the two children in early 1911, hoping to see her ill father. Unfortunately, he died before they arrived, but Mrs. Johnson and the children spent the next year visiting other relatives in Finland and some of her husband's family in Sweden. After booking third-class tickets on *Titanic* for their return, Mrs. Johnson wrote to her husband directing him to meet the family in New York. In anticipation of their return, he refurnished their house as a surprise. On *Titanic* the Johnsons shared a cabin with two Swedish women who were also headed to Illinois and would play a role in the Johnson family's survival.

Because no Swedish embarkation papers exist for Hulda Veström (14), Gertrud Klasén (16 months), or their guardian on the voyage, Hulda

The second-class promenade area of the boat deck.

Klasén, it is most likely they travelled first to Copenhagen and then on to Southampton. All three were headed to Los Angeles, where Mrs. Klasén was a widowed dressmaker. After a visit to Sweden, she brought with her on the return voyage two of her nieces: her namesake Hulda Veström, whose dad had already immigrated to the US, and Gertrud Klasén. Gertrud's mom, thought to be unmarried, had earlier left her infant daughter behind in Sweden to start a new life in Los Angeles. The travelling party also included Klasén's brother-in-law and uncle of Gertrud.

The last Swedish family with no record of departure from Sweden was the Pålssons, mother Alma and four children, Torborg (8), Paul (6), Stina (3), and Gösta (27 months). Mr. Pålsson had been a miner in Sweden, but after a strike and a period of unemployment, immigrated to the US in 1910—and changed the spelling of his last name to Paulson. Working as a tram conductor in Chicago, where two of Mrs. Pålsson's brothers also lived, he had saved enough money to send for his family. They also probably arrived in Southampton via Copenhagen. Like the Goodwin family, the Pålssons were lost in the disaster and, like Sidney Goodwin, Gösta also was a significant figure in one of *Titanic*'s greatest mysteries. Of the twenty-nine Swedish children aboard *Titanic*, only seven would arrive in New York.

Among approximately sixty Finnish passengers on *Titanic* were nine children, five from one family alone. All except one boarded the Finland Steamship Company's SS *Polaris* which left Hanko, Finland, on April 3. Maria Panula and her five sons were headed to Coal Center, Pennsylvania, where her husband had lived since 1911 and worked as a coal miner. Mrs. Panula had gone back and forth between the United States and Finland several times since her initial immigration to Michigan in 1893. Ernesti (16), Arnold (15), Juho (7), and Urho (35 months), had all been born in the United States but the youngest, Eino (13 months), had been born in Finland in the spring of 1911. Their father returned to the United States that fall and, in the spring of 1912, Mrs. Panula sold their farm and left Finland once again. To help with the boys, she also brought along the daughter of a neighbour. Once on board *Titanic*, the family split up— Mrs. Panula and the three youngest were in a third-class cabin in the stern; Ernesti and Arnold joined the unmarried men near the bow. The entire Panula party perished in the sinking, while Eino would go on to have a key role in one of *Titanic*'s longest mysteries.

The other Finnish children also had strong family connections in the United States. Erna Andersson (16) hoped to join her brother in New York and find work as a domestic. Helga Hirvonen was bringing her daughter Hildur (26 months) to Monessen, Pennsylvania, where Mr. Hirvonen, who had immigrated the year before, now worked in a steel factory. Helga's brother and another young man from their hometown joined them on the journey.

The only child in second class who arrived from Finland was Viljo Hämäläinen (14 months). Viljo had been born in Massachusetts to Finnish parents who later moved to Detroit. He and his mom were returning to their Detroit home after a visit to her native country. Viljo's father awaited their return. Accompanying them was an eighteen-year-old girl who was to become their housekeeper, having obtained permission to work in the US for five years.

The one Finnish family that did not travel to Southampton on *Polaris* was the Rosbloms. Mrs. Rosblom, her son Viktor (18)—named after his dad—and daughter Salli (25 months) had left the port town of Hanko aboard the SS *Titania* on March 27, a week prior to *Polaris*'s departure. The Rosbloms had planned to travel on the RMS *Olympic*, but Salli got sick, which caused them to miss that sailing and switch to *Titanic*. Like the Panula family, their immigration to the United States had not followed a smooth path. Mrs. Rosblom had married in 1893, and sons Viktor and Eino were born in Finland. Mr. Rosblom went to the United States in 1905, returned to Finland in 1908, and left for the US again in 1910, only a month after the birth of his daughter Salli. Now Mrs. Rosblom was bringing Salli and her eldest son to join him in Astoria, Oregon. Twelve-year-old Eino refused to leave his homeland, a decision which proved wise. Of the nine Finnish children, only three would reach their destination.

The only two children from Norway sailing on *Titanic* both survived the voyage, but only one of their stories has a happy ending. Kalle (Karen) Abelseth (16) had three sisters who had immigrated to the United States, and now she planned to join her sister in Los Angeles. Since family friend (but no relation) Olaus Abelseth lived in the US and was now returning after a visit to Norway, he agreed to watch over young Karen. She shared a third-class cabin with a fellow Norwegian and some Swedish women.

Nine-year-old Artur (Arthur) Olsen's young life had not been easy. He was born to Norwegian emigrants in Brooklyn, but his mom had died when he was only three, so his dad took him to Norway to live with his grandmother. Meanwhile, back in the US, his father remarried and had another son. When Arthur's grandmother died in 1911, his father went back to Norway to fetch his freckle-faced, red-headed son. Mr. Olsen originally booked their passage home on *Philadelphia*, but fate intervened again, and they were transferred to *Titanic*.

Although several Scandinavians left from Denmark, only one Danish child boarded *Titanic* in Southampton. Svend Jensen (16) was travelling with his older sister, her fiancé, and her fiancé's uncle to Portland, Oregon, where the uncle had lived previously. Like many males in steerage, he would never arrive.

Continental Europeans

Several continental Europeans arrived in Southampton on cross-channel ferries from the north of France. Among them were members of seven immigrant families with eleven children. Louis M. Hoffman had a secret, a secret that went on to become one of *Titanic*'s most well-known stories. The man travelling under that name, Michel Navratil, had taken his two sons, three-year-old Michel Jr. (nicknamed Lolo) and twenty-five-month-old Edmond (nicknamed Momon) from their mother. Originally from Slovakia in Austria-Hungary, Navratil had moved to Nice, France, in 1902. Five years later, he married Italian Marcelle Caretto, who was ten years younger than him. By 1912, the tailoring business he had established in Nice was in difficulty, Mrs. Navratil was having affairs, and her mother continued to criticize him as an unfit match for her daughter. As a result, the couple separated, and Lolo and Momon went to live with their mom. The boys stayed with their dad on Easter weekend, April 6–7, 1912, but when Mrs. Navratil went to get them afterward, her estranged husband had disappeared with their sons.

Navratil had decided to take the boys to the US, in what may be the first documented case of international parental child abduction or kidnapping (the response to such action was only codified in 1980 by the Hague Convention on the Civil Aspects of International Child Abduction).

Michel Navratil, a.k.a Louis Hoffman.

He took a train to an English Channel port, boarded a ferry, and sailed to England, where he and the boys stayed in London. Navratil purchased second-class tickets for *Titanic* under the assumed name of Hoffman, the real name of a friend who had helped them get away, while the boys were booked as Loto and Louis.

In 1910, Franck Lefebvre, along with four of his children, all in their early twenties except for an eleven-year-old, moved from the coal-mining area of northern France to Mystic, Iowa, where he hoped to become a miner. His wife and the couple's four other children, Mathilde (12), Jeanne (8), Henri (5),

LETTER IN A BOTTLE: MESSAGE FROM THE PAST OR ELABORATE HOAX?

In 2017, a family exploring the shoreline at Hopewell Rocks Provincial Park in New Brunswick made an interesting discovery. Famous for its giant sea stacks, affectionately called "flowerpots," the park is noted for the dramatic Bay of Fundy tides, which make the shore accessible only at low tide. From the muck, the family pulled what appeared to be an old bottle with a piece of paper inside. Unfortunately, to retrieve the message, they had to break open the bottle. Dated April 13, 1912, the message, handwritten in French, reads in English, "I am throwing this bottle into the sea in the middle of the Atlantic. We are due to arrive in New York in a few days. If anyone finds it, tell the Lefebvre family in Liévin." The message is signed Mathilde Lefebvre.

Could a message in a bottle really have resurfaced 105 years after being hurled into the North Atlantic? Multinational experts considered three areas of authentication: the location of the find, the physical properties of the bottle and the message, and, lastly, the style of both expression and handwriting in the note. First, how plausible is it that a bottle thrown from a deck on *Titanic* would end up on the shores of the Bay of Fundy, which separates New Brunswick from Nova Scotia? Prevailing currents flow west to east, making it more likely that such a bottle would end up on the coast of Ireland. Moreover, the bottle would have had not only to float west along the south shore of Nova Scotia but also make a dramatic U-turn into the Bay of Fundy. While possible, oceanographers both in Canada and Norway agreed that the odds of such an event are very small.

Next, were the physical elements—bottle, cork, wax, paper, and ink—over a century old? A multidisciplinary team at Université du Québec à Rimouski issued a press release in May 2021, stating that, through techniques such as radiocarbon dating, those items are consistent with what was available in 1912.

This intriguing story was picked up by media outlets on both sides of the Atlantic, including in France. There, relatives of the Lefebvre family were hopeful that the message was authentic. However, it is also from France that the strongest evidence against the authenticity of the note

more...

...cont'd from previous page

emerged. Although no examples of Mathilde's handwriting exist for comparison, French expert Coraline Hausenblas, who specializes in the development of writing in children, examined the script based on online photographs. She determined that the language used in the letter was much closer to that of a modern adult than to that of a twelve-year-old child in 1912. She especially noted that the spacing between letters was not consistent with the way a French schoolgirl would have been taught to write at that time. In April 2022, she published her conclusion: hoax.

and Ida (3), remained behind in Liévin and were to join the rest of the family later. Lefebvre must not have known that *Titanic* would depart from nearby Cherbourg—which would have saved him money and his family time and inconvenience—and instead purchased third-class tickets from Southampton. Sadly, the intended family reunion never took place as his wife and their four children were lost.

There were members of three Belgian families travelling to the US aboard *Titanic*. The father of Alfons (Alphonse) De Pelsmaeker (16) had been killed in a work accident, leaving his wife to raise six children. Alphonse intended to join his older brother in Gladstone, Michigan. Leo Vanderplancke (15) was travelling with his sister, his newly wedded brother, and his brother's wife. The group planned to first visit relatives in Detroit before joining another brother in Fremont, Ohio. Ten-year-old Catharina Van Impe and her parents were also travelling to Detroit. All eight Belgians were in third class; all were lost.

Several Europeans from other continental countries were also travelling third class. Luise (Louise) Kink-Heilmann (4), her parents, and a sister and a brother of her father were emigrating from Switzerland to Milwaukee, Wisconsin. Louise, her mom, and her aunt shared a cabin with three other women at the stern, while her dad and his brother occupied a cabin toward the bow with four other men.

Meier Moor (7)—later Meyer Moore—had been born in Romania, which was then part of the Russian Empire. Meyer and his widowed mother were reputedly fleeing due to anti-Jewish pogroms and the threat of Meyer's eventual conscription into the Russian army. They had been turned back the previous year on their first attempt to flee, after making it as far as Quebec City, en route to an uncle in Portage la Prairie, Manitoba. In the interim, they remained in London before deciding to immigrate to join Meyer's aunt and uncle in Chicago.

Departure

Titanic's transatlantic voyage almost ended in disaster as soon as it started. At noon on April 12, as six tugs towed the massive liner away from its new dock, the vessel's displacement—coupled with a low tide—caused a wave of water to surge out from both sides of *Titanic*. While the wave on the river side flowed harmlessly away, on the dock side, it

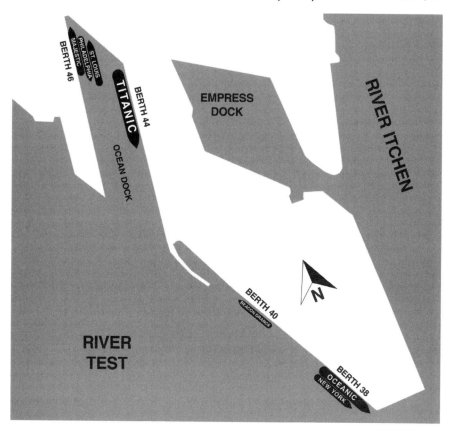

The Southampton docks showing the positions of Titanic *and* New York *before their near-collision.*

was another story. The wave rolled toward the SS *New York*, put additional strain on its mooring lines, and caused them to break. *New York* started to drift downriver and into *Titanic*. Only quick action by a tugboat's captain and *Titanic*'s captain halted its drift. An hour late, Captain Smith was able to finally proceed on his 163-kilometre (101-mile) voyage across the English Channel to Cherbourg.

As Sylvia Caldwell, mother of ten-month-old Alden, boarded *Titanic*, she had a question for a nearby crewman.

"Is this ship really unsinkable?" she asked.

"Yes, lady," he replied immediately. "God himself could not sink this ship."

CHAPTER 3

CHERBOURG & QUEENSTOWN

My sister was 14 years old and I was 12 when we boarded the Titanic. We were saddened to leave father behind [in Syria], but were excited about being on board the RMS *Titanic*, the largest, fastest and most luxurious ship of its time and also said to be unsinkable! The anticipated arrival in New York was to be Wednesday, April 17. The water was calm, the weather typically chilly for April.

—Ilyās Nīqūla Yārid (Louis Garrett), 12 on *Titanic*

Titanic passengers are often divided into two categories: victims and survivors. But there is, in fact, another group which fits into neither category. These are the passengers who boarded *Titanic* not planning to cross the Atlantic Ocean but only to cross the English Channel and, in some cases, continue to Ireland. While this might seem like a mere footnote to the historic voyage, we have some of these cross-channel passengers or day trippers (and overnighters) to thank for valuable insights into life aboard *Titanic*.

Among the families who boarded at Southampton were the Lenox-Conynghams. Eleven-year-old Eileen and her ten-year-old brother Dennis were travelling with their mother and their aunt. The group was embarking on a month-long tour of France, while their dad, Rev. George Lenox-Conyngham, would take the other two children to Ireland. Eileen and Dennis were to spend the school holidays practising their French while visiting French cultural attractions. Knowing that her children were prone to seasickness, Mrs. Lenox-Conyngham chose the largest ship available to cross from Southampton to Cherbourg and paid £3 (C$746) to book passage for the three of them, which included lunch but not accommodation. A bonus was the opportunity to experience what was by all accounts an exciting new ship. The four-hour crossing of the English Channel gave Eileen and Dennis ample time to explore. As Eileen later recounted to her great-nephew, "We were absolutely staggered by the beauty and size of this great ship." She described the ship as "elegant beyond description."

Bound for Cherbourg as well were thirteen-year-old William Noel and his father, a retired army major. The pair, who had brought along their bicycles, planned to continue to Finistère in Brittany, where the English family owned a home.

The family of eleven-year-old Jack Odell also boarded in Southampton, but their voyage was to extend overnight to Queenstown, Ireland. Their first-class passage of £24 (C$5,978) for the group included meals, cabins, and access to all *Titanic* had to offer for the next twenty-four hours. The Odell party included young Jack, his mom, his two maternal uncles, and his paternal aunt. Absent was Jack's dad, who had been detained in

Jack Odell leans against the rail on A Deck forward.

England on business. Their overnight crossing was a prelude to a driving tour of Ireland. Jack intended to document his holiday by taking photographs along the way, including on board *Titanic*.

Cherbourg

Cherbourg, like its neighbour across the channel, Southampton, also has a rich maritime history, although more in the realm of conflict than commerce. Only about 150 kilometres (93 miles) from the nearest point on the south coast of England, its position at the tip of the Cotentin Peninsula made it a strategic location in the ongoing battles between the English and the French. As part of the Duchy of Normandy during the time of William the Conqueror, its ownership changed multiple times during the ensuing Hundred Years' War, until finally it was ceded to France in the mid-fifteenth century.

Three centuries later, it was briefly occupied by the British during the Seven Years' War. At the beginning of the nineteenth century, Napoleon Bonaparte ordered work on a sea wall at Cherbourg, hoping the port could become the location to launch an invasion of England. In 1840, it was Cherbourg that greeted his remains from their burial place on the island of St. Helena, where he had been exiled. During the American Civil War, thousands of spectators in Cherbourg watched as, just offshore, the Union warship *Kearsarge* battled and sank the Confederate raider *Alabama*. (Although he was not an eyewitness to the battle, Édouard Manet used press reports of the time to immortalize the battle in his painting *The Battle of the Kearsarge and the Alabama*, now in the Philadelphia Museum of Art.)

In 1907, when the White Star Line announced that Southampton would be the terminus of its transatlantic liners, it also noted that Cherbourg would become its European port of call. With a six-hour-long regular train service from Paris, the port was an ideal location for both tourist and business traffic. At the time, it was also the largest artificial harbour in the world. Despite its size and, unlike Southampton's, Cherbourg's dock could not accommodate large ocean liners like *Titanic*, so the White Star Line commissioned two tenders: *Nomadic*, to ferry first- and second-class passengers, and *Traffic*, to carry third-class passengers, mail, and cargo back and forth. On the afternoon of April 10, when Le Train transatlantique arrived from Gare Saint-Lazare in Paris, the passengers received disappointing information: *Titanic* would be late and, therefore, they needed to amuse themselves for an additional hour.

An interesting mix of 281 travellers waited in Gare Maritime or strolled along the Grande jetée. Representing over two dozen countries, they included 151 first-class, 28 second-class, and 102 third-class passengers. Thirty-one children were among them. First class was overwhelmingly comprised of American tourists and businessmen (more than 100), while third class was mostly Middle Eastern emigrants (80). Oddly enough, French citizens were not well-represented among the passengers, and six of the twenty French were, in fact, servants of wealthy Americans.

Among the four children in first class to board at Cherbourg was Washington Dodge Jr. (4), the only child of Dr. Washington Dodge and his wife. Although Dr. Dodge was a qualified physician, for several years his main interest was local politics, and he became very wealthy. His most recent position was city assessor for San Francisco. The family had journeyed from their mansion in the city's wealthy Lafayette Park area to France, where Dr. Dodge had received treatment for a blood disease, and was now returning home.

Douglas Spedden (6) was eager to board this grand new ship. This was not, however, his first transatlantic crossing. He was a seasoned traveller on ocean liners, including *Caronia* and *Adriatic*. Moreover, the list of places to which he had travelled was long: Panama to view a great canal under construction, Bermuda to frolic on beautiful beaches, Madeira to enjoy warm breezes. All these trips had one thing in common—respite from the cold winters in Tuxedo Park, the gated enclave where he lived just outside New York. Summers, by contrast, were spent in Maine, seeking relief from the heat and humidity. The family's rented cottage on Grindstone Neck, near Winter Harbor, was just across Frenchman Bay from Bar Harbor, where many prominent families summered.

Douglas was the much-loved only child of Frederic Spedden and Margaretta (Daisy) Spedden. His father was a wealthy banker and avid yachtsman; his mother, who doted on her son, enjoyed photography and kept a daily journal. In the first decade of the twentieth century, the family led a life of privilege and frequent travel. Their most recent travel adventure began with a voyage aboard *Caronia* to Algiers. Douglas's nanny, Margaret Burns, whom Douglas called "Muddie Boons," and Mrs. Spedden's maid accompanied the family. Also along was Douglas's constant companion, a white Stieff bear that he had named Polar. From Algiers, the Spedden family crossed the Mediterranean to Monte Carlo for a month-long stay in Cannes. After two train rides, first to see the sights in Paris and then on to the port of Cherbourg, the Speddens were ready to go home.

John (Jack) Ryerson (13) came from a similarly wealthy background. The Ryerson party of Haverford, Pennsylvania, and Cooperstown, New York, included his father and mother, two older sisters, a maid, and a governess. They too summered in Maine. Wealth did not shield them from grief, however; they were forced to cut their European tour short when they learned that their oldest son, a Yale student, had been killed in an automobile accident back in Pennsylvania on Easter Monday. They needed to return home as soon as possible, so they booked passage on the first available ship: *Titanic*.

Mary Lines (16) and her mom were travelling to the United States for a much happier occasion—the graduation of her older brother, Howard, from Dartmouth College in New Hampshire. Dr. Ernest Lines was president and medical director of the New York Life Insurance Company. Due to business, he could not take time off and was not joining them on this trip. Dr. Lines, his wife, son, and daughter had lived in Paris since the early 1890s and were frequent transatlantic voyagers. Mary was a student at the prestigious girls' school Lycée Fénelon (noted alumnae include philosopher Simone de Beauvoir and artist Louise Bourgeois). Mary described *Titanic* as "a very delightful ship," but noted the British "completely neglected to afford any means of escape from the ship," presumably influenced by its "system of bulkheads."

Only three children were in second class. The Mallet family was from France but living in Montreal, where their son André had been born almost two years prior. Mr. Mallet worked as a cognac importer for a Montreal liquor company, but the reason for this recent two-month visit had been to see family in Paris. On the train from Paris, they struck up an acquaintance with the Laroche family: Joseph Laroche, his pregnant wife, Juliette, and their daughters, Simonne (3) and Louise (21 months).

Mr. Laroche had been sent to France from Haiti to study engineering by his prosperous and well-connected family (an uncle was president of Haiti). Upon graduation he had married a French woman, but discovered there were few opportunities for employment. As a Black man with biracial children, he hoped the family would be more comfortable back in Haiti. His mother sent the family tickets to return on the new French liner *France,* which was scheduled to make its maiden voyage from Le Havre on April 20. But when the Laroches learned that children on the SS *France* could not dine with their parents, they exchanged their tickets for *Titanic.*

Although most immigrant children who boarded at Cherbourg were Lebanese, there were a couple of other nationalities represented in third class. Manca Karun (4), her dad, and her father's brother-in-law were travelling together. They were en route from Šenčur, Austria-Hungary (today in Slovenia), to Galesburg, Illinois, to join the rest of the family. Mr. Karun ran a boarding house for railway workers there and was returning after a visit home. Romanian Uscher Pulner (16) left his job as a plumber in Paris (where he had moved earlier) to join his older brother in New York. Although not known for certain, he may have been travelling with a family friend.

Middle Eastern Pipeline...of Emigrants

Third-class families who boarded at Cherbourg were predominantly Middle Eastern emigrants (out of 102 passengers in third class, 80 were Lebanese, including 23 children). They were part of a diaspora that brought more than 55,000 Lebanese people to the United States and Canada by 1910. Indeed, the Syrian-Lebanese families on board not only came from the same villages, but were also often travelling to the same cities in North America, where others from their families or neighbourhoods had previously settled. Several families, for example, were from the village of Hardin in what is now Lebanon. Many were en route to Pennsylvania, especially the Wilkes-Barre area, and to Ontario. Most were Maronite Christians. Leaving their villages by whatever means possible—on foot, in horse-drawn carts, or even in camel caravans—they first made their way to Beirut, then by freighter to Marseille, and finally by train to Cherbourg.

Although they came from what is now Lebanon, in 1912 that country did not exist, but was a region within Greater Syria. At the time, the Mount Lebanon Mutasarrifate was an autonomous precursor of an expanded, modern Lebanon. The later secret Sykes–Picot Agreement of 1916 divided Syria between Britain and France and created Lebanon in the process. While most of their descendants identify as Lebanese, on the ship's manifest those passengers were all labelled "Syrians." In addition to confusion over nationality, there was often uncertainty about the spelling of their names. White Star Line employees and immigration officials often misspelled or anglicized unfamiliar names at the time of booking or boarding. The Arabic speakers who settled in North America did not usually resist those changes and often accepted these instantly

NAME CHANGES FOR LEBANESE PASSENGERS AND THEIR CHILDREN

Original Names in Arabic	Anglicized Versions
Latīfah, Mārīyā, Ūwjīnīyā, & Hilānah al-Ba'qlīnī	Latifa, Maria, Eugenie, & Helen Baclini
Sultānah, Nūr al-'ayn, & Akar Būlus	Sultana, Laura, & Akar Boulos
Husayn Mahmūd Husayn Ibrāhīm	Houssein Hassan
Yūsuf Ilyās	Joseph Elias
Tamīnah & Hilānah Jabbūr	Tamini & Hileni Jabbur
Amīnah, Halīm, & Jirjis Mubārik	Amenia, William, & George Borek
Adāl Qiyamah	Adele Kiamie
Sa'īd, Wadi'ah, & Mariayam Nakid	Sa'īd, Mary, & Maria Nackid
Ilyās & Jamīlah Nīqūla Yārid	Louis & Amelia Garrett
Butrus Sim'ān	Betros Seman
Yūsuf Sim'ān	Youssef Samaan
Bashīr, Thamīn, & As'ad Tannūs	Charles, Thelma, & Assed Thomas
Tannūs Hannā Mu'awwad Tannūs	John Thomas
Hinnah, Jirjis, & Mariyam Tu'mah	Anna, George, & Mary Thomas
Kātrin, Nabīah, & Shafīq Yūsuf	Katherine, Mary, & Michael Joseph

anglicized names or formally changed to them later. Like vast numbers of immigrants before them, they just wanted to fit in. Anglicized versions of their names will be used here for continuity and clarity.

As in other agrarian societies around the world at the time, a year in Lebanon was measured by the seasons: sowing, growing, harvesting. For the many Lebanese who were Christians, major religious celebrations, such as Easter and Christmas, were the only important specific dates. As a result, birth certificates were not customary in a region where people measured their age by the number of seasons, and the children's ages are estimates at best.

The father of the three Baclini sisters, Maria (5), Eugenie (3), and Helen (33 months), had left their homeland before the youngest had even been born, fleeing religious persecution. By 1912, Mr. Baclini was running a dry-goods business in Brooklyn and could afford to send for his wife and daughters. Similarly, the neighbour with whom Mr. Baclini had emigrated wanted his fifteen-year-old daughter to also join him in New York, so Latifa Baclini was looking after Adele Kiamie as well as her own three. The group had not originally been booked on *Titanic*; Maria's case of conjunctivitis had delayed their departure.

Sister and brother Amelia (14) and Louis (12) Garrett left their village of Al Hakur with the intention of joining their mother and older siblings in Jacksonville, Florida, where they had previously immigrated. Their father was supposed to accompany them on the trip but, as with the Baclinis, an eye infection thwarted that plan. Instead, the young teens boarded *Titanic* alone, speaking no English, hopefully to be watched over by their fellow Lebanese travellers.

Among the group from Hardin were sixteen-year-old Thelma Thomas and her five-month-old son, Assed. Her husband had already immigrated to Wilkes-Barre, Pennsylvania, where his brother had a dry-goods business. When the brother went back to Hardin for a visit, he agreed to return with his sister-in-law and nephew. Several other Hardinites were making the same trip. Amenia Borek and her sons, George (7) and William (4), were on their way to Clearfield, Pennsylvania, where her husband had set up a small grocery store a few years earlier. The family was travelling in the company of Mrs. Borek's newly married sister and her husband.

Darwish Thomas left his wife and two children behind in Tibnin to immigrate to Michigan in 1905, with the goal to earn enough to buy his own farm. Now, his wife and two children, Mary (9) and George (8), were coming to join him on that farm in Dowagiac, Michigan, thanks to his brother, who had sent their passage. Although she did not understand the words, Mrs. Thomas clutched a piece of paper bearing the address: Dowagiac, Michigan, U.S.A. With several other villagers, she and the children left Tibnin in a camel caravan bound for Beirut. The arduous journey of more than one hundred kilometres (sixty-two miles) took several days. The families slept in tents and ate meals of yogurt, cheese, olives, and pita bread, all provided by the caravan company. Despite the fatigue, Mrs. Thomas recalled with fondness evenings of music and dancing provided by her fellow travellers.

Michael (4) and Mary (32 months) Joseph had been born in Detroit, Michigan, to Syrian-Lebanese immigrants. In 1910, their mother took them back to Lebanon for an extended family visit, and now they were returning to Detroit with her. The Nackid family, Sa'īd, Mary, and their thirteen-month-old daughter, Maria, was from Ehden, a town in northern Lebanon with Biblical connections. It is said to be where Adam and Eve lived after they left the Garden of Eden, as well as the home of Noah's grandchildren. Mr. Nackid, a labourer, and his family were on their way to Waterbury, Connecticut, to join his mother, who had lived there for several years.

Sultana Boulos was travelling with her daughter Laura (10) and son Akar (7) to join her husband in Chatham, Ontario, where he was a bus driver for a hotel. Mr. Boulos had been in Canada for several years and returned to Lebanon in 1908, where he remained for two and a half years to operate his farm. When he returned to Chatham, Mrs. Boulos remained behind to run the farm and likely sold it before going to Canada. Six weeks before *Titanic* sailed, Mr. Boulos sent his wife money for their travelling expenses, including the cost of a ticket for the voyage. Although Mr. Boulos did not know on which ship they sailed, his brother in Lebanon sent him a letter advising that his wife and children left their village on March 15 and departed Marseille on April 11. Mrs. Boulos and the children were lost in the disaster, a fact not confirmed to Mr. Boulos until April 22.

Hileni Jabbur (16) and her older sister were housekeepers about whom little else is known. Some sources state they were travelling to New York from their village of Serhel, while others note they were on their way to join their father somewhere in Canada. The family name is often written as "Zabour," apparently from a misinterpretation of a cursive *J* for a *Z* by someone copying a passenger list. The surname "Zabour" is not found in any contemporary Arabic newspapers that list the victims, although "Jabbur" is.

A LETTER'S VOYAGE

During the crossing from Southampton to Cherbourg, after exploring the ship and enjoying an elegant luncheon, Eileen Lenox-Conyngham followed her mother's suggestion and retreated to the ship's library. There she quietly wrote a note to her nanny, who was looking after Eileen's infant brother in Little Bray, Ireland. That letter, written on *Titanic* stationery, with the schoolgirl penmanship of an eleven-year-old, survives to this day. Indeed, the voyage of the letter is a story in itself. The Lenox-Conynghams disembarked at Cherbourg as planned, while the letter carried on to Queenstown where it was posted to the nanny. In the aftermath of the sinking, she cherished this letter from her young charge and kept it for her entire lifetime.

Eventually, the letter passed to the nanny's daughter who, realizing its value as a piece of *Titanic* memorabilia, put it up for auction in 1983. The story of a recently discovered *Titanic* artifact attracted international attention, including an article in the *Washington Times*. The report, however, falsely claimed that the author of the letter had died in the sinking. The article was read by Eileen, who had married an American and was, coincidentally, living just outside Washington. She dispatched family members to buy it back at the auction for £1,000 (C$7,385) and kept it until her death in 1993. She bequeathed the letter to her son, who in turn left the letter to the Lenox-Conyngham ancestral home, Springhill House, in Northern Ireland, now managed by the National Trust. The letter arrived there in 2012, one hundred years after Eileen wrote, "This is the first long voyage the *Titanic* has ever made. It is quite calm."

There were other Lebanese children who boarded *Titanic* at Cherbourg, none of whom arrived in New York: Houssein Hassan (11), travelling with a relative to visit his dad in Fredericksburg, Virginia; Joseph Elias Jr. (15), immigrating to Ottawa with his father and older brother; Betros Seman (10), travelling with an uncle to join his widowed mom in Wilkes-Barre, Pennsylvania; Youssef Samaan (16), a labourer from Hardin, also on his way to Wilkes-Barre, with his dad and brother, to join his wife; and John Thomas (16), travelling with his father to Columbus, Ohio, to complete his education, along with two male relatives (who were heading to Youngstown to work in the steel mills) and two female relatives.

Even before *Titanic* was sighted in the English Channel, tenders began loading passengers, baggage, and mail for the transfer to the ship, and by 6:00 P.M. they were ready and waiting out in the harbour. *Titanic* was an hour behind schedule, so no time could be wasted. Between the time *Titanic* dropped anchor at 6:30 P.M. and left just after 8:00 P.M., twenty-four cross-channel passengers, like the Lenox-Conynghams and Noels, disembarked and their baggage was unloaded.

At the same time, 281 passengers boarded with their luggage. One passenger alone, Mrs. Charlotte Cardeza, sailed with fourteen trunks, four suitcases, and three crates of baggage. (Her detailed claim of £36,567 [C$9,141,936] for her group's lost possessions was the largest of all claims submitted after the disaster.) In addition to the bags of mail, *Titanic* also received luxury French provisions for its first-class dining saloons, including champagne, wine, cheese, meat, and mineral water.

According to American passenger Edith Rosenbaum, the transfer from tender to ship while bobbing on the choppy seas was difficult: "The gangplank was held down by ten men on either side, as it shook and swayed in every direction. I was the last one to leave the tender, hating the idea of crossing that gangplank."

With boarding complete by 8:00 P.M., *Titanic*, now brightly lit up against the darkening sky, bid adieu to Cherbourg and began its overnight passage to Ireland.

Queenstown

> I am enjoying the trip immensely and am now looking forward to see the coast of old Ireland. They say we shall have some fun at Queenstown, for as soon as we arrive people flock out in skiffs and sell their goods.
>
> —William Mellors (19), in a letter to his mother from *Titanic*

The final stop for *Titanic* before leaving the coast of Europe behind was Queenstown (known as Cobh since 1920), Ireland. The purpose of this last stop was four-fold: disembark the seven remaining cross-channel passengers, board new passengers, drop off bags of mail, and pick up more mail bound for New York. Although this stopover brought on board fewer passengers than Southampton or Cherbourg, traditionally Queenstown was one of the busiest departure ports for Irish emigration. In the nineteenth and twentieth centuries, over six million had emigrated from Ireland, and Queenstown was the departure point for two and a half million of them.

The White Star Line office in Queenstown was ready. *Titanic* would drop anchor off Roches Point, 3 kilometres (1.9 miles) from the dock. At the dock, the tenders *Ireland* and *America*, paddle-steamers dating from 1891, were waiting to carry 123 passengers (3 first-class, 7 second-class, and 113

The statue of Annie Moore and her brothers in Cobh represents Irish migrants.

third-class) and more bags of mail. In addition to the tenders, smaller boats were assembling to bring vendors of Irish lace and linen out to the ship to sell their wares. The passengers began queuing to board the tenders, along with reporters who had been invited to tour the new liner. The train from Cork had arrived, slightly late, with more passengers and mail. Colourful signal bunting added a festive air to the dock—the arrival of *Titanic* was a special occasion. After an overnight sail from Cherbourg, the ship dropped anchor at 11:30 on Thursday morning. It was a typical Irish spring day, partly cloudy and cool, with a moderate breeze.

Among the seven cross-channel passengers disembarking at Queenstown, three carried cameras, and it is the film in those cameras that carried the last known photos taken on board *Titanic*. When Jack Odell (11) and his extended family stepped from the tender onto the dock, a motor car was waiting to take them on a driving tour of Ireland. On the voyage from Southampton, Jack had proudly worn his camera

A PHOTOGRAPHIC LEGACY

Fr. Francis Browne was an academic and Jesuit novitiate when his uncle, the Bishop of Cloyne, gave him the gift of a first-class ticket for cross-channel passage on *Titanic* from Southampton to Queenstown. Occupying stateroom A-37, he spent much of the voyage wandering around the ship and indulging his passion for photography. His photographic legacy of candid shots of life on the deck, in the dining saloon, and in the wireless room has been invaluable to historians and *Titanic* enthusiasts. His images include the near-collision with *New York* in Southampton and the last-known photograph of Captain Smith. Although Fr. Browne sold several photographs to newspapers immediately after the sinking, it was not until 1985, twenty-five years after his death, that a fellow priest, Eddie O'Donnell, discovered a cache of negatives in the Irish Jesuit archives. The photographs were published in 1997 as *Father Browne's Titanic Album*, with Fr. O'Donnell writing the text. Since that time, numerous other books of Fr. Browne's photos have followed.

around his neck, while his aunt Kate recorded the Odell family vacation in photos. Also departing at Queenstown with his Kodak camera was their cross-channel shipmate, Fr. Francis Browne.

As the passengers were tendered out, the mournful sounds of uilleann pipes carried across the water. According to a reporter for the *Cork Examiner* who was present that day, "Mr. Daly is a well-known performer on the war-pipes...and as the tender on which he left Queenstown cast off, he played up 'A Nation Once Again,' his performance being received with delight and applause by his fellow-travellers." The departure must have been bittersweet, however, for the 113 steerage passengers, immigrants who were leaving their homeland, perhaps never to see it again. Their sadness at separation from family and friends was tempered by hope for a better life across the Atlantic. Some on board would have spent the previous evening at a "living wake" or "American wake," a party held in their honour to mourn their leaving. Most of the passengers were young—average age just over twenty-six—and were not the first in their families to leave. Like the Scandinavians and Lebanese already on board, these passengers were links in the chain of migration, joining family members who had already established themselves in the United States. Although the group was young, there were few children among their ranks on this trip. The Rice family alone accounted for five of the ten youngest to board that day.

Thirty-nine-year-old Margaret Rice had crossed the Atlantic before. Born in Athlone, Ireland, in 1872, Margaret married Englishman William Rice, a soldier stationed in the nearby army barracks. Their first child, William, was born in 1899 but lived less than two months. He had swallowed his pacifier and died four days later after several convulsions. The couple relocated to London, where a second son, Albert, arrived in 1902. The Rices immigrated to Montreal in early 1903, where George was born late that fall. The family next moved to Ontario, where Mr. Rice worked as a shipping clerk for the Grand Trunk Railway. Two more sons were born in Canada: Eric in 1905 and Arthur in 1907.

In January 1909, the family left Canada for Spokane, Washington, where Mr. Rice got a job as a machinist with the Great Northern Railway and son Francis was born. Only a year after their arrival, tragedy struck again, when Mr. Rice was crushed by an engine and died shortly afterward in the hospital. With the compensation she received for her husband's death, Mrs. Rice returned to Athlone with her five boys. It is not known if she originally intended to stay in Ireland or not but, perhaps encouraged by a few locals who had decided to emigrate, she also opted to return to the US. Mrs. Rice and her sons boarded *Titanic* at Queenstown as third-class passengers, at a cost of nearly £30 (C$7,500).

Five fifteen- and sixteen-year-olds, travelling without their parents, were leaving Ireland for New York. Maurice O'Connor (15) had already left school and was no longer living with his family in Ballinloughane, County Limerick. Listed as a general labourer, he planned to join his older brother. Also from Limerick was sixteen-year-old Patrick Lane. Paddy, likewise, had left school and was working in a marine store, but was recorded as a farm labourer on the ship's manifest. He was headed to Manhattan. Accompanying him on the journey was family friend Nellie O'Dwyer, who had immigrated to Brooklyn six years earlier as a teenager. Now twenty-two years old, she could lend her ocean travel experience to the young man from her native county.

Many Irish immigrants were young women hoping to find domestic work in the United States, girls like Mary Burns (15) from Kilmacowen, County Sligo. The oldest of eight children, she was travelling to the home of her paternal aunt, who lived in Brooklyn. Hanora O'Leary (16) from Kingwilliamstown, County Cork, had watched several of her siblings emigrate from Ireland. Now it was her turn to join her sister in New York. Nora, as she was called, was part of a group of half a dozen young men and women from her region, led by Daniel Buckley. Ellen Corr (16) from Corglass, County Longford, listed as a "farmer's daughter" in the 1911 census, was one of ten children. She was leaving to join two older sisters who had previously immigrated to New York. Although she had no family on board, she was likely part of a slightly older group who were also from Longford. Sadly, Mary would never arrive in Brooklyn.

Just before 2:00 P.M., when all transfers of passengers and mail had been completed, the tenders headed back to dock. *Titanic* drew up its anchor and set off for its next landfall, New York. Only two of the ten Irish children on board would make it.

When *Titanic* left Queenstown, it sailed with just over half of its full passenger capacity (51 percent: some 1,317 out of 2,566). There are

The tender America *alongside* Titanic, *Queenstown, April 11, 1912.*

several reasons for this. For many, early spring was a slow season for travel, with summer and winter preferred. The coal strike had also dissuaded some potential passengers who, tired of the whole affair, decided to wait until regular scheduled services could resume. Finally, *Titanic* was a new ship and still relatively unknown at the time; its fame rests upon its sinking. The slightly older *Olympic* was much more famous, as were White Star Line's rivals, the Cunarders *Mauretania* and *Lusitania*. In hindsight, it was fortunate that the liner was not filled to capacity, as many more deaths would undoubtedly have been caused and added to the scope of the tragedy.

Children...or Not?

Titanic sailed with 156 children aboard either as passengers or crew. But were there more? *Titanic* historians by necessity deal with uncertainty. Modern technology in areas as diverse as DNA testing and metallurgy has resolved some questions, but specifics of passenger and crew counts, lifeboat assignments, and identities of recovered bodies may never be finalized. One remaining area of uncertainty is the exact age of several people on board. Michael Findlay, the co-founder of the American-based Titanic International Society and a frequent contributor to Encyclopedia Titanica, edited a comprehensive passenger list based on official documents, such as contract ticket lists and US immigration records, and less official sources, such as interviews with *Titanic* survivors and their descendants. As another researcher wryly noted, the more sources consulted, the more discrepancies found. (See Afterword – When Does Childhood End? for the basis of using sixteen as the upper age limit for inclusion in this book.)

Here, then, is a table of young people who were considered for inclusion, but ultimately rejected because of the uncertainty of their ages.

NAME	AGE	NATIONALITY	TICKET CLASS	SOURCE
Adāl Nasr Allāh (Adal Nasrallah)	13	Lebanese	Second	Death Certificate
	15			*The Dream & Then the Nightmare: The Syrians Who Boarded the Titanic*
	16			1920 & 1940 US Censuses
	17			Encyclopedia Titanica
	18			1930 US Census

List of young people not included in this book due to uncertainty about their ages (continued on next page).

NAME	AGE	NATIONALITY	TICKET CLASS	SOURCE
Bannūrah Ayyūb-Dāhir (Banoura Ayoub)	12	Lebanese	Third	*The Dream & Then the Nightmare*
	15			Cemetery headstone
	17			Encyclopedia Titanica; husband's naturalization records
Kate Gilnagh	15	Irish	Third	*A Night to Remember* ("a pert colleen not quite 16")
	16			1957 BBC interview ("I was sixteen, going on 17")
	17			Encyclopedia Titanica
Annie McGowan	14	American	Third	Social Security application; death record
	17			Encyclopedia Titanica; American Red Cross
Alfred Rush	16	English	Third	Titanic International Society
	17			Encyclopedia Titanica

Sīlānāh Yazbak (Celiney Yazbak)	14	Lebanese	Third	*Monroe Journal* ("A widow 14 years old")
	15			*The Dream & Then the Nightmare*
	17			Encyclopedia Titanica; *The Wilkes-Barre Times Leade*r

For the next three days, life was idyllic aboard *Titanic*. Without pre-arranged activities (except for meals and church services), adult passengers were free to explore the massive new liner—or at least as much as class barriers would allow—on their own. In between sleeping and eating, pleasant days were filled with walks, chats, games, smoking, reading, and other activities.

Life for children aboard *Titanic*, like everything else, depended upon their class of ticket. Those in first class had ample space to frolic and were often attended by their nannies. This was not a Disney cruise, however, with planned activities for children. The nine in first class had free access to the first-class promenade deck, where they could be out in the fresh air, the lounge for quieter pursuits, such as reading and writing notes, and the gymnasium, where the hours from 1:00 P.M. to 3:00 P.M. were set aside for children. In addition, the Verandah Café became a de facto playroom for some first-class families to chat while their children engaged in free play with whatever toys they had brought on board. In addition to his stuffed bear, Douglas Spedden (6) played with a spinning top on deck. Fr. Browne's photograph of Douglas spinning his top is one of the most iconic images of the voyage. James Cameron recreated the scene in his 1997 epic, *Titanic*, attesting to the director's attention to detail.

Douglas Spedden (6) spins his top on the aft promenade of A Deck under the watchful eye of his father, Frederic, April 11, 1912.

The twenty-eight children in second class did not have quite as much space to roam but did have access to a library and second-class outdoor promenade spaces. Marshall Drew, an adventurous eight-year-old, found there were few boys his age in second class, so he went exploring alone. Marjorie Collyer later recalled that, from an eight-year-old's perspective, the loss of her beloved doll was the most distressing part of the evacuation from the ship. She told a reporter in New York that in the lifeboat, "I cried hardest when I thought of my dolly back there in the water with nobody to mind it and keep it from getting wet."

Eva Hart (7) described her family's second-class accommodation, "We had ample cupboards for all our clothes and the cabin had its own wash hand basin and a dressing table as well as a couple of comfortable chairs. My bunk was below the one used by my father and much of the time it was occupied by my doll and teddy bear which I had taken to keep me company." Once Eva and Nana Harper (6) discovered each other, they played on deck together. Eva also looked forward to her daily visits with a French bulldog owned by another passenger. She recalled:

> When I wasn't playing with the dogs or sight-seeing around the ship, my special playmate was another girl of about my own age. Her name was Nina [Nana] Harper and she was particularly fond of my large teddy bear which my father had bought from the middle of a Christmas display at Gamage's large store in Holborn [London] only a few months previously. We must have made quite a spectacle for the other passengers as we dragged this big teddy bear with us all over the ship.

For Edith Brown (15) and her mom, second-class tickets were a bit of a comedown, but their accommodation proved quite satisfactory and their fellow second-class passengers amiable. On that final Sunday night, they attended a hymn sing-along before retiring.

In a letter to her dad, Mrs. Laroche described the comfortable accommodation for her family: "We have two bunks in our cabin and the two babies sleep on a sofa that converts into a bed." She went on, "At this moment they are on the enclosed deck with Joseph. Louise is in her pram and Simonne is pushing her."

In addition to communal dining halls, third-class passengers and their children had a general gathering room with a piano, often the spot for late-night singing and dancing. Many of the 114 third-class children had great latitude to roam within third-class boundaries, run up and down long corridors, and find playmates. In larger families like the Sages and the Skoogs, the older children also had responsibilities to care for their younger siblings. Frankie Goldsmith (9) soon befriended half a dozen other boys in third class, including Arthur Olsen, also nine. The small gang explored the ship—swinging from baggage cranes and glimpsing soot-covered firemen in the boiler room. Similarly, George Thomas (8) remembered descending three flights of stairs to reach their cabin, which still smelled of fresh paint. "During the trip my sister and I were always playing...sometimes when no one was looking, we'd slide down the banisters or run up and down the corridors." In fact, George later recalled,

"There was nothing else to do but play." Some children also remembered sneaking into unoccupied rooms, of which there were many, as the ship carried only slightly more than half of its potential passenger capacity. Second-class passenger Eva Hart recalled her initial happy-go-lucky days: "Our thoughts as children aboard the *Titanic* were a long way from disaster and tragedy."

Then, on Sunday, April 14, as the temperature plummeted, activities moved indoors, and families retreated to their cabins. A colossal mountain of floating ice was about to prematurely end the voyage. Even for the lucky children who survived the collision, the carefree days of childhood would be lost forever.

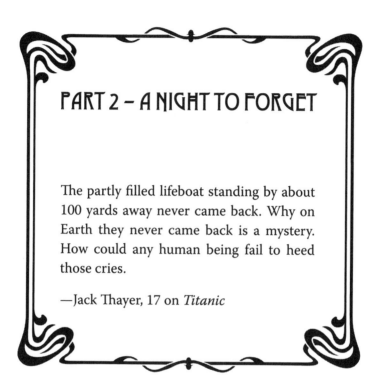

PART 2 - A NIGHT TO FORGET

The partly filled lifeboat standing by about 100 yards away never came back. Why on Earth they never came back is a mystery. How could any human being fail to heed those cries.

—Jack Thayer, 17 on *Titanic*

CHAPTER 4

THE FIRST TWO HOURS

"Iceberg, right ahead!"

At 11:40 P.M. on Sunday, April 14, lookouts Frederick Fleet and Reginald Lee had only twenty minutes left in their shift. For the last hour and forty minutes, they had stood shivering in the cold night air in *Titanic*'s crow's nest high on the foremast, as the temperature dropped to just below freezing. They were warned to look out for icebergs, but their job was complicated by the moonless night and the lack of binoculars. Unknown to anyone, the binoculars intended for the crow's nest were secured in a locker in Second Officer Charles Lightoller's cabin.

Suddenly, Fleet saw a black mass materialize out of the ocean dead ahead of the liner. He lunged for the bell in the crow's nest, rang it three times to signal ice to the front, and called the bridge on the ship's telephone. "Iceberg, right ahead!" he shouted into the mouthpiece to Sixth Officer James Moody. Moody immediately repeated the warning to First Officer William Murdoch, who instantly ordered quartermaster Robert Hichens to turn the wheel "Hard astarboard!"

In response, Hichens spun the wheel to starboard, which turned the bow to port. Thirty-seven seconds after Fleet first spotted the iceberg, *Titanic*'s starboard bow scraped along the submerged side of the massive mountain of floating ice. The rock-hard ice opened six separate gashes below the waterline, each along a riveted seam. The ocean began to pour in.

Within the next ten minutes, the ship had a starboard list of fifteen degrees.

Titanic was sinking.

In less than three hours it would be gone forever.

Launching the Lifeboats

Titanic carried twenty-four lifeboats of three different types, which could carry a total of 1,178 people. Fourteen standard lifeboats had a

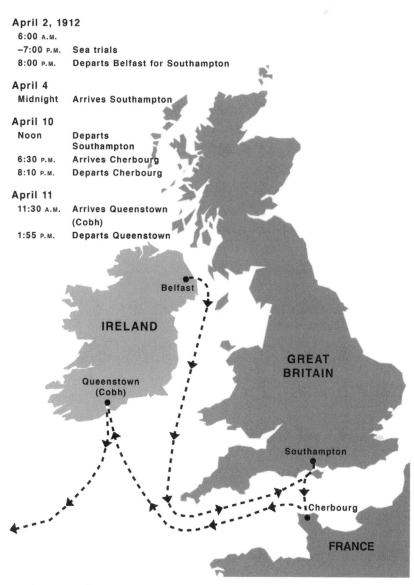

April 2, 1912
6:00 A.M.
–7:00 P.M.   Sea trials
8:00 P.M.   Departs Belfast for Southampton

April 4
Midnight   Arrives Southampton

April 10
Noon   Departs
Southampton
6:30 P.M.   Arrives Cherbourg
8:10 P.M.   Departs Cherbourg

April 11
11:30 A.M.   Arrives Queenstown
(Cobh)
1:55 P.M.   Departs Queenstown

Belfast

IRELAND

Queenstown
(Cobh)

GREAT
BRITAIN

Southampton

Cherbourg

FRANCE

Titanic's *voyage begins.*

A contemporary artist's depiction of Titanic *hitting the iceberg.*

capacity of 65 each, two emergency cutters could carry 40 people each, and four Englehardt collapsible lifeboats with folding canvas sides could each hold 47. The two cutters were always swung out over the port and starboard sides next to the bridge wing, ready for immediate use in case of an emergency, such as someone falling overboard.

Indicating the initial lack of urgency or panic aboard *Titanic*, it took one hour after the liner hit the iceberg before crewmen launched the first lifeboat. Part of this was due to the reluctance of many passengers to leave a huge and seemingly safe passenger ship for a small lifeboat bobbing about in mid-Atlantic on a cold, dark night. In addition to being chilly out on deck, it was also noisy. For at least the first half hour after *Titanic* stopped, the noise of steam being vented from the engine room as a safety measure created a deafening roar.

As with much of *Titanic* lore, a great deal remains unknown about the ship's lifeboats. This includes the exact timing of the launch of each one, which is based on the often-unreliable memories of surviving passengers and crew, but which has been estimated by dedicated *Titanic* buffs after years of research. Similarly, it also involves the sequence of their launching. Almost unbelievably, it also includes how many passengers and crew were aboard each boat and the names of those who were in them. While considerable research has been done in this area, definitive answers remain elusive.

The loss of many of the men and boys in the disaster depended on a simple fact: whether they were on the starboard or port side of the ship when they got on deck. It boiled down to personal interpretation of the term "women and children first" by the two officers in charge of loading. On the starboard side, where odd-numbered lifeboats were launched, First Officer Murdoch followed the rule explicitly and only allowed male passengers to enter a lifeboat *if* there were no other women or children nearby. If there was still room, he then allowed men to get in. On the port side, where even-numbered lifeboats were launched, Second Officer Lightoller's interpretation was different—he believed he was to load women and children *only*. His more rigid understanding of the rule resulted in several lifeboats leaving with empty seats, when there were men and even boys nearby. In total, more than three times as many men and boys got away in starboard lifeboats than did in port ones. Paradoxically, while Lightoller survived, many men and boys were needlessly denied the opportunity to enter partially filled lifeboats.

Lifeboat 7 (first starboard) – 12:40

Lifeboat 7 was the first to go into the water. Due to the crew's unfamiliarity with the new Welin davits, they lowered the boat unevenly, causing some passengers to fear they would be tipped into the ocean. First Officer Murdoch, in charge of the launch, ordered the lowering to stop so the boat could be levelled out before resuming. No. 7 carried only twenty-eight people when it was lowered away, three of whom were crew. All passengers were first-class, except for one second-class. None of them were children. Twenty-four-year-old New York heiress Margaret Hays (along with her Pomeranian, Lady), one of the passengers to figure prominently in the later saga of the Navratil brothers, was aboard.

Lifeboat 5 (second starboard) – 12:43

Lifeboat 5 was the first one to be launched with a child, although it was the second boat to go into the water. Dr. Dodge, who had boarded in Cherbourg after receiving medical treatment in France, helped his wife and four-year-old son Washington Jr. into it, kissed them goodbye, and then managed to find a place in Lifeboat 13. No. 5 is thought to have carried forty-one people, including seventeen female and sixteen male passengers. Eight were crew members, including Third Officer Herbert Pitman and a female. Some occupants estimated other numbers, ranging between thirty-five and more than fifty. Lifeboat 5 carried only first-class passengers. Young Washington, clad lightly in his pyjamas and wearing a life preserver, shivered in the cold night air. Later, when Mrs. Dodge described the scene, she noted some women became hysterical, which caused Washington to cry and ask, "Where's papa?"

Lifeboat 3 (third starboard) and Lifeboat 8 (first port) – 1:00

Bright lights and the hushed voices of his parents woke Douglas Spedden from his sleep in the cabin he shared with his nurse, Muddie, and his ever-present companion, Polar, the teddy bear. Mrs. Spedden and her husband had been awakened earlier by "a sudden shock, a grinding noise and a stopping of the ship's engines." A visit to the deck made them realize the seriousness of the situation, and they went back down to rouse the rest of their entourage. Muddie hurriedly dressed Douglas, grabbed his bear, and told him, "Come, we're taking a trip to see the stars."

The Spedden family donned life jackets and proceeded to the top deck where Mrs. Spedden, the nurse, the maid, and young Douglas were eventually loaded into Lifeboat 3. Once all women and children in the vicinity of the boat were loaded, Mr. Spedden was allowed to join his family. Mrs. Spedden later recalled the jerking as the lifeboat was lowered, the splash as it hit the water, and the rockets lighting up the sky. After a while, the waves lulled Douglas to sleep. Lifeboat 3 carried forty people: twenty-five first-class passengers (one of whom brought his dog) and fifteen crew.

The first boat launched on the port side, Lifeboat 8, went into the water without any children. By now, half of *Titanic*'s 160 minutes afloat after it hit the iceberg had passed. Yet a mere four lifeboats had been launched, carrying about 50 percent of their capacity: perhaps 127 to 133 people out of a potential 260. Only two of them were children. Like its predecessors, No. 8 carried only first-class passengers. Not one of them was a man.

Lifeboat 1 (fourth starboard) – 1:05

Lifeboat 1 was one of two emergency cutters carried on *Titanic*. It was permanently swung out over the starboard side, ready for emergency use. Although it had a capacity of forty, it carried the smallest number of people of any *Titanic* lifeboat: five first-class passengers and seven crewmen. Not one of them was a child.

Lifeboat 6 (second port) – 1:10

Lifeboat 6, the second one lowered over the port side, carried between twenty-four and twenty-eight people, all but one of them first-class women. The two crewmen aboard were lookout Fred Fleet and Quartermaster Robert Hichens. Although there were no children in the boat, Elizabeth Rothschild carried her Pomeranian.

Lifeboat 16 (third port) – 1:20

When Lifeboat 16 was launched, it was the first of the next eleven boats that carried children. Among its forty-five second- and third-class passengers and eleven crew were three third-class children, two of whom were sixteen-year-old immigrants seeking a better life in the United States: Norwegian Karen Abelseth and Irishwoman Ellen Corr.

Five-month-old Lebanese infant Assed Thomas had a remarkable escape. His sixteen-year-old mom, Thelma, was on her way to join her husband in Pennsylvania, escorted by her brother-in-law. Thelma and her brother-in-law climbed to the upper decks but became separated in the confusion, with the brother-in-law carrying baby Assed. Thelma made it into Lifeboat 14, but without her baby. Her brother-in-law ran into a woman on deck and asked her if she would take the baby into a lifeboat. Edwina Troutt, who had already resigned herself to going down with the ship, quickly understood that she was likely the baby's only hope for survival and took Assed. Lifeboat 16 was lowered so poorly that some of its occupants later commented that they thought they would end up in the ocean.

Lifeboat 14 (fourth port) – 1:25

Lifeboat 14 carried thirty to thirty-two passengers, plus ten or eleven crewmen and two female stewards, with Fifth Officer Harold Lowe in charge. This total included eleven children—the largest number of children on a lifeboat at the time, as well as the second largest number of children in any lifeboat. Ten of the children got into the boat with their mothers, while the eleventh was herself a mom: sixteen-year-old Thelma Thomas.

A member of the only South African family aboard, Edith Brown had been asleep when she "heard a crash and felt a slight jar." She immediately awakened her mom, who called to her husband in another compartment of their second-class cabin. Mr. Brown went up on deck and returned to report that the ship had struck an iceberg, but "there was no danger." Edith and her mom went back to bed. Then, only a few minutes later, Mr. Brown returned, somewhat shaken and ashen-faced, and told them to get dressed as there were concerns about the ship's safety. Edith and her mom dressed quickly, and Edith put on "extra warm garments." Mr. Brown returned again, this time with three life preservers, which they put on before making their way to the boat deck. Up on deck, he helped Edith and his wife into Lifeboat 14 before he turned away. "That was the last I ever saw of him," Edith recalled. "He never turned round while we could see him." Despite being in a lifeboat, Edith maintained that she and others did not believe that *Titanic* could sink, as such an idea "was quite incomprehensible."

Eight-year-old Marjorie Collyer, a member of an active church-going family from Hampshire on their way to Idaho, was in her second-class cabin with her mom when *Titanic* struck the iceberg. Mrs. Collyer was in bed, as she was nauseous from her dinner being too rich for her that night. Mr. Collyer went on deck to investigate and returned to advise:

"There's no danger. An officer told me so!" When the situation became worse, the family went to the boat deck, where Marjorie was wrenched from her mom and thrown into No. 14, while her mom was pulled into the boat. Mrs. Collyer later stated she would have preferred to stay with her husband and die with him, but she "lived for her [daughter's] little sake otherwise she would have been an orphan."

Agnes Davies, who had been widowed twice, and her eight-year-old son, John Jr., were in their second-class berths when Mrs. Davies felt a jar as *Titanic* hit the iceberg. Although she could not imagine anything serious had transpired, she rang for a steward, who assured her that "nothing of consequence had happened" and they could remain in their berths "without fear." Twenty-one-year-old Alice Phillips, who shared a cabin with Mrs. Davies and John Jr., remembered it differently and later wrote of feeling a "tremendous shock." Alice ran outside, but immediately encountered a steward—perhaps the same one Mrs. Davies had met—who assured her that everything was all right and she should return to her cabin.

Shortly afterward, Alice's father came to the cabin and told her to dress. She did so and then went out on deck. When she returned, she said orders had been given for everyone to get dressed and put on life jackets. By this time, Mrs. Davies had already dressed, but John Jr. was still sleeping. The steward came to their cabin again and repeated his earlier statement that there was no danger. Erring on the side of caution, Mrs. Davies dressed her little boy. Her other son by a previous marriage, nineteen-year-old Joseph Nicholls, then showed up from his cabin and helped them put on lifebelts before they all went to the boat deck at about 12:15 A.M. On deck, Joseph helped to place Mrs. Davies and John Jr. into Lifeboat 14, but was denied entry himself and threatened with being shot if he tried to get in. Mrs. Davies pleaded with the crew to let him in, but in vain. As the boat was lowered away, she saw some men slide down the ropes and get into it. Even then she noted there were "about fifty in the boat, but there was room for more." Joseph died in the sinking; his body was recovered and buried at sea as an unknown victim. He was later identified by possessions found on his body.

The three members of the Hart family from Essex were among the few immigrants going to Canada. When *Titanic* hit the iceberg, Eva (7) and her father were asleep in their second-class cabin. Her mother was awake, having had visions of something bad happening since boarding. Mrs. Hart was fully clothed and dozing, sitting on a suitcase with her head resting on the side of her bunk. Suddenly, "there came the most awful sound" she had ever heard: "a dreadful tearing and ripping sound… the sound of great masses of steel and iron being violently torn, rent, and cut asunder." Mrs. Hart later stated she could never understand how passengers who were not asleep at the time claimed they hardly felt anything. She shook her husband awake and, although Mr. Hart was upset at his wife, he dutifully went up on deck as she requested, dressed only in his nightshirt. He returned shortly and told his wife that there was a lifeboat drill taking place, to which she replied, "They don't have lifeboat drills at 11 at night." The couple dressed quickly, then her father dressed Eva, and the family went up to B Deck.

The next few minutes were a blur to Mrs. Hart. She heard cries of "She's sinking" and "Women and children first" as the family was hurried along the deck from boat to boat, trying to find a spot. After passing four lifeboats, they found room in the fifth. Eva was tossed in first—hitting her stomach on the gunwale on the way—and her mother followed. Just then, a man succeeded in getting into No. 14 on his second attempt, but Fifth Officer Lowe ordered him out and fired his revolver into the air to show he was serious and threatened to shoot the next man who got into the boat "like a dog." Trouble started on the boat deck around Lifeboat 14 before it was lowered. Lowe believed the crowd was getting rowdy, with some men pushing closer and threatening to jump into the boat. As the boat was lowered away past A, B, and C Decks, he fired his pistol along the side of the ship three times to warn people to keep back. Mr. Hart turned to Lowe and quietly said that he was not going to get into the boat and added, "but for God's sake look after my wife and child." Eva then shouted out to Lowe in fear, "Don't shoot my daddy, you shan't shoot my daddy!" She later recalled her experience in the lifeboat:

> The worst thing I can remember are the screams. It seemed as if once everybody had gone, drowned, finished, the whole world was standing still. There was nothing, just this deathly, terrible silence in the dark night with the stars overhead.

According to Juliette Laroche, there was widespread panic, which included pushing and shoving, after *Titanic* hit the iceberg. Mrs. Laroche and her husband, the only Black man aboard the liner, who was taking his family to live in his native Haiti, were surrounded by a crowd as they tried to get to a lifeboat. Suddenly, Mrs. Laroche could feel that her elder daughter, Simonne (3), had been snatched from her and flung into No. 14, hanging above the water. As she cried out for Simonne, she felt herself being grabbed and lifted towards the boat

Juliette and Joseph Laroche with Simonne (left) and Louise.

before being tossed into it beside her daughter.

Mrs. Laroche looked back into the crowd and could see her husband holding Louise (21 months) above his head, trying to force his way through the throng. As with Simonne, someone grabbed Louise and passed her forward to her mom. Then, as Lifeboat 14 started to descend, Mrs. Laroche heard her husband shout, "See you soon, my dear! There will be room for everyone...watch over our little girls...Goodbye!" He died in the sinking.

Madeline Mellenger (13), who was travelling second class with her mother on their way to a new job on the Colgate estate in Vermont, later recalled in an interview for the *Toronto Star* that she and her mom were asleep when "a man banged on our door and told us to put on warm clothes and lifebelts and to get on deck." Once on the boat deck, Madeline and Mrs. Mellenger were "hurled" into No. 14.

On their way to join their father in Ohio, who had been there for two years, Joan (4) and Ralph (28 months) Wells were asleep in their second-class cabin with their mother, when *Titanic* struck the iceberg. Reacting to a roommate's shouted directions, Mrs. Wells quickly dressed herself and her children. She later claimed it was hard to get to the upper decks because many of the passages she had used previously were locked, a strange statement coming from a second-class passenger. Once on deck, the three Wellses were put into Lifeboat 14.

Russian-born seven-year-old Meyer Moore and his mom were making their second attempt to flee to North America, after making it as far as Quebec City the previous year before being sent back. In later years, Meyer recalled his mother waking him after she had been spilled out of her third-class bunk by the impact. She left to find out what had happened but returned quickly and dressed him. They somehow made their way to the upper decks through "chaotic" passageways. On the boat deck, Meyer remembered seeing a "distinguished-looking" woman in No. 14, who, after

---

TIME AND MEMORY

Meyer's obituary in the *El Paso Times* of April 17, 1975 (he had died two days earlier, on the sixty-third anniversary of the disaster), referred to this incident. It noted the woman who got off the lifeboat said her station in life had always been at the side of her husband. The woman, it went on, "was Mrs. John Jacob Astor who went down with the great 'Unsinkable Titanic,' at the side of her life's companion."

This is an example of the many erroneous stories about *Titanic*. Madeleine Astor was not in Lifeboat 14; she was escorted into Lifeboat 4 by her husband, who stepped back when told he could not enter the boat. Madeleine remained in Lifeboat 4 and was rescued. As far as Mr. Astor being "her life's companion," the Astors had been married only seven months earlier.

---

she asked where her husband was, left the lifeboat when she received the answer. Meyer and his mom took the place vacated by the woman.

One other child made it into Lifeboat 14. As noted above, it was Thelma Thomas, but without her five-month-old baby son, Assed, who escaped in No. 16. As Lifeboat 14 approached the water, the stern rope stopped lowering, while the forward one kept going until the bow of the lifeboat reached the water. With the stern dangling about two metres (six and a half feet) above the water, some crewmen aboard had to release the ropes, which caused the stern to crash down onto the surface so forcefully that it sprang a leak, perhaps by pushing the drain plug out. Water filled the bottom of No. 14, some twenty centimetres (eight inches) deep until "some ladies" took care of it with lingerie and other items of clothing.

Lifeboats 9 (fifth starboard) and 12 (fifth port) – 1:30

Launched five minutes after Lifeboat 14, Lifeboats 9 and 12 carried forty-one and forty-three persons respectively. Surprisingly at this late stage of the sinking, only three of them were children. Mary Lines, who was only half dressed, was on her way to her older brother's graduation from Dartmouth College. Bertha Watt, who was travelling the farthest of any passengers, all the way to Oregon, wore only a long-sleeved nightgown under a fur-lined tweed coat. Both Mary and Bertha escaped with their moms in No. 9. Laura Cribb was the lone child in No. 12, having become separated from her father, whose luck had run out on his twenty-fourth voyage across the Atlantic.

Lifeboat 11 (sixth starboard) – 1:35

Lifeboat 11 hit the water five minutes after Lifeboats 9 and 12. Indications are it was overloaded and carried as many as seventy people, perhaps reflecting a growing sense of panic among those left on board. Two sets of siblings were among the seven children in No. 11. Jane Quick and her daughters were returning to Detroit after a visit with relatives in Plymouth. Winnie (8) and Phyllis (32 months) went to bed at about 9:00 P.M. in their second-class cabin and slept through the crash. The noise of a woman from the next cabin shouting about the accident woke Mrs. Quick, which was soon followed by a steward banging on her door. "For

God's sake, get up!" he told her. "Don't stop to dress. Put your life jackets on. They've hit an iceberg and the ship is sinking!"

Mrs. Quick got up, put on a skirt over her nightgown, and dressed her girls. With Phyllis wrapped in a shawl and holding Winnie by the hand, Mrs. Quick struggled to get on deck while carrying their lifebelts. Once outside, a male passenger helped get life jackets on Winnie and Phyllis, while Mrs. Quick put on her own. He then led them up a ladder to the boat deck. Crewmen helped the family into the lifeboat, although Winnie recalled being "literally tossed into the boat and losing my slippers in the ordeal." As the lifeboat lowered away, Winnie screamed in terror and began to cry, believing she would have to jump or be chucked into the water. When the boat hit the water, she calmed down and stopped crying. Phyllis soon fell asleep, while Winnie sat beside a German lady who offered to share her large coat with her against the cold night air.

The other pair of siblings in Lifeboat 11 was Marion and Richard Becker, who were travelling with their mom and older sister all the way from India to obtain medical treatment for baby Richard. After being awakened and told by a steward there was no time to dress, their mom managed to grab shoes and stockings before she guided Ruth (12), Marion (4), and Richard (21 months), dressed only in their nightclothes, from their second-class cabin to an upper deck. They waited there in one of the common areas. After a time, the family climbed a ladder to a higher deck—possibly from B (second-class promenade) to A (first-class promenade)—where several lifeboats were being filled. Mrs. Becker was worried that it was too cold and told Ruth to go back to their cabin for more blankets. Before Ruth returned, crewmen chucked Marion and Richard into No. 11, and their mother rushed to get in with them as the boat lowered away. Suddenly, Ruth reappeared, and her mother yelled at her to get into the next lifeboat.

Leah Aks and her baby son, Frank, were on their way to join Mr. Aks, a tailor, in Virginia. A fellow passenger awakened Mrs. Aks in her third-class cabin and asked if she knew *Titanic* had struck something. Replying that she did not, Mrs. Aks dressed and went out on deck to see for herself. A crew member told her there was no danger and to go back to bed. When she told fellow passengers she intended to take her ten-month-old son up on deck, they told her to let the baby sleep. But she ignored their advice and carried Frank outside.

On deck, Mrs. Aks saw lifeboats on the water with people in them and more boats being filled on the first- and second-class decks. She later stated in a newspaper interview that, when she tried to get into a boat with Frank, she was not allowed onto the second-class deck. Mrs. Aks says she had given up all hope when some young men came to her rescue. They held their arms together and made a ladder to lift her from the steerage deck to the second-class deck, "on the outside of the ship." On the second-class deck, passengers were pushing and shoving so much, trying to get into the lifeboats, that Frank was knocked from her arms and pitched into Lifeboat 11 as it was lowered to the water. Mrs. Aks searched frantically for her son aboard the sinking ship without success and tried to get into Lifeboat 13, but it was full. Then a woman stepped out to look for someone and Mrs. Aks took her place.

Six-year-old Nana Harper was asleep in her second-class stateroom with her cousin, Jessie Leitch, when Nana's father, a Scottish minister who was on his way to a series of revival meetings in Chicago, banged on their door and told them *Titanic* had struck an iceberg. While Jessie dressed, Mr. Harper left to get further details and returned to state that lifebelts were to be worn. He then carried Nana out onto a deck, where the women were told to go to the upper deck. Jessie climbed an iron ladder, with Mr. Harper following and carrying Nana. Assured that *Titanic* could not sink, the women and children were told to get into the lifeboats as a precaution and the men would follow. Jessie and Nana got into Lifeboat 11 and were lowered away. Nana's only recollection of the event was of sitting on Jessie's lap as they watched *Titanic* go under.

The eight-person Allison party from Montreal was returning from a holiday in England and was split between first and second class. While parents Hud and Bessie shared a first-class stateroom, Loraine (34 months) was in a cabin next door with the family maid, and Trevor (11 months) was in another with the nanny. When *Titanic* hit the iceberg, a female bedroom steward told the maid to get dressed. She ignored the warning and returned to bed as soon as the steward left. A fellow passenger finally woke her up and she got away in Lifeboat 8, which was launched at 1:00 A.M. As Loraine was not with the maid, it is assumed that the maid had first delivered Loraine to her mother, Bessie.

In the meantime, Mr. Allison had left the stateroom to find out what was going on. Meanwhile—and apparently without telling anyone—the nanny took baby Trevor down to second-class, probably to wake up the cook and the chauffeur. Once Mr. Allison returned, he put his wife and Loraine into Lifeboat 6 and then left, possibly to look for the nanny and Trevor. Shortly afterward, Mrs. Allison was so worried about Trevor when she could not see him that she took Loraine and left the lifeboat. Unfortunately, unknown to Mrs. Allison, the nanny was already safely in No. 11 with Trevor—on the other side and at the other end of *Titanic*. As she searched frantically for her baby, did it finally dawn on Mrs. Allison that Trevor must be in a lifeboat with his nanny?

Lifeboat 13 (seventh starboard) – 1:40

Lifeboat 13 had been lowered to A Deck to take on passengers. It carried only one less than its rating of sixty-five, possibly because of rising feelings of panic. Someone who did not panic was Ruth Becker, one of eight children aboard. With her mom and two younger siblings, Marion and baby Richard, safely away in Lifeboat 11, she calmly approached the next boat in line, Lifeboat 13, and asked if she could get in it. A sailor promptly lifted her up and dropped her into the boat.

Returning to San Francisco after a visit to Sweden, Mrs. Sandström occupied a third-class cabin on *Titanic* with her American-born children, Marguerite (4) and Beatrice (20 months). Also in the cabin were Mrs. Ström and her American-born daughter, Telma (28 months), who were returning to Indiana. When a steward awoke Mrs. Sandström, she did not believe anything could happen but went up to the boat deck in any case. The Ströms followed her, led by Mrs. Ström's brother. On deck, Mrs. Sandström passed two full lifeboats and thought she and her daughters would not make it into a boat. Then she came to a third lifeboat with her cabin steward already in it. He saw the Sandströms, calmed Mrs. Sandström down, and helped them into the boat. Meanwhile, Mrs. Ström, her brother, and her daughter, Telma, had become separated from the Sandströms in the crowded confusion and made it to the stern at 2:15 A.M. By then, all the lifeboats were gone, and they agreed to "accompany each other into the deep." Then the liner made a sudden lurch, and the brother was tossed into the water with his sister and Telma, who were quickly lost to sight. He was able to scramble aboard a collapsible, but Telma and her mom died in the sinking.

Four other third-class children escaped in Lifeboat 13. The youngest was Virginia Emanuel (6), the daughter of American actress and would-be singer Elise Martin, along with her nursemaid. Brooklyn-born Arthur Olsen (9), who had been brought up in Norway by his grandmother after his mother died six years earlier, was travelling with his dad and a Norwegian sailor. Mr. Olsen woke Arthur up and told him to get dressed, but when they exited their cabin, the companionways were already knee-deep in water. At the bottom of a stairwell, Arthur saw a woman holding her baby tightly and howling in distress. The sight so upset him that he began to cry; it was an image he retained for the rest of his life. Mr. Olsen fought his way to the upper decks and, when denied entry into a boat, asked a young woman to look after his son. He then placed Arthur in the lifeboat, saying, "It may be a long time before I see you. Be a good boy, Artie." Mr. Olsen remained on board and was lost, but his sailor friend managed to get into the boat and survived.

The eldest son, Swedish teenager Johan Svensson (14) was travelling alone to join his father and a sister in South Dakota, while his mother and five other siblings were to follow later. As *Titanic* sank, Johan managed to sneak onto the first-class boat deck and finally made it into Lifeboat 13, after being denied entry into two other boats. After a struggle through the crowd, Irish immigrant Nora O'Leary, who was in a party led by Daniel Buckley, made it to the boat deck and got into the lifeboat. In her group of seven, only four made it into boats: Nora, both older females, and Buckley as the lone male. Once in the lifeboat, Nora and her Irish travelling companions started to say the rosary.

Two passengers in Lifeboat 13 were there without their children. Dr. Dodge had seen his wife and son into Lifeboat 5, the second boat to be launched, and somehow managed to find a seat in No. 13. Similarly, Mrs. Aks, whose son Frank was in Lifeboat 11, also found a place in it.

Returning to the United States after teaching in Siam for two years, second-class passenger Sylvia Caldwell (who had earlier asked a steward if the ship was unsinkable), climbed in, while her husband, Albert, had to carry ten-month-old Alden. Sylvia suffered from neurasthenia and could not hold her baby. Mr. Caldwell then handed the boy, wearing only a nightgown, to a steward so he could get in. Alden was passed back to his dad in the stern, who then passed him to another woman passenger so he could help row. The Caldwells were the last ones to get into Lifeboat 13.

Lifeboat 15 nearly drops onto Lifeboat 13. The Graph, *April 27, 1912.*

As Lifeboat 13 was being lowered away, Lifeboat 15 nearly dropped onto it from above, which would have swamped No. 13. Fortunately, a sailor had a knife and quickly cut the ropes, allowing the lower boat to hit the water and get away just before No. 15 would have come down on top of it. When Lifeboat 13 was launched, two hours had passed since the collision, and twelve of *Titanic's* twenty lifeboats had been launched, all in the last hour. They carried to safety 34 of the 156 children aboard the ship. More than five and a half times as many adult males—some 192—were also scattered throughout these dozen boats.

CHAPTER 5

THE LAST FORTY MINUTES

Mother and I then were permitted through the gateway, and the crewman in charge reached out to grasp the arm of Alfred Rush to pull him through because he must have felt that the young lad was not much older than me, and he was not very tall for his age, but Alfred had not been stalling. He jerked his arm out of the sailor's hand and with his head held high said, and I quote, "No! I'm staying here with the men." At age 16 [17], he died a hero.

—Frankie Goldsmith, 9 on *Titanic*

By 1:40 A.M. there was no doubt that *Titanic* was going to sink. Any hope that anyone may have had that the liner would stay afloat had disappeared in the face of the inevitable. Everyone still onboard knew that *Titanic's*—and possibly their—end was at hand. Yet officers and crewmen remained in control, although the situation on deck, especially near the remaining lifeboats, was described by some as "chaotic."

The only two reported cases of groups of men attempting to get into lifeboats without permission occurred within the last forty minutes. The first group simply got into a boat before it was due to be launched, while the second one rushed a lifeboat. The men who got into the first one meekly obeyed when ordered out, while the mob in the second boat was successfully beaten back by crewmen, assisted by other passengers.

Lifeboat 15 (eighth starboard) – 1:40

Lifeboat 15 was full, having taken on mostly third-class passengers from both the boat deck and A Deck. It was at the stern of the ship and was the last regular lifeboat to be lowered over the starboard side. Among its sixty-five to seventy occupants were six children, as well as twenty crewmen and a female crew member. Five of the children had escaped with their mothers, while one got away with her dad. The seven-member Swedish-American Asplund family: father, mother, Filip (13), Clarence (9), twins Carl and Lillian (5), and Felix (3), was travelling third class, returning to Massachusetts after a five-year absence. Mr. Asplund passed Lillian and Felix through a window on A Deck (which had been opened to let first-class passengers out) and into the lifeboat as it was lowered past. Mrs. Asplund wanted to remain with her husband but was flung into the same boat. The others in the family perished. For the rest of her life, Lillian maintained she was haunted by the faces of her dad and brothers peering over the rail at her. In the boat, the three huddled together for warmth, with Felix on his mom's lap and Lillian between her knees.

Like Lillian and Felix Asplund, Harold (4) and Eleanor (20 months) Johnson made it into No. 15 with their mom. After a year-long stay in Finland, besides her two children, Mrs. Johnson was escorting two Swedish girls in their twenties—Helmina Nilsson and Elin Braf—to the United States. After *Titanic* hit the iceberg, Mrs. Johnson took her children and her travelling companions to the upper decks, where she climbed into the boat with Eleanor, followed by Helmina. But the other girl, who was holding Harold, was frozen with fear and remained on the deck, unable to move. Mrs. Johnson called out repeatedly for Harold to join her, without success. Finally, someone pulled Harold from Elin's arms and passed him into the boat. Elin remained on deck and died.

Elin had brought a doll with her on the voyage to give to her niece in the United States. According to Helmina, Elin carried the doll with her onto the upper deck. During one of the many underwater expeditions to the *Titanic* wreck site, a haunting image of a doll's head was photographed in the *Titanic*'s debris field. It is located near the wreck's stern, where No. 15 was launched. Could it be Elin's?

Twenty-six-month-old Finn Hildur Hirvonen was travelling third class with her mom on their way to join Mr. Hirvonen in Pennsylvania, where he had secured employment in a steel factory a year earlier. Mrs. Hirvonen's brother and a family friend accompanied mother and daughter. As *Titanic* sank, the brother and the friend managed to get from the single men's quarters in the forward part of the ship to the stern, where the women resided. The brother put his sister and Hildur into Lifeboat 15 and then got in with the friend.

Manca Karun (4), as noted earlier, was travelling from the part of Austria-Hungary that is modern-day Slovenia with her dad. One of the few non-Lebanese immigrant families who boarded at Cherbourg, they were on their way to Illinois with Mr. Karun's brother-in-law to join Mrs. Karun and four of Manca's siblings. Manca and her father made it into Lifeboat 15, but the brother-in-law perished.

As mentioned previously, Lifeboat 15 was the boat that nearly dropped onto Lifeboat 13 as it was being lowered away. Only the quick actions of a sailor who cut through the ropes of No. 13, reacting to the panicked screams of passengers in both boats, allowed it to hit the water and move out of the way just before No. 15 came crashing down.

Lifeboat 2 (sixth port) – 1:45

Lifeboat 2 was the second emergency cutter and was permanently swung out over the port side. By now, water had climbed over the top of *Titanic*'s bow and the liner had a noticeable list to port. Second Officer

Titanic's *port side with Lifeboat 2 in the distance.*

Lightoller needed to launch the cutter in a hurry so that its davits could be used to launch Collapsible D, stored on deck beside it. Although numbers claimed aboard it vary greatly, from seventeen to thirty (it could carry forty), it included four crewmen and four children. Fourth Officer Boxhall was in charge, having been directed aboard by Lightoller. Before that happened, Lightoller ordered a group of about twenty-five crewmen and male passengers, who had gotten into the boat, "Get out of there you damned cowards! I'd like to see everyone of you overboard!" The pistol in his hand emphasized the seriousness of his threat, even though it was not loaded. The men quietly obeyed, and Lightoller told the women and children to get into the boat. Returning to their home in St. Louis after a holiday in Europe, Georgette Madill, her recently widowed mother, her cousin, and her mother's maid all got into No. 2.

Minnie Coutts and her boys were emigrating from London to New York to join Mr. Coutts, who had gone ahead and obtained employment in his engraving trade. Although awakened by the crash, Mrs. Coutts lay awake in her third-class bunk for about fifteen minutes before she got up to see what had happened. She returned, dressed Willie (9) and Neville (3), and put lifebelts on them, although she could not find one for herself. Not wanting to waste any precious time, Mrs. Coutts made it to the steerage common area with Neville and Willie but could not find a way to the upper decks. Just then, a crewman came along and led the family to the boat deck.

When Mrs. Coutts told the sailor she did not have a lifebelt, a nearby American passenger overheard her and gave her his, saying, "If I go down, please pray for me." Willie was wearing a straw boater hat at the time and was initially refused entry into the lifeboat, probably because the hat made him look older. When his mother proclaimed, "If he doesn't go, we aren't going," the family was allowed in the boat.

Swiss four-year-old Louise Kink-Heilmann was travelling third class with her father, mother, an aunt, and an uncle, on their way to a new life in Milwaukee, Wisconsin. When the collision occurred, her dad and his brother went up four decks to see what was happening. They quickly returned to their cabin, dressed, put on life preservers, and remained there until water began pouring in. They then left to find the rest of the family before proceeding to the boat deck. Somehow during the confusion, Mr.

Kink's brother and sister became lost in the crowd. He never saw them again. Her father put Louise and her mom into No. 2 but was forced to stay back. As the lifeboat was about to be lowered away, his wife and daughter shouted for Mr. Kink, so he jumped into it. Boxhall did not eject him.

Lifeboat 4 (seventh port) – 1:50

Although Lifeboat 4 was the second-last standard one to be launched, it was originally intended to be first. It had initially been lowered to A Deck to cater to first-class passengers, who had been directed there. When a special tool to open the windows could not be found, somehow in the confusion the lifeboat was forgotten about and left hanging in its falls just outside the windows. Several first-class passengers, including some millionaires, waited patiently—and somewhat annoyed—for the windows to be opened, until a steward came along and directed them to the boat deck.

When Second Officer Lightoller discovered them there, he promptly sent them back down to A Deck as the tool to open the windows had been found. Because *Titanic*'s list to port had caused No. 4 to swing too far from the liner's side for easy access, grappling hooks were used to pull it closer, while a deck chair was used to form a small gangway for women and children to cross safely. Even at this late stage, only about thirty-three or thirty-four people were in the boat, including four crewmen.

Six children were among the people in No. 4, three in each of first and second class. Jack Ryerson, his family, and two servants were returning from a European holiday to the United States due to the death of his older brother, a student at Yale, in a car accident. Lightoller stopped thirteen-year-old Jack from getting into the boat, claiming he was too old. When Jack's father protested loudly, Lightoller relented and allowed the boy in, along with his mother, two older sisters, a maid, and a governess. Mr. Ryerson died.

After the crash, wealthy Philadelphian William Carter woke his wife, Lucile, told her to get dressed and go to the upper deck. Mrs. Carter and her maid took the children to A Deck and were loaded into Lifeboat 4. Mr. Carter was nowhere to be seen. Young William, who had earlier been amazed at *Titanic*'s elegance, cried at being forced to leave his beloved Airedale behind, until John Jacob Astor, whose pregnant wife, Madeleine, was also in No. 4, assured the boy he would look after the dog. One story states that when Mrs. Carter observed the exchange between Lightoller and Ryerson over Jack, she immediately took her hat off and put it on her son, who was just a little more than a year younger than Jack, ostensibly against the cold night air—or to disguise him as a girl. Another account states that Mrs. Carter "found" the hat in the boat.

Finn Anna Hämäläinen, the mother of American-born fourteen-month-old Viljo, recalled that, on A Deck, the officer who was loading Lifeboat 4 "looked around and saw me, with the baby in my arms...he shoved me into the boat.... We were only a short distance away when the ship sank." According to Mrs. Hämäläinen, she became separated from her travelling companion due to the "crowd and so much excitement" on deck. Her companion did not survive.

Emily Richards's mom rushed into her cabin after the collision to rouse her, saying "something has gone wrong." After venturing out on deck in her nightgown and being told by a crewman to put on a life preserver, Mrs. Richards returned to her cabin, got dressed, and took William (3) and Sibley (10 months) onto A Deck, where they were pushed through a window into Lifeboat 4. While the boys' grandmother, aunt, and great-aunt survived, the boy's uncle, Mrs. Richards's brother, perished in the disaster.

Lifeboat 10 (eighth port) – 1:55

Although Lifeboat 10 was the last standard one to be launched, it was only half full and carried about thirty-four people, almost three-quarters of them women. Four of the women had their children with them: two with one child each and two with two children. All were in second class except the Deans, who were travelling third class. The chief baker, Charles Joughin, had been assigned to command No. 10, but he became so absorbed in loading children—in fact, tossing them into the lifeboat—that he failed to get in himself. He later ended up in the water and, liberally fortified by alcohol just before *Titanic* went under, survived long enough to be picked up by Collapsible B.

James Drew happened to be on deck having a smoke when *Titanic* hit the iceberg. He returned to his cabin to have his wife and surrogate son, Marshall (whose mother had died shortly after his birth), dress and put on their life preservers. Mr. Drew escorted them to Lifeboat 10, said his goodbyes, and stood back. Marshall later remembered the difficulties in lowering the lifeboat, with the ropes jamming in the pulleys several times and causing a sudden drop each time they were freed until they reached the water.

French natives Antoinine and Albert Mallet were travelling with their twenty-two-month-old son, André, returning to Montreal, where Mr. Mallet worked for a liquor company, after a two-month visit to both their mothers in Paris. Although details are not known, mom and son got away safely in No. 10, while Mr. Mallet died in the sinking, along with a family friend who had been travelling with them.

The West family, father (who was emigrating to start a fruit farm in Florida), mother, and daughters Constance (4) and Barbara (10 months), was asleep when the collision occurred. It only woke Mrs. West, who was pregnant. Initially, she thought little of it, until she heard passengers scurrying past outside her cabin. Then a steward knocked on the door and told the family to get up and dress warmly. Mr. West put life preservers on Barbara and Constance and carried them to the boat deck, while his wife followed. After ensuring they were safely in No. 10, he went back to their cabin to get a flask of hot milk. When he returned, the lifeboat was already being lowered away, so he descended a rope to the boat, passed the thermos to his wife, said his farewells, and climbed back up to the boat deck. While Mr. West voluntarily returned to a sure death, a couple of men were already hidden under women's skirts in the bottom of the lifeboat, where they had to be asked to put out their cigarettes, in case they set the skirts on fire.

The Deans were en route to Kansas, where Mr. Dean planned to operate a tobacco shop. Bert (23 months) and Millvina (2 months—the youngest person aboard) were the only third-class children to get into Lifeboat 10. Mr. Dean felt the crash, woke his wife, and went on deck to see what had happened. When he returned, he told his wife to dress herself and the children warmly before they all proceeded to the lifeboats. At this point, accounts vary as to what happened next. One version has Mrs. Dean and the children safely entering No. 10, while the other has Bert becoming separated from his family in the crowd and ending up in another lifeboat, only to be reunited with his mom on the rescue ship *Carpathia*. But no records exist of Bert being on any other lifeboat. Both versions agree on one thing: Mr. Dean died in the sinking.

Widow Margaret Rice was returning to the United States with her five boys after an unsuccessful attempt to settle in her native Ireland. One of Margaret's fellow Irish travelling companions, who survived the sinking in Lifeboat 10, stated later she saw Margaret on the port side, holding Francis (31 months) to her breast, with Albert (10), George (8), Eric (6), and Arthur (4) clutching her skirts. It is easy to imagine the heart-rending scene of Margaret and her boys huddled together, watching in terror as the waters rose higher about them and—certainly for the older ones—horribly aware there was no escape. As a Catholic, no doubt Margaret was saying her prayers and encouraging the older boys to pray with her.

Lifeboat C (ninth starboard) – 2:00

Widow Rhoda Abbott and her boys, Rossmore (16) and Eugene (13), were also returning to the United States after their unsuccessful effort to settle in Rhoda's home county of Hertfordshire. The three somehow made it to the stern of the boat deck and then moved slowly forward through an area strewn with ropes and other debris from earlier lifeboat launchings. By the time they reached the starboard side of the bridge, only the collapsibles were left. Collapsible C was being loaded, but Rhoda believed her sons would not be allowed in it because of their ages, so stepped back when her turn came. Several of Rhoda's new acquaintances were already in Collapsible C. One of them later recalled the twinge of sadness she felt, knowing all three would likely perish.

Lifeboat C was the first of the collapsibles to be launched, carrying forty-seven people. It was one of only two boats that had more women than men in it. There were also thirteen children in the collapsible, all third class, and all but one of them Lebanese.

Nine-year-old Frankie Goldsmith, who was immigrating to Detroit from Kent with his parents, was the only non-Lebanese child in the lifeboat. After the collision, Frankie (who stuffed gumdrops into his pockets "like seasickness pills"), his parents, and their two male travelling companions made it to the forward part of the boat deck, where crewmen were preparing to launch the collapsibles. After Mr. Goldsmith escorted his wife and child to Collapsible C, Frankie vividly recalled his chum, Alfred Rush (17), voluntarily stepping back to stay with the men. All three men died.

One of the most amazing stories of securing places in a lifeboat concerns Latifa Baclini, her three daughters, Maria (5), Eugenie (3), and Helen (33 months), and the family's neighbour Adele Kiamie (15). After the collision occurred, Mrs. Baclini woke the children, dressed them, and put on their lifebelts before proceeding to the lifeboats with Adele. Somehow, Mrs. Baclini, only twenty-three years old herself and speaking no English, managed to navigate her way from steerage through a maze of passageways and stairs to reach the boat deck, while she and Adele carried the younger girls. On deck, they all got into Collapsible C. Mrs. Baclini's dogged determination resulted in the largest third-class family group to survive the disaster without a loss.

When *Titanic* hit the iceberg, Anna Thomas had already put George (8) to bed but was anxiously awaiting the return of his older sister, Mary (9), who spent much of her time running around the ship and hiding in empty cabins with other children. Mrs. Thomas was standing at the open door to her cabin when the jolt slammed the door shut on her hand, injuring it. While Mrs. Thomas looked after her hand, several Lebanese men went to see what was wrong. When they returned, they said they had been told the ship was in danger—but to stay in their cabins and pray. Despite this direction, curiosity got the better of Mrs. Thomas and she dressed George before making her way up to the boat deck.

When she got there, she told George to stay by a lifeboat and returned to look for Mary. As Mrs. Thomas arrived at her cabin, Mary came out of a nearby vacant one where she had been sleeping. Mrs. Thomas quickly dressed Mary and grabbed a few valuables, including an all-important piece of paper with her intended destination in the United States. Mother and daughter made their way to the boat deck, where they found George at the spot his mom had left him. By this time, George was quite anxious, as several people had tried to put him into a lifeboat without his mom and sister. But young George stood firm, and all three got into Collapsible C.

Sa'id and Mary Nackid were travelling with their thirteen-month-old daughter, Maria. After Mr. Nackid heard a loud noise, he got his family dressed, and they then made their way to the boat deck. Somehow all three managed to get into Collapsible C. As Mr. Nackid was in fear of being forced out, he hid in the bottom of the boat undercover.

After feeling a bump when *Titanic* scraped along the iceberg, fourteen-year-old Amelia Garrett convinced her twelve-year-old brother, Louis, to investigate the noises outside their cabin door. Louis eventually complied and, on seeing fellow passengers streaming by, the two youngsters (who had left their dad behind in Cherbourg) proceeded to the boat deck. Suddenly, Amelia remembered the $500 (C$21,185) her father had entrusted to her before departure, so the two returned to their cabin. By the time they got there, water was already filling the passageway, and Amelia could not open the door. The two teenagers went all the way back to the boat deck and secured places in Collapsible C.

Michael (4) and Mary (32 months) Joseph were sleeping in their cabin with their twenty-three-year-old mom when *Titanic* hit the iceberg. The impact awakened Mrs. Joseph and, persuaded by the noise outside the cabin, she got up, dressed, and then woke and dressed the children. She carried Mary in her arms and told Michael to hold onto her skirt as she manoeuvred her way through a crowd of confused steerage passengers toward the upper decks. Somewhere in the chaos, Michael lost his grip on his mom's skirt and became separated from her. A male stranger grabbed Michael's hand and rushed him toward the lifeboats. Mrs. Joseph could see them disappear into the crowd ahead of her and hurried along as best she could while carrying Mary but arrived at Collapsible C without seeing them again. A sobbing Mrs. Joseph got into the boat with Mary, not knowing what had happened to Michael.

The Boreks—mother Amenia and sons George (7) and William (4)—were a family from Hardin. The collision jolted Mrs. Borek's brother-in-law and his new bride, Celiney (Amenia's younger sister, described as either fourteen, fifteen, or seventeen), out of their bed. The newlyweds decided to investigate, and Celiney—still in her nightclothes—followed her husband through the ship to the engine room, where a quick glance at the chaos amid the rising water sent them scurrying back to steerage to alert their family and friends.

Shouting "Yallah!"—meaning "Let's go!" or "Come on!"—they told the others to leave their belongings behind and make their way to the upper decks. Celiney (even now still in her nightclothes) and her husband helped Mrs. Borek and her boys make their way along corridors and up staircases and ladders. George and William could only move so fast, so the other three half-dragged and half-carried them through the below-decks maze, sometimes running into blocked passageways and having to backtrack. Eventually, they came out on deck, by now a scene of chaos. A mob of men tried to rush the collapsible and some even succeeded in getting in. First Officer Murdoch fired his pistol into the air and ordered them, "Get out of this! Clear out of this!" Attracted by the shots, first-class passengers Hugh Woolner and Mauritz Björnström-Steffansson arrived and helped the crew to forcibly remove the interlopers from the boat. The two men then left to find a lifeboat they could board.

Amenia and George got into Collapsible C, while Celiney's husband embraced her before lifting her into the collapsible. He then passed William to her. Celiney waved to him to get in, but as he tried to do so, an officer put a pistol to his head and said, "Women and children first." Her husband, who spoke English, tried to reason with the officer, while Celiney shouted in Arabic that the boat still had room. When it became obvious that the officer was not going to change his mind, Celiney tried to climb out but was held back by others. Her husband moved away.

Remarkably, although eight third-class Lebanese children died, fifteen got away. In many cases, they were led by a young mom who did not speak English and had to traverse a labyrinth of corridors and stairwells before coming out onto the boat deck. Shortly afterward, just before Collapsible C was lowered, White Star Line Chairman J. Bruce Ismay quietly climbed into the boat and survived, as did Mr. Carter, who had earlier put his family into Lifeboat 4. Surely Rhoda Abbott and her boys should have taken priority over them? And while Collapsible C was being rowed away from *Titanic*, four male Chinese steerage passengers were found in the boat.

Lifeboat D (ninth port) – 2:05

Collapsible D was the last lifeboat to leave *Titanic* with children. Second Officer Lightoller and some men managed to get the collapsible into the empty davits of Lifeboat 2 so it could be launched. Even though it was obvious the ship would sink in a few minutes, the collapsible was not filled to its capacity of forty-seven. Estimates vary greatly, but when lowered away, it likely carried only eighteen persons, including four children. Four-year-old Michael Joseph, who had been separated from his mom and sister as they got into Collapsible C and was left standing alone on the deck, had a miraculous escape. A male stranger took him by the hand and placed him safely into Collapsible D. Michael always believed it was his guardian angel who had stretched out his hand and hurried him into the collapsible. Michael was the last Lebanese passenger to escape from the sinking ship.

On her way to join her brother in New York, sixteen-year-old Erna Andersson was travelling third class in the company of four fellow Finns: a married couple and the wife's two brothers. Erna got into Collapsible C along with the wife, while their three male travelling companions died.

After the collision, tailor Michel Navratil dressed his two boys, Michel Jr. (3) and Edmond (25 months)—whom he was secretly taking from his divorced wife—in their warm chinchilla coats with the assistance of another passenger. They went up to the boat deck, where Navratil saw the bow was already under water and only three collapsibles were left. By now, Second Officer Lightoller had formed a ring of crewmen around Collapsible D to hold back any men, allowing in only women and children. Navratil passed his boys through the human chain to some women, who wrapped them up warmly.

Meanwhile, Hugh Woolner and Mauritz Björnström-Steffansson had descended to a now-deserted A Deck just as Collapsible D was being lowered past the windows. The two decided to take their chances and jumped. Björnström-Steffansson landed in the bow, but Woolner ended up clinging onto the gunwale with his feet hanging in the water. Björnström-Steffansson pulled him aboard. The two first-class male passengers were saved, while there was still room for at least another twenty-five children in the collapsible.

Lifeboats A (tenth starboard) and B (tenth port) – 2:15

The last two boats launched carried no children. As the crew worked frantically to launch the only lifeboat left on the starboard side, Collapsible A, *Titanic* made its final plunge. The collapsible was washed overboard in an upright position and had a few centimetres of cold water in its bottom. Standing on the deck nearby, Rhoda Abbott and her sons were abruptly swept into the icy waters. She grabbed her boys' hands but could not hang on in the turbulence created by *Titanic* as it went under.

As she attempted to keep herself afloat, Rhoda desperately tried to find the boys among others thrashing about and shouting in the swirling waters but failed. Just as she was about to give up, a strong arm reached out and pulled her into Collapsible A. Rhoda survived, but her boys died. Although Eugene's body was not found, Rossmore's was recovered. Collapsible B had been washed overboard upside down.

Once *Titanic* struck the iceberg, Alma Pålsson spent quite a bit of time dressing her four children against the frigid night air, so long, in fact, that when she arrived on deck, all the lifeboats had been launched. Outside, Alma ran into August Andersson (a fellow Swede travelling under the assumed name of Wennerström), whom she had met earlier. She often played the mouth organ to entertain her children, and Andersson recalled she did that now to keep them calm. Alma also asked Andersson to help her by holding two of the children, but when the waters flooded over them, he lost his grip, and the children disappeared. He managed to get into Collapsible A, but Alma and her four children could not be found.

Titanic *sank bow first, with lights blazing. Drawn for* The Sphere *by F. Matania.*

Collapsibles C and D were the last lifeboats launched with children onboard; those seventeen children represent 23 percent of all seventy-three children who survived. In other words, almost one-quarter of the children who were saved escaped just minutes before the ship sank. Still on board were another eighty-three children, consisting of seventy-eight passengers and five crew members, left to go down with the ship or succumb to the frigid waters. Meanwhile, some three hundred males over the age of sixteen, either passengers or crew, escaped in the lifeboats.

Three of *Titanic*'s standard lifeboats could have carried all the children to safety—as well as an accompanying parent or guardian for each child or set of siblings.

Women and *children* first?

CHILD SURVIVAL RATES			
All Classes & Crew	Male	Female	Total
Survived	32	41	73
Lost	55	28	83
Total	87	69	156
Percentage saved	37%	59%	47%

No entire family of any size was lost in first or second class. Yet eight third-class families that perished in their entirety accounted for thirty-nine out of eighty-three children who died—almost half of the total. In fact, only one quarter of all families who boarded *Titanic* arrived intact in New York. Families lost along with four or more children are shown in the table below (where only one parent is mentioned, either the husband was not on *Titanic* or, in the case of Margaret Rice, there was no husband).

Lifeboats by Launch Time

When *Titanic* hit the iceberg at 11:40 P.M., it took one hour before the first lifeboat was launched. Port side loading was overseen by Second Officer Lightoller, who believed his directions meant to load women and children only. On the starboard side, First Officer Murdoch was in charge of loading and interpreted the direction to mean women and children first, but men if room was still available. While it is known which children got into which lifeboat, the same cannot be said for all adult passengers and crew. Despite years of research by dedicated enthusiasts, among

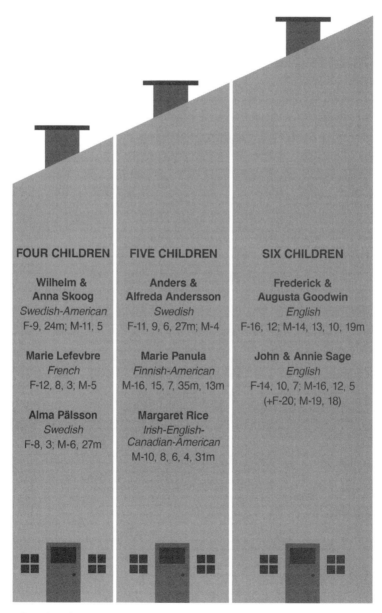

FOUR CHILDREN

**Wilhelm &
Anna Skoog**
Swedish-American
F-9, 24m; M-11, 5

Marie Lefevbre
French
F-12, 8, 3; M-5

Alma Pälsson
Swedish
F-8, 3; M-6, 27m

FIVE CHILDREN

**Anders &
Alfreda Andersson**
Swedish
F-11, 9, 6, 27m; M-4

Marie Panula
Finnish-American
M-16, 15, 7, 35m, 13m

Margaret Rice
*Irish-English-
Canadian-American*
M-10, 8, 6, 4, 31m

SIX CHILDREN

**Frederick &
Augusta Goodwin**
English
F-16, 12; M-14, 13, 10, 19m

John & Annie Sage
English
F-14, 10, 7; M-16, 12, 5
(+F-20; M-19, 18)

Large families lost on Titanic, *by sex, age, and nationality.*

the 640 or so adults who escaped, it is unknown in which lifeboat some of them got away. While this may seem strange to our data collection–driven age, it was a fact of life in the pre-computer and -smartphone era. While the numbers in each lifeboat varied greatly—from a low of twelve to a high of seventy—in overall terms, the lifeboats were filled to only 60 percent of their capacity of 1,178. Among the pregnant women, only Ada Doling and Hannah O'Brien cannot be placed in a lifeboat. (For more about them, see Chapter 11.)

Est launch time (A.M.)	Life-boat no. Port	Life-boat no. Stbd	Cap-acity	No. of chil-dren	Names	Notes
12:40		7	64	0		Margaret Hays, who later kept Navratil boys, & dog
12:43		5	64	1	Washington Dodge Jr. (with mother, father in LB 13)	
1:00		3	64	1	Douglas Spedden (with parents)	
1:00	8		64	0		
1:05		1	40	0		
1:10	6		64	0		pregnant Eloise Smith
1:20	16		64	3	Karen Abelseth (with friend), Ellen Corr, Assed Thomas (mother in LB 14)	Edwina Troutt looked after Assed Thomas

Est launch time (A.M.)	Life-boat no. Port	Life-boat no. Stbd	Cap-acity	No. of chil-dren	Names	Notes
1:25	14		64	11	Edith Brown (with mother; father lost), Marjorie Collyer (with mother; father lost), John Davies Jr. (with mother), Eva Hart (with mother; father lost), Simonne & Louise Laroche (with mother; father lost), Madeline Mellenger (with mother), Meyer Moore (with mother), Thelma Thomas (son in LB 16), Joan & Ralph Wells (with mother)	pregnant Juliette Laroche
1:30	12		64	1	Laura Cribb (father lost)	
1:30		9	64	2	Mary Lines (with mother), Bertha Watt (with mother)	
1:35		11	64	7	Frank Aks (mother in LB 13), Trevor Allison (with nurse), Marion & Richard Becker (with mother; sister in LB 13), Nana Harper (with cousin; father lost), Winnie & Phyllis Quick (with mother)	pregnant Argene del Carlo pregnant Kate Phillips

Est launch time (A.M.)	Life-boat no. Port	Life-boat no. Stbd	Cap-acity	No. of chil-dren	Names	Notes
1:40		13	64	8	Ruth Becker (mother in LB 11), Alden Caldwell (with parents), Virginia Emanuel (with nanny), Nora O'Leary, Arthur Olsen, Johan Svensson, Marguerite & Beatrice Sandström (with mother)	Dr. Washington Dodge Leah Aks
1:40		15	64	6	Lillian & Felix Asplund, (with mother; father & siblings lost), Hildur Hirvonen (with mother), Harold & Eleanor Johnson (with mother), Manca Karun (with father)	
1:45	2		40	4	Willie & Neville Coutts (with mother), Louise Kink-Heilmann (with parents), Georgette Madill (with mother)	

Est launch time (A.M.)	Life-boat no. Port	Life-boat no. Stbd	Cap-acity	No. of chil-dren	Names	Notes
1:50	4		64	6	Lucile & William Carter II (with mother; father in LB C), Viljo Hämäläinen (with mother), William & Sibley Richards (with mother), Jack Ryerson (with mother & siblings; father lost)	William Carter did not want to leave his dog behind pregnant Madeleine Astor
1:55	10		64	6	Bert & Millvina Dean (with mother; father lost), Marshall Drew (with aunt; uncle lost), André Mallet (with mother; father lost), Constance & Barbara West (with mother; father lost)	pregnant Ada West pregnant Mary Marvin
2:00		C	47	13	Maria, Eugenie, & Helen Baclini (with mother), Adele Kiamie (with the Baclinis), George & William Borek (with mother), Amelia & Louis Garrett, Mary Joseph (with mother), Maria Nackid (with parents), George & Mary Thomas (with mother), Frankie Goldsmith (with mother; father lost)	J. Bruce Ismay William Carter

Est launch time (A.M.)	Life-boat no. Port	Life-boat no. Stbd	Cap-acity	No. of chil-dren	Names	Notes
2:05	D		47	4	Erna Andersson, Michel Jr. & Edmond Navratil (father lost), Michael Joseph (mother in LB C)	pregnant Maria Backström
2:15		A	47	0		Washed overboard, Rhoda Abbott later transferred to D
2:15	B		47	0		Washed overboard upside down
Totals			1,178	73		

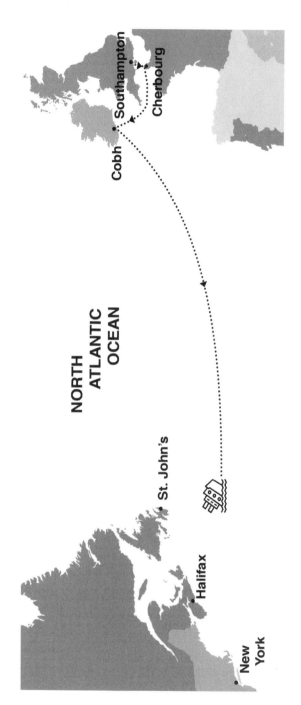

Titanic's *route, April 10 to April 15, 1912.*

CHAPTER 6

DELIVERANCE

I woke up in daylight and 360 degrees around us there were icebergs. You would think you were in the Arctic Circle. We were so close to some of the icebergs the crewmen could have touched them with the oars.

—Marshall Drew, 8 on *Titanic*

The Cunard liner *Carpathia* was on its way from New York City to Fiume, Austria-Hungary (now Rijeka, Croatia), with 240 crew and 743 passengers aboard. Shortly after midnight on Monday, April 15, Harold Cottam, the lone wireless operator, was tired after seventeen straight hours on duty with only a short break for lunch. While waiting for acknowledgement of the receipt of a Morse code message he had sent to the liner *Parisian* earlier, Cottam checked other frequencies for any interesting transmissions. On Cape Cod's frequency, he picked up several messages for *Titanic* that had gone unanswered. Cottam switched frequencies again, this time to *Titanic*, and asked if the liner's operator (Jack Phillips) knew there was a batch of messages for him from Cape Cod. Without waiting for Cottam to finish his transmission, Phillips broke in and asked *Carpathia* to come at once as *Titanic* had "struck a berg." When Cottam asked if Phillips required assistance, the reply was instant: "Yes. Come quick."

Cottam ran to the bridge and passed the message to First Officer Horace Dean, who immediately entered the cabin of *Carpathia*'s captain, without knocking and with Cottam in tow. Captain Arthur Rostron was initially upset at such a rude interruption—especially just as he was about to drop off to sleep—but when *Titanic*'s situation was explained to him, he instantly grasped its seriousness. Before he even got out of bed, Rostron ordered *Carpathia* turned around. He then went to the nearby chart room and calculated the course, distance, and time to *Titanic*. It was ninety-three kilometres (fifty-eight miles) away; how long would it take his ship to get there?

ROSTRON TO THE RESCUE

Captain Rostron's actions were a dazzling example of a term not even in use at the time: multi-tasking. Among his many rapid-fire instructions:

• to the chief engineer: pile on as much coal as possible, call out off-duty stokers to assist, cut off all heat and hot water in the cabins to keep as much steam as possible in the boilers.

• to the first officer: cease all routine work to organize the ship for rescue operations; all seamen to be on deck as lookouts and to swing lifeboats out; rig electric lights at each gangway and over the side.

• to the second officer: station yourself on the starboard bridge wing to look out for lights or flares, as well as icebergs.

• to the chief steward: call out staff and make coffee for all crew members; have hot soup, coffee, tea, brandy, and whisky available for survivors; pile blankets at every gangway; station a purser at every gangway to record survivors' names to send by wireless; make officers' cabins available for survivors.

• to the surgeon: collect all stimulants and restoratives on the ship; set up first-aid stations in each dining room; put the other two doctors aboard in charge of the second- and third-class dining rooms, with the surgeon in charge of the first-class one.

• to all crew members: open all gangway doors; sling bosun's chairs out at each one; drop pilot ladders over the side; drape portable lights and nets over the side; have oil ready to be dumped into the ocean (to settle any waves encountered near *Titanic*'s lifeboats); be as quiet as possible to avoid disturbing passengers; tell any passengers encountered in hallways that *Carpathia* was not in trouble and to return to their cabins; station extra lookouts on the bow, in the crow's nest, and on the port bridge wing to fire a green rocket over the bow every fifteen minutes, with Roman candles in between.

• to the master-at-arms: keep steerage passengers under control with a detail of stewards in case of any difficulty with being moved around.

Within minutes of Rostron's directions, *Carpathia* was steaming through the North Atlantic at seventeen knots, above the ship's maximum rated speed of fourteen knots. If *Carpathia* could maintain that speed, *Titanic's* location would be reached in four and a half hours. Rostron later described his experience of racing to the reported site where *Titanic* had foundered:

> Icebergs loomed up and fell astern and we never slackened. It was an anxious time with the *Titanic's* fateful experience very close in our minds. There were 700 souls on *Carpathia* and those lives as well as the survivors of the *Titanic* depended on the sudden turn of the wheel.

Adrift

Among all human characteristics, the instinct for survival is perhaps pre-eminent. On the night *Titanic* sank, this trait was displayed in its rawest form by many of the survivors.

When the great ship went under, an unknown number of people, such as steerage passengers and engineering crew—likely somewhere in the low hundreds—went down with it. This left more than a thousand men, women, and children struggling hopelessly in the bitterly cold water of the North Atlantic. Death due to hypothermia was inevitable. Temperatures around freezing result in unconsciousness in as few as fifteen minutes and death within forty-five, depending on body size, clothing (including life vests), age, and movement. Yet only one lifeboat reacted to the screams and gasps for help. The rest stayed away, ostensibly due to fears that desperate souls in the water would overwhelm and capsize the boats as they attempted to climb aboard. There was also an unfounded fear that the sinking ship would cause a massive suction, drawing lifeboats under with it.

Sadly, by the time Bessie Allison likely realized that baby Trevor must have escaped with his nanny, all the lifeboats had left. Mr. and Mrs. Allison, along with thirty-four-month-old Loraine, died in the sinking. Bessie was only one of four first-class women to be lost in the disaster, while Loraine was the only first-class child. True to the melodramatic newspaper articles published in the wake of the disaster, stories of Bessie refusing to leave her husband's side and get into a lifeboat filled their pages. A report in one newspaper, supposedly from the nanny (erroneously labelled as Bessie's sister) stated:

> The boat was full and she grasped Lorraine [*sic*] in one arm, her husband with the other, and stood waving her hand [three arms?], and it seemed to me smiling as she saw us rowing away. The last I saw of her, just as the boat started to plunge to the bottom, was Bessie turning to her husband for a farewell kiss. As the water washed to their knees, Lorraine was holding to her mother's skirts.

Before *Titanic* sank, Lifeboat 5 came alongside Lifeboat 7, and Third Officer Pitman directed that the two boats be lashed together, as No. 7 did not have an officer in it. Mrs. Dodge took four-year-old Washington Jr. and transferred to the other boat, "to get away from the hysteria of the others." As Washington, the only child in the two lifeboats, drifted on the ocean, he observed *Titanic* slowly settle into the water before it "busted in two" and disappeared. Although he was sorry so many people had died, he was more upset he had lost all his toys.

Lifeboat 3 also only had a single child in it: six-year-old Douglas Spedden, who was well wrapped up against the frigid night air. Freezing water slowly seeped into the boat as it rocked on the gentlest of swells, which may be part of the reason Douglas quickly fell asleep cuddling his teddy bear. It is just as well that he did sleep, as he was spared the horrific sight of bodies floating around the lifeboats after *Titanic* finally sank.

Madeline Mellenger (13) and her mother shivered in Lifeboat 14, surrounded by the cries of the drowning. In a later interview, she recalled:

> I could see the lights of the ship starting to go under water, then soundlessly, perhaps a mile away, it just went down. It was gone. Oh yes, the sky was very black and the stars were very bright. They told me the people in the water were singing, but I knew they were screaming.

In the same boat, fifteen-year-old Edith Brown remembered:

> As the boat was lowered the band was playing a hymn; hardly had the strains of the hymn died away from our ears before we could see that the mammoth vessel was sinking slowly... Finally the bow seemed to sink more rapidly and we could

see the little forms on the deck running to the other end of the vessel, the instinct of self-preservation making them fight for those last minutes of life. Then we turned our heads away.

In later years, Edith contradicted herself and said that she saw *Titanic* break in two and the stern section settle almost level with the surface of the ocean before it sank. Her memory of those struggling in the water never changed, however:

> I could see nothing, but the shrieks and the screams that filled the air were terrible. I presume that it was just as she went under water that the most horrible moans as from a thousand lips came over the water as that many men and I believe some women were hurled into the water and struggled about trying to find something on which to save themselves. After the awful moan it was quiet for a moment and the screams broke out again, but I heard no cries for help. They were more like the agonized cries of men that knew there was no help for them.

Eva Hart (7) retained vivid memories of the sinking. "I can remember the colours, the sounds, everything," she once related, "The worst thing I can remember are the screams." She did concede, however, that the silence that followed was even worse.

Sixteen-year-old new mom Thelma Thomas was hysterical at having left her five-month-old son, Assed, behind in the hands of her brother-in-law when Lifeboat 14 was suddenly lowered over the side. The sight of bodies floating in the water added to her delirium, as she imagined him being placed in another boat, which in turn might capsize. Addie Wells and her children were so crowded in No. 14 that she was forced to stand and wrap her skirts around Joan (4) and Ralph (28 months) to keep them dry. Mrs. Wells struck up a conversation with Mrs. Davies, who had escaped with her eight-year-old son, John Jr. The two women were confused, and Mrs. Davies asked Mrs. Wells what it was all about.

In Lifeboat 12, Laura Cribb (16) remembered, "It did not seem long after we were taken off until the big vessel went down. It was terrible to realize that there were people drowning." But her thoughts were mostly

Lifeboat 14 tows Collapsible D toward Carpathia.

about her dad: "Of course, I could not help, but hope and almost feel sure that my father was safe aboard another boat. It did not seem possible that anything so serious could happen."

Rescued in Lifeboat 9, Bertha Watt (12) remembered, "We heard many pistol shots, and could see people running hopelessly up and down the decks," but "there was nothing anyone could do. We just kept on going." Mary Lines (16) was in the same lifeboat. On board *Carpathia,* she wrote a six-page letter in French to her schoolmate at their school in Paris, describing her *Titanic* experience: "What a horrible thing, this enormous ship engulfed in the little space of two hours. And the cries of the dying as it sank!!!" Today, the letter is a prized part of the *Titanic* collection at the Mariners' Museum in Newport News, Virginia.

Six-year-old Nana Harper did not remember much about her escape in Lifeboat 11 but did recall the noises of those thrashing hopelessly about in the icy water. Winnie Quick (8) later stated:

I remember seeing the boat sinking, the lights going out and hearing the engines and the screams. I was crying most of the time but I suddenly stopped after the cries started to die away. I said to my mother "I am not afraid any more. I asked God and He said we're going to be saved."

Arthur Olsen (9) was confused by what was happening and did not understand why he was in a lifeboat without his dad. As he shivered in the cold, some women in the boat hugged him to help keep him warm, while a sailor who was travelling with him and his dad put his coat over him. Still, the boy cried in the bitter cold.

Twelve-year-old Ruth Becker missed getting into Lifeboat 11 with her mom and brother because her mother sent her back for blankets, but she made it into Lifeboat 13. Her description of the sinking is one of the most vivid:

Titanic survivors disembark from Lifeboat 12.

We rowed away from the *Titanic* as fast as we could, and there were five or six decks and they were just lined with people—standing there at the edge looking over. I suppose they were wishing and hoping someone would come and rescue them. When we were about a mile away the boat was just beautiful, it was a very dark, black night and the ocean was very calm. It was just like a mill pond, just like we were going out for a ride on the pond. It was going down very slowly, not fast at all and the night was dark, no moon, a very dark, black night and that boat was just beautiful, all the lights were on. But it was going down quietly and the lights were just going under the water. I remember that very plainly—I thought it was a beautiful night and a terrible sight because you could see that the boat was going under the water...There fell upon the ear the most terrible noises that human beings ever listened to—the cries of hundreds of people struggling in the icy cold water, crying for help with a cry we knew could not be answered. That was a terrible, terrible time, I can still hear them.

Lillian Asplund (5) recalled that as she sat in Lifeboat 15 and watched *Titanic* sink, "It looked like a big building going down." Willie (9) and Neville (3) Coutts, huddled together with their mom in Lifeboat 2, did not suffer as much as several others in their partially filled boat. Before leaving their cabin, Mrs. Coutts had taken the time to dress the boys warmly against the frigid night air, while others were dressed only in light nightclothes.

In Lifeboat 10, Mrs. West nestled for warmth with baby Barbara and four-year-old Constance. She was not concerned about her husband's safety until *Titanic* went down and she heard the screams of those struggling in the water. A steward in the boat remarked that the people in the other boats were singing and encouraged everyone to do likewise. Their voices drowned out the cries of those in their final death throes. Marshall Drew (8) was in the same lifeboat and noted:

> I remember seeing the rows of porthole lights sink into the sea, row after row, until the first deck was awash. And then came a tremendous explosion, steam, smoke, a flash of light. And then everything blacked out. I didn't see anything after that, but I heard the cries of the people across the water. Then all was quiet. That was it.

Marshall also saw the liner's stern rear out of the ocean, causing machinery and people to hurdle toward the bow, as other passengers tumbled from the decks. Then, once the ship went under, and as only the young can, he fell asleep.

Collapsible C carried several Lebanese children. Mrs. Thomas tried to shield the eyes of Mary (9) and George (8) from the sinking by putting them under her cloak. Twelve-year-old Louis Garrett saw *Titanic* sink: a memory that haunted him for the rest of his life, along with the spine-chilling sound of people crying frantically for help as they were dumped into the frigid water. It was not only people in the water who were screaming. Louis's fourteen-year-old sister, Amelia, yelled so long and so loudly—coupled with the trauma of the tragedy—that it took three months before she could talk again. Throughout the night, Amelia and Louis kept slapping each other to keep their blood circulating.

Frankie Goldsmith (9) was the only non-Lebanese child in Collapsible C. For him, the experience was "exciting at first." Then, when *Titanic* sank, he was terrified at the thought that his dad might have been lost. His mom held him tightly as the liner's boilers exploded and the ship went down.

Collapsible D carried four children.

Collapsible D was the last lifeboat to be launched that contained children. Michel Navratil Jr. and his younger brother Edmond were passed into the boat without their father. Although just under four years old at the time, Michel Jr. claimed:

> I don't recall being afraid, I remember the pleasure, really, of going plop! into the lifeboat. We ended up next to the daughter of an American banker who managed to save her dog—no one objected. There were vast differences of people's wealth on the ship, and I realized later that if we hadn't been in second-class, we'd [have] died. The people who came out alive often cheated and were aggressive, the honest didn't stand a chance.

Then, with their back to *Titanic*, the Navratil brothers went to sleep. They have the dubious distinction of being the only children to survive the disaster without a parent.

Once safely ashore, Karen Abelseth wrote a letter to her father back in Norway, in which she described her memories of the incident as she escaped in Lifeboat 16 (which she incorrectly claimed was the second last to leave the ship). The sixteen-year-old's memories were not in accord with those of any other survivors. "First *Titanic* sank," she wrote, "then she resurfaced close to where we were, and overturned twice." She also wrote, "We heard the cries for many hours."

Transfers

To balance the loads in the lifeboats, during the night some passengers and crew were redistributed between boats at the direction of a couple of the surviving ship's officers. Fifth Officer Lowe in Lifeboat 14 wanted very much to go back for any survivors in the water. He transferred all his passengers to other boats, including eleven children, took on a few seamen, and was the only one to go back. He probably picked up four people in the water. Lifeboat 4 also picked up about eight men from the water, but only because they were in the boat's immediate vicinity.

As part of the transfers, Lowe moved Madeline Mellenger and her mom to Lifeboat 12. Later that morning, the occupants of Lifeboat 4 and Madeline's boat heard Second Officer Lightoller's whistle blasts as he and about twenty-five remaining exhausted men balanced precariously on the keel of overturned Collapsible B. They all transferred to Lifeboat 12. Once in No. 12, Mrs. Mellenger helped to revive a very wet and frozen Lightoller by putting her brown-and-white-checked hooded wool cape over him and rubbing his hands and arms to restore circulation. Lifeboat 12 was the last one to reach *Carpathia*. To thank her, Lightoller gave Mrs. Mellenger a small token: his tin whistle. After she died in 1962, the whistle was passed to Madeline. She in turn gave it to Walter Lord when he interviewed her for *A Night to Remember*, while Mrs. Mellenger's cape is on display in the National Maritime Museum in Greenwich, London, England.

Eva Hart had been vomiting for quite some time—the result of hitting her stomach on the edge of Lifeboat 14 when she was thrown into it as it left *Titanic*. In the transfer to Lifeboat 12, Eva and her mom became separated, and the mother was not able to reach "the poor little thing... to wipe her mouth."

Rhoda Abbott, the mother of Rossmore (16) and Eugene (13) had been picked up by Collapsible A and later transferred to Collapsible D. During the night, three of her fellow passengers died. Rhoda has the depressing distinction of being the only woman to go into the water, be pulled into a lifeboat, and survive after being in the ocean. Hers is also a unique instance of a parent surviving while children were lost.

By the time night turned into dawn, Douglas Spedden's Lifeboat 3 contained freezing water, which came up to the passengers' knees. As the morning grew lighter, it illuminated the icebergs surrounding the boat, which carried Douglas as its only child. Upon waking, he exclaimed to his nursemaid, "Oh, Muddie, look at the beautiful North Pole with no Santa Claus on it." Mary Lines, who escaped in Lifeboat 9, described a similar scene in a letter to a friend: "I'll never forget this sunrise; the sky clear as a glass of water, the sea calm as a mirror, and the enormous icebergs surrounding us, white as swans."

Carpathia Arrives

After three and a half hours of steaming at the fastest speed of which it was capable, *Carpathia* reached its destination at about 4:00 A.M. Captain Rostron later described the experience: "When day broke, I saw the ice I had steamed through during the night. I shuddered and could only think that some other hand than mine was on that helm during the night." Survivors from *Titanic* had first spotted one of *Carpathia*'s rockets arcing into the night sky at 3:30 A.M., and forty minutes later, the first women started to climb ladders up the rescue ship's side. *Carpathia* moved slowly through the scattered lifeboats, picking up their grateful occupants, at the same time as more distant boats started to row toward the ship.

Lifeboat 2 was the first to be rescued at 4:10 A.M., with Fourth Officer Boxhall in charge and the Coutts brothers, Louise Kink-Heilmann, and Georgette Madill in it. Rostron called a shivering, shocked Boxhall to the bridge, where his suspicion was confirmed: *Titanic* had gone down; "about 2:30," according to Boxhall. In reply to Rostron's next question, Boxhall said that "perhaps a thousand, perhaps more," had perished. Rostron sent him below for hot coffee and warmth.

At dawn, Winnie Quick in Lifeboat 11 saw *Carpathia* coming toward them. She also remembered, "My sister and I were lifted on [*sic*] burlap sacks to the deck," while her mother "was strapped to a special chair and pulled on board." Lifeboat 5 was also one of the first to reach *Carpathia*. Like other young children, Washington Dodge Jr. was hauled aboard in a sack, an incident he recalled as "lovely." When Lifeboat 3 reached *Carpathia*, because of his small size, Douglas Spedden was also lifted aboard in a sack. Michel Navratil Jr. was pulled up in the same way and later expressed his indignation: "I thought it was extremely incorrect to be in a burlap bag!" The sack in which William Richards was hoisted aboard was made into a makeshift coat for him. He was photographed wearing it on arrival in New York.

When Lifeboat 4 came alongside *Carpathia*, William Carter was already aboard the rescue ship, having escaped in Collapsible C. As he stood on deck looking down, father did not recognize son with a lady's hat on, so he called out for him but did not identify him until William looked up. For Mary Lines, climbing a rickety rope ladder from Lifeboat 9 up to *Carpathia*'s main deck was a "terrifying ordeal." Others who were too cold to make the climb were hauled up by ropes. On board, Mary's mom was given a bunk, while Mary slept on the floor along with another girl of similar age.

Aboard *Carpathia*, Bertha Watt's mother made both her and Marjorie Collyer a skirt out of an extra blue blanket from the ship, one of which had been provided to every survivor. "She put pleats in to help hide the word 'Cunard,'" Bertha later recalled. "I can see those skirts yet.... I had that skirt until the moths got it."

Lifeboat 12 was the last one to be rescued at 8:15 A.M. The lone child in it, Laura Cribb, remembered she was "almost frozen before we were finally taken aboard the *Carpathia*, for I had only this dress, and none of the others had any more clothing."

By 8:45 A.M. all lifeboats had been unloaded, and the survivors were being cared for with hot drinks, food, and blankets. With full daylight, Rostron steamed slowly through the whole area, searching for more survivors. There were no more, although there was lots of wreckage and—according to Rostron—only one body, which he left in the ocean. *Carpathia* did not have enough supplies to continue her eastward journey, so Rostron decided to return to New York. Before he left, he had thirteen of *Titanic's* lifeboats winched aboard, leaving three lifeboats and all four collapsibles in the water. Collapsible A still had three bodies in it. As *Carpathia* was about to depart, two other ships appeared, *Mount Temple* and *Californian*. Rostron asked their captains to continue searching, but neither found any survivors—or bodies.

At four o'clock that afternoon, Rostron stopped his ship, conducted a brief religious service in the main lounge, and buried four people—one of whom was brought aboard already dead and three who died later.

Laura Cribb recounted that, aboard *Carpathia*, her steerage accommodation was not up to the standard she had experienced on *Titanic*. Jane Quick and her two girls, Winnie and Phyllis, were given bunks in the cargo hold deep inside the overcrowded *Carpathia*. Winnie recalled they were well fed and looked after by the crew. She also remembered the dead being put on a plank before sailors tipped them into the ocean, while "we stood around and prayed."

Madeline Mellenger and her mom became separated on *Carpathia* when her mother was taken to the ship's hospital, where she remained unconscious for the rest of the day. Meanwhile, Madeline was shut in a cabin with a woman who was "almost insane" over the loss of her husband. Madeline cried all day but could not leave the cabin as she had only a short underskirt to wear and could not even get out of the still-warm bunk into which the crew had put her. She was reunited with her mom that night when Mrs. Mellenger was able to leave the hospital.

On board *Carpathia*, French speakers Michel Jr. and Edmond Navratil were looked after by New Yorker Margaret Hays, a first-class passenger who spoke French fluently. As the only children to survive without a parent, no one knew their identity.

Leah Aks searched frantically for her ten-month-old son, Frank, on *Carpathia*, but without luck. On the verge of a complete mental breakdown, she lay on a mattress for two days. A fellow survivor urged her to come up on deck for some fresh air and, when she did, she heard a baby crying and recognized the cry as Frank's. Mrs. Aks ran up to the woman, a pregnant Italian named Argene del Carlo, who had lost her husband in the sinking. Mrs. del Carlo refused to give up Frank, somehow believing he had been sent by God as a replacement for her lost husband and a brother for her expected child. The identification was only resolved through the intervention of Captain Rostron, after Mrs. Aks stated that her son had been circumcised in accordance with their Jewish faith— while an Italian baby would not have been.

Aboard *Carpathia*, South African Edith Brown and her mother searched in vain for her father, despite being told by another survivor that he had seen him in another boat. Lillian Asplund recalled:

> A woman took all my clothes off me. My clothes had gotten very dirty and wet in the lifeboat. My mother was trying to find me. She was saying, "I have a daughter!" Well, she found me. And eventually my clothes were dry, and I put them back on. They took us, the children, to the place where they take people who are sick. Well, not sick, but people who needed a little more attention. The people on the *Carpathia* were very good to us.

During the next four days, the Spedden family quickly set about assisting in any way they could. Mrs. Spedden and Douglas's nanny cut up blankets to make clothes for survivors and dispensed hot drinks; Mr. Spedden joined a committee of *Titanic* survivors to draft a resolution of gratitude to *Carpathia*, its captain and crew, and to raise funds for those who had lost everything. Even young Douglas, according to his mom, tried to help by giving his handkerchief to a weeping woman. In a letter written on board on April 15 to a friend in Madeira, Mrs. Spedden decried, "people who were cruel enough to say that no steerage should have been saved, as if they weren't human beings." On April 18, Mr. Spedden sent a brief telegram from *Carpathia* to family in Connecticut, "All safe on *Carpathia*. Notify family and friends."

The survivors on *Carpathia* collected $15,000 (C$635,170) for the crew to thank them for their rescue efforts. The Cunard Line refused to let its employees have the money and instead turned it over to charities for the survivors. Cunard also refused to accept money from the White Star Line for any expenses incurred in the rescue, although out of its own funds Cunard paid *Carpathia*'s crew an extra month's wages. A parsimonious White Star Line, on the other hand, stopped paying *Titanic*'s surviving crew members as of the minute their ship sank, and never gave them anything for their distress and suffering. The same survivors' committee that collected the money later presented Rostron with a loving cup.

New York

Carpathia entered New York harbour shortly after 9:00 P.M. on April 18 with its flag at half mast, steamed past Cunard's Pier 54, and stopped further on at White Star's Pier 59, where Rostron had *Titanic*'s thirteen empty lifeboats unloaded. For Madeline Mellenger, the landing at New York was "much more exciting to me than the accident" as "the noise, commotion and searchlights terrified me." She "stood on the deck directly under the rigging on which Captain Arthur Rostron climbed to yell orders through a megaphone. Those orders were to let no one on and off and close all openings."

Rostron then returned to Pier 54, where some thirty thousand people were waiting. The crowd included relatives and friends of *Titanic*'s survivors and *Carpathia*'s passengers, plus representatives of relief agencies and several thousand curious people intrigued by news of the sinking. Rostron had *Carpathia*'s passengers disembark first, as he believed that, as soon as *Titanic*'s survivors appeared, control might be lost. In recognition of the disaster, normal immigration regulations, which would have included a stop at Ellis Island, were waived. This courtesy did not apply to the six Chinese survivors, who were expelled within twenty-four hours of their arrival and put on a boat to Cuba under the Chinese Exclusion Act of 1882. The class propriety of the time was also followed during disembarkation: first- and second-class passengers were let off first, followed by third-class passengers at about eleven o'clock. In anticipation of a formal inquiry, all of *Titanic*'s crew were held on another ship until they were no longer needed.

Meanwhile, in New York, several federal, municipal, and private organizations began to receive *Titanic*'s survivors and render any assistance they could. The Women's Relief Committee (quickly formed by fifteen of the city's best-known society women a day after the sinking), Travelers' Aid Society, American Red Cross, Salvation Army, Council of Jewish Women, and various churches, all stepped in to provide assistance. Initially, it was assumed that first- and second-class survivors would not require any help, and that assistance efforts would be devoted to third-class passengers, especially immigrant women who had lost their husbands. That quickly changed when it was realized how many husbands of second-class women were lost. In fact, second-class men had by far the lowest survival rate of any group, followed by third-class

Arrival of the "ship of sorrow" at New York by Boston Globe *artist L. F. Grant, May 4, 1912.*

men. Representatives of the aid groups met the survivors at Pier 54, provided food and clothing, transported those who required medical treatment to hospitals, took anyone needing accommodation to shelters or private homes, and assisted distraught relatives in locating their loved ones.

While only 13 percent of *Titanic's* 1,317 passengers were children, 15 percent of the 500 or so passengers who survived were children. This seems to indicate the unwritten rule of women and children first was followed to a small degree. But in total numbers, only 48 percent of children on board *Titanic* survived. This is still far less than would be expected if the rule had been strictly followed, where figures approaching 100 percent should have been achieved. And by class, the child survival rate difference is even starker: in round numbers, 89 percent of first-class children survived, 93 percent of second-class, and 34 percent of third-class. Of those who sailed from Queenstown, one child was lost in first class and two in second. For the five children who were members of the crew, the results were calamitous: 0 percent survived.

The rescue operation was over; now the gruesome task of recovery was about to commence.

A FOREIGN AFFAIR

When news was received that there were survivors from *Titanic*—and before their names were widely publicized—many people lived in hope that their family and friends were among those rescued. When Franck Lefebvre learned that two French children had been saved from the sinking, his local Mystic, Iowa, community collected money to cover his expenses to go to New York to see if he could identify them as his own. By the time he got to Chicago, however, he learned from the French consul there that the boys had already been identified; they were not his but the Navratil brothers.

And there the matter might have rested had Lefebvre not decided to pursue compensation from the Red Cross Relief Committee. When committee authorities wrote to Mystic city officials to verify his claims, it was determined he was already living with another woman. The case was turned over to the US Immigration Bureau, who discovered he had entered the country illegally, by making "false and misleading statements" to Ellis Island immigration officials. In fact, Lefebvre had entered the US with another woman, Mary Dupont, whom he claimed was his wife, but she was already married to another man and had deserted him. Because he had brought a woman into the country for "an immoral purpose," both Lefebvre and his "wife" were in an "excluded class of immigrants." The two were jailed, pending further investigation.

In an interview with immigration officials, Dupont stated she had paid the fares for herself and her son, as well as those of Lefebvre and a daughter, and they had travelled together as a family under the assumed name of Du Mountier. She claimed that, after three months of living together, Lefebvre had "turned her adrift," having spent $2,000 (C$85,500) of her money and leaving her with just sixty cents. Lefebvre, Dupont, and two of their children were deported to France in July 1912, while his three oldest sons remained in the United States.

CHAPTER 7

RECOVERY & BURIAL

It was between four and five o'clock, Saturday, April 20th, when our ship sighted an iceberg off the bow to starboard... looking down over the rail we distinctly saw a number of bodies so clearly that we could make out what they were wearing and whether they were men or women. We saw one woman in her night dress, with a baby clasped closely to her breast. There was another woman, fully dressed, with their arms tight around the body of a shaggy dog. The bodies of three men in a group, all clinging to one steamship chair, floated nearby, and just beyond them were a dozen bodies of men, all of them encased in life-preservers, clinging together as though in a last desperate struggle for life...we could see the white life-preservers of many more dotting the sea, all the way to the iceberg.

—Mrs. Johanna Stunke, first-class passenger on SS *Bremen*

Despite the heartfelt pleas and outright demands of many of his passengers, Captain Wilhelm of the SS *Bremen* refused to stop and retrieve any of the estimated 150 to 200 corpses he saw floating in the water. His ship had just received a message, which stated another vessel had been sent from Halifax to recover the bodies of *Titanic*'s victims and was only two hours away from the wreckage. The German liner continued its transatlantic voyage to New York. The shocking experience of the men and women aboard *Bremen* constitutes some of the earliest descriptions of *Titanic*'s victims and remains among the most vivid of all accounts.

Initially, White Star Line officials refused to believe *Titanic* had gone down. A combination of hubris, complacency, confidence, superiority, and other factors (but perhaps most of all, denial) had conspired to convince the men who ran the International Mercantile Marine Company, American owners of the White Star Line, that it was simply impossible for *Titanic* to have sunk. The matter was not helped by two wireless messages from other ships that unfortunately were combined into one. A message stating *Titanic* had sunk was morphed with another that advised a disabled oil tanker was being towed to Halifax. The resulting headline and variations of it, such as the one in the *Washington Times*—"Liner *Titanic* kept afloat by water-tight compartments being towed into Halifax, N.S."—blared from the front pages of hundreds of evening editions on April 15.

Based on such incorrect early information, Philip Franklin, the vice-president of the International Mercantile Marine Company, denied to reporters that *Titanic* had sunk. At the same time, he contracted trains with thirty sleeping cars and three dining cars for approximately 610 first- and second-class passengers, plus enough day coaches for 710 third-class passengers. They were to travel from New York to Halifax and pick up the passengers he expected to land there. Optimistically, he also ordered "a sufficient number of baggage cars for all classes." By 7:00 that night, after the evening editions had already gone to press, the truth came out, and *Carpathia* was steaming toward New York with survivors. Franklin cancelled the trains, some of which had already begun their journey northward.

When the enormity of the disaster hit home, there was an immediate outcry for the White Star Line to do something to recover bodies of the victims and give them a proper burial. Many "experts" publicly stated there would be few remains to recover. They believed most would have been drawn down into a mighty vortex when *Titanic* took its final plunge or trapped inside the liner, unable to escape. Soon, reports of floating corpses from *Bremen* and other passing ships put those theories to rest. White Star Line officials now realized they must act and chartered four vessels in succession to sail to the debris field to recover as many victims as they could.

The CS *Mackay-Bennett*

The first ship chartered by the Halifax agent of the White Star Line, A. G. Jones and Company, was the 79-metre-long (260-foot) Cable Ship *Mackay-Bennett* (pronounced "Mackie-Bennett"), which spent much of its time operating out of Halifax laying or repairing undersea transatlantic telegraph cables. White Star Line paid US$550 (C$23,300) per day for the use of the ship, commanded by Captain Frederick Larnder of Halifax and crewed by seamen who had volunteered for "work that was unsettling." The morning of Wednesday, April 17, saw a flurry of activity, as a hundred tons of block ice, 125 rough-hewn coffins, all the embalming fluid in the city, canvas for shrouds for those to be buried at sea, and scrap iron to weigh them down were loaded aboard. The ship's officers and men were joined by John Snow Jr., the chief embalmer of John Snow & Company, the largest funeral home in Nova Scotia, along with undertaker and stonecutter George Snow. Anglican Canon Kenneth Hind of the Cathedral Church of All Saints also went aboard to conduct any burial services at sea.

Mackay-Bennett—dubbed the "Death Ship" by several reporters—left Halifax shortly after noon and arrived at the search area about thirteen hundred kilometres (slightly more than eight hundred miles) away on the evening of Saturday, April 20. By then, it was too dark to start searching for bodies, so that gruesome task began the next morning. It very quickly became obvious there were far more bodies than expected floating on the surface. Captain Larnder described the scene as "like nothing so much as a flock of sea gulls resting upon the water…All we could see at first would be the top of the life preservers. They were all floating face upwards, apparently standing in the water."

Mackay-Bennett's crew quickly developed procedures to locate, recover, and document each body found. When lookouts on the bridge or bow spotted one or more bodies, two or more of the ship's cutters, with five seamen aboard each one, rowed to the spot. Then perhaps the most unpleasant part of the sailors' task began. While some used hooks to pull a corpse closer to their small boat, others moved to the opposite side to prevent the cutter from overturning as the cold, wet, heavy body was manhandled aboard. Once a few bodies were recovered (never more than nine), each cutter returned to *Mackay-Bennett* to deliver its sorrowful load before heading back out again.

A boat crew from the CS Minia *recovers the body of a* Titanic *victim.*

Once a body was aboard *Mackay-Bennett*, a set procedure was followed. A numbered tag was tied to the body and the same number put on a small canvas bag, known as a mortuary bag. Frank Higginson, *Mackay-Bennett's* purser, described in sworn testimony afterward what his duties were during the recovery operation, as the crew and others attempted to identify the victims:

> I supervised searching the pockets and clothing of bodies and saw that all valuables were put into bags and every mark of identification preserved...First I put down approximate age and any marks noticed and effects found on the clothing of or on the body. The effects were put directly into a bag tallying with the number I was entering in the book and the bag was then checked over by the Doctor.

Once the examination was complete, a choice had to be made: burial at sea or transport to Halifax. Although records do not exist for the basis of this decision, it may have been based on positive identification of the body from personal effects and condition of the remains (some were too damaged to be embalmed). Other factors *may* have had a bearing, such as whether the body was passenger or crew, the person's social class, and their class of ticket. Too much should not be read into this, however, as crew members and some passengers from all classes were buried at sea, while others were taken to Halifax. At the time, health laws mandated that only preserved bodies could be brought ashore. Once additional embalming supplies were received from the CS *Minia*, no more burials at sea occurred after April 24, regardless of class.

Although a total of 337 bodies was eventually recovered from the sea, only 5 of them were children. This figure is a mere 1.5 percent of all bodies found, while 22 percent of the bodies of all those who perished were eventually recovered. As noted earlier, only 1 first-class child died—Loraine Allison—the result of an unfortunate misunderstanding, as well as 2 children in second class—fourteen-year-old George Sweet and sixteen-year-old Thomas Mudd. Most books about *Titanic* maintain no second-class children died, but they use twelve as the upper age limit, while sixteen is used here. Seventy-five third-class children died, some 66 percent of the class and 96 percent of all child victims.

Could it be third-class children and their families remained below decks for too long, patiently waiting to be called to the lifeboats? Did the five crew members sixteen or under who died "hang around" inside waiting for orders that never came as the ship sank? Or is it possible smaller bodies were simply harder to spot floating on the surface than adult ones?

Whatever the reason, five seems like a very small number. All five children's bodies recovered were found by chartered ships, four by *Mackay-Bennett* and one by the Canadian Government Ship *Montmagny*. Two were buried at sea, one was shipped outside Canada for burial, and two were buried in Halifax. The fate of these children's bodies will be covered in this order, rather than in the chronological order of recovery.

Will Sage – Body No. 67

On Monday, April 22—Day 2 of the recovery operation—*Mackay-Bennett's* crew picked up twenty-six bodies and buried fifteen of them at sea. One of the fifteen was twelve-year-old Will Sage, who had been travelling to Jacksonville, Florida, with his father, mother, and nine siblings, aged four to twenty. As happened so often with bodies immersed in water for a few days, the crew over-estimated his age as fourteen. A few surviving witnesses reported the family was seen on the boat deck some time after the collision, and one of the girls—either Stella (20) or Dorothy (14)—was offered the chance to enter a lifeboat but refused to go without the rest of her family. Tragically, the entire Sage family of eleven died; the single biggest loss for one family aboard *Titanic*. Was their loss a case of the well-known British penchant for standing politely in line, waiting to be told what to do—until it was too late? Will's was the only Sage body recovered.

Captain Larnder and Cannon Hind conducted burials at sea in the evenings. Chief electrician Fredric Hamilton described the burials of the first bodies on April 21 in his diary:

> The tolling of the bell summoned all hands to the forecastle where thirty bodies are to be committed to the deep, each carefully weighted down and carefully sewn up in canvas. It is a weird scene, this gathering. The crescent moon is shedding a faint light on us, as the ship lays wallowing in the great rollers…for nearly an hour the words "For as [much] as it hath pleased…we therefore commit his body to the deep" are repeated and at each interval comes, splash! As the weighted body plunges into the sea, there to sink to a depth of about two miles. Splash…splash…splash.

Fittingly, Will's body was returned to the deep where he joined the rest of his family.

Rossmore Abbott – Body No. 190

On Day 3—Tuesday, April 23—*Mackay-Bennett's* crew recovered 128 bodies but could not bury any of them at sea due to a shortage of canvas for shrouds. The radio operator sent a wireless message to nearby ships asking for additional supplies of canvas, which was heard by the passing Allan Line ship *Sardinian*. The ship stopped to hand over all the canvas it carried at 7:00 P.M. This allowed the crew to bury 77 bodies at sea the next day, the final occasion on which the crew of *Mackay-Bennett* committed bodies to the ocean. In all, 116 victims had been buried at sea. Body No. 190—identified as Rossmore Abbott—was one of them. Although he was sixteen, the crew sorting out his belongings estimated his age as twenty-two, another example of water immersion making victims appear older than they were.

Rossmore's identification was aided by a medal attached to his watch, which was engraved on one side with:

Oxford Street Grammar School
Awarded to Rossmore Abbott
For Excellence in Reading 1910.

And on the other side with:

The Senator Anthony Prize
1812–1884
Providence Public Schools.

After Rhoda Abbott returned to Providence, Rhode Island, friends of the family held a memorial service for the boys, but she did not attend. She never recovered from the loss of her sons and continued to grieve for them until her death in 1946.

Walter van Billiard – Body No. 1

Even though only five children's remains were recovered, a child's body was the first. Early on the morning of Sunday, April 21—just a little more than five days after *Titanic* sank—the crew of *Mackay-Bennett* hauled aboard the body of a young boy with light brown hair. Later identified as Walter van Billiard, he had been dressed warmly as protection against the cold night air. But his grey overcoat, two other coats, a woollen sweater, and a shirt could do nothing to save him from the freezing water. As with so many bodies, his age was overestimated, but not by much. Crew pegged him at ten to twelve, while he was nine. Walter was supposedly identified from his personal effects: a purse containing a few Danish coins and a ring, as well as two handkerchiefs embroidered with the letter *A*.

A handwritten note scrawled across the bottom of the description on the fatality card for Body No. 1 states, "Unable to identify from clothing or effects," yet "W. Van Billiard" was added sometime later above this annotation. The questions remain: why and by whom? Walter had been travelling with his father, Austin, and ten-year-old brother, James. The father's body was the 255th recovered, but James's was never found. The family was American, not Danish, and the only connection to the A-embroidered handkerchiefs was the father's first name—Austin—but why would Walter be carrying two of his dad's hankies?

Mr. van Billiard's body was identified from his personal effects, including twelve uncut diamonds. At his parents' request, his body was shipped to North Wales, Pennsylvania, on May 4. Despite the doubtful evidence of Walter's identification, Body No. 1 was shipped as well. Father and son were buried on May 8. The next year, Mrs. van Billiard and the two surviving children moved to North Wales to join her parents-in-law, whom neither she nor her children had met. Over the years, there has been some doubt expressed as to the reliability of the identification of Walter, especially given the presence of Danish coins. This has led some researchers to believe the body could have been another child. Only the handkerchiefs bearing the letter A—possibly his father's—seem to be the questionable basis for this identification. Dedicated *Titanic* buffs and researchers have been unable to identify the body based on the handkerchiefs.

Hileni Jabbur – Body No. 328

Besides *Mackay-Bennett*, the White Star Line contracted three other ships to assist in the search, even though it was rapidly becoming obvious there were few bodies left to recover. Between them, *Minia*, *Montmagny*, and *Algerine* recovered twenty-two bodies. One of the last bodies found by the contracted search ships was the only female child found. The CGS *Montmagny*, a lighthouse supply and buoy tender operated by the Department of Marine and Fisheries, made two voyages to the search area. On May 10, the crew found three victims—one of them a female child clinging to a life preserver along with a male adult—before departing for Louisbourg on Cape Breton Island. The three remains were then shipped to Halifax by train, and the child's body was buried in Roman Catholic Mount Olivet Cemetery, where nineteen *Titanic* bodies are buried together in two rows.

Body No. 328 was the second-last body recovered by the four con-tracted search vessels, and was described as probably a third-class pas-senger with "refined features," golden-brown hair, very dark skin, and estimated to be fourteen or fifteen years old. She was described as weigh-ing thirty-six to thirty-eight and a half kilograms (eighty to eighty-five pounds) and standing 137 centimetres (four-foot-six) tall. Her clothing consisted of a lace-trimmed red-and-black overdress, black underdress, green-striped underskirt, black woolen shawl, and black slippers. Her body bore no marks. Anglican clergyman Rev. Samuel Prince, one of two clerics aboard *Montmagny*, noted in his diary the body was that of a "young Syrian girl." She was buried in Mount Olivet Cemetery. Today, many believe Body No. 328 is sixteen-year-old Hileni Jabbur, who was travelling with her nineteen-year-old sister, Tamini, to join their dad.

THE LEBANESE CONNECTION

The Lebanese community in Halifax also believes Hileni is Body No. 328 and conducts an annual service at her headstone. Mount Olivet Cemetery authorities are prepared to inscribe the headstone with her name, but first they must solve the issue of the effects of automobile pollution from nearby Mumford Road on the headstones. The fumes of passing traffic have removed the white paint from the engraved letters and made it impossible for any new paint to adhere.

The Unknown Child – Body No. 4

The Sunday, April 21, diary entry of Clifford Crease, a mechanic aboard *Mackay-Bennett*, noted "one baby" was recovered. The story of this child led to one of *Titanic's* most enduring tales and a mystery that was not finally solved until late 2007—ninety-five years after the sinking. Described as a beautiful little boy with fair hair, whose age was estimated as two, the child was carefully dressed against the cold in a grey coat with fur on the collar and cuffs, a brown serge frock, petticoat, flannel gar-ment, pink woollen singlet, and brown shoes and stockings. There were no marks on the body. Uniquely, the body was the only one recovered without a life jacket.

After two weeks at sea, *Mackay-Bennett* sailed into Halifax Harbour early on Tuesday, April 30. Among the 190 bodies aboard were those of the young boy. As the identity of the child was not known at the time, he was buried in Halifax. With nothing to identify the baby, he quickly became branded as the "Unknown Child." Several people offered to pay for the child's funeral and headstone, but the crew of *Mackay-Bennett* was given the honour.

The funeral took place on May 4 at St. George's Anglican Church, with *Mackay-Bennett*'s entire crew in attendance. It was the only funeral held that day. Canon Hind, who had been on the ship, conducted the service. Afterward, a sombre procession marched from the church to the Fairview Lawn Cemetery. Hundreds of Haligonians lined the streets to see the horse-drawn hearse carrying a small white coffin.

From the beginning, the identity of the Unknown Child was a matter of conjecture. Scrutiny of passenger lists soon led authorities to conclude the child had to be from third class, where six male children under three years old were lost. They were, from Sweden, Gösta Pålsson (27 months) and Gilbert Danbom (5 months); United States (but living in Ireland), Francis Rice (31 months); England, Albert Peacock (7 months) and Sidney Goodwin (19 months); and Finland, Eino Panula (13 months).

Gösta Pålsson

Eventually, all six were investigated to see which one was the Unknown Child, and at one time or another, three of the six were identified as him. The first—and the longest assumed to be the Unknown Child—was the Pålsson boy. On May 13, White Star Line officials had listed Body No. 4 as "Baby? Paulson" on a list circulated to their offices and to relatives hoping to identify members of their families. Shortly afterward authorities referred to him as Leonard Paulson. Alma Pålsson had been travelling from Sweden to Chicago with Gösta (27 months) and her three older children to join her husband. In the Windy City, Mr. Paulson held out hope some of the rescued children might be his, but a White Star Line official in Chicago told him none had been saved. The agent noted his "grief was the most acute of any who visited the offices...but his loss was the greatest."

Although Gösta fit the description of the Unknown Child, the elaborate headstone (paid for by the crew of *Mackay-Bennett*) placed on the grave does not carry his name and reads: "Erected to the Memory of an Unknown Child Whose Remains Were Recovered After the Disaster to the 'Titanic' April 15th 1912." Unlike the other headstones, there is no number on it. To many, this is fitting, as the stone has come to symbolize all children who died and whose remains were not recovered. Alma's body (No. 206) was recovered and carried the tickets for all five family members. Her headstone bears her name and those of her four children in descending order of age. Whether by design or chance, Alma's headstone is located close to that of the Unknown Child.

The matter might have rested there forever, had it not been for a 2001 request to have the body of the Unknown Child exhumed to extract DNA from the remains, in conjunction with two other exhumations. Although not without controversy, authority was granted. Unfortunately, nothing remained in the other two graves because of the combined action of slightly acidic soil and groundwater over the years. Researchers were more fortunate with Body No. 4, which was buried higher up the slope. They found three teeth (two of them molars) and a six-gram (about ¼-ounce) fragment of poorly preserved arm bone.

Researchers sent these remains to the department of anthropology at Lakehead University in Thunder Bay, Ontario, for DNA analysis. Under Dr. Ryan Parr, a team extracted mitochondrial DNA (mtDNA), which is passed from mother to child and is more reliable to establish heredity than simple DNA. Meanwhile, *Titanic* researcher and author Alan Ruffman had tracked down relatives of Gösta in Sweden and obtained samples of mtDNA from them. None of it matched Gösta. The Lakehead team then expanded their search to include mtDNA from relatives of five other male children: the Rice, Danbom, Peacock, Panula, and Goodwin boys. Ruffman succeeded in the monumental task of tracking down historians, genealogists, and relatives of these children to obtain mtDNA samples.

Francis Rice

The story of Margaret Rice and her family is one of the most tragic that occurred as *Titanic* sank. Body No. 12, one of the females recovered by *Mackay-Bennett*, was buried on Friday, May 3. She was Catholic, as noted by the medallion around her neck marked B.V.M. ("Blessed Virgin Mary") and "one jet and one bead necklace," with either one or both likely a rosary. She also appeared to be Irish, based on her shoes, marked "Parsons Sons, Athlone," and some Irish money. Additionally, she had a box of pills with the name and address of a chemist's shop in Athlone. Authorities in Halifax wrote to the shop and received a letter in response from chemist James Fleming that identified the owner as a "Mrs. Rice," who had the prescription filled on April 9, which led to her positive identification. Margaret and her five boys died in the sinking and only Margaret's body was recovered. It was the single biggest loss of any of the Irish immigrant families aboard *Titanic*.

In July 1998, a memorial to the Irish victims who perished in the disaster was unveiled in Cobh (formerly Queenstown), *Titanic's* last port of call. The memorial, a bas-relief bronze plaque mounted on a granite plinth, depicts a few *Titanic* passengers aboard the tender *America* as they head out to board the liner anchored in the background. The Rice family stands in the centre. Margaret and four of her sons have their backs to the viewer, while she cradles baby Francis in her arms.

It is a scene reminiscent of the family's final minutes.

It took researchers until April 2003 to find maternal descendants of Francis Rice—in a Protestant branch of the family in Scotland. Three more years of part-time research followed, based on mtDNA, which resulted in Francis being eliminated as the Unknown Child.

Gilbert Danbom

Mr. and Mrs. Danbom were returning to the United States with their five-month-old son, Gilbert, after a lengthy honeymoon in Sweden. Mr. Danbom recruited immigrants from Sweden as passengers for the White Star Line and was carrying a cheque for $1,315.79 (C$55,740), $276 (C$11,695) in cash, and $30 (C$1,271) in gold on *Titanic*. Although the family reached the boat deck, all three perished in the disaster. Only Mr. Danbom's body (No. 197) was positively identified. It was brought to Halifax by *Mackay-Bennett* and shipped to Iowa for burial. Gilbert was the youngest male *Titanic* victim. Based on mtDNA analysis, by the end of summer 2002, researchers were able to eliminate Gilbert Danbom as the Unknown Child.

Albert Peacock

Edith Peacock, her four-year-old daughter, Treasteall, and seven-month-old son, Albert, were travelling from Southampton to join her husband in Newark, New Jersey. After the collision, a steward assisted Mrs. Peacock and her children in finding a lifeboat. A seventeen-year-old scullion met the small group and took one of the children from the crying woman, while the steward carried the other. When they neared one of the collapsibles, the men handling it shouted for them to go aft. As they turned, a wave swept them off the deck and into the ocean. Although the small child the scullion was carrying was pulled from his arms by the surging water, the crew member made it into Collapsible B. Mrs. Peacock and her children were lost in the sinking, and their bodies were never identified. Albert was *Titanic's* second youngest victim. As in the case of Gilbert Danbom, by the end of summer 2002, mtDNA analysis eliminated Albert Peacock as the Unknown Child.

Eino Panula

With Rice, Danbom, and Peacock ruled out, this left only Panula and Goodwin as potentially being the Unknown Child. Meanwhile, analysis of the teeth suggested an age somewhere between nine and fifteen months, based on shape, size, and condition. This eliminated Goodwin (nineteen months), leaving Panula as the lone possibility. On November 6, 2002, Ruffman and Parr announced that the results of mtDNA testing and teeth analysis pointed to Eino Panula as the Unknown Child. Shortly afterward, relatives of the Panula family journeyed to Halifax to visit the grave of the Unknown Child.

Thirteen-month-old Eino Panula had been travelling with his mom, a neighbour's daughter, and his four older brothers, ranging in age from two to sixteen. The family was travelling to Coal Center, Pennsylvania, to join Mr. Panula. Aboard *Titanic*, Arnold and Ernesti had berths assigned with unmarried men toward the bow of the ship, while Mrs. Panula, her other three sons, and the neighbour's daughter shared a cabin in the stern with an eighteen-year-old Finnish passenger. The neighbour's daughter survived and later stated one of the older boys had awakened them and said the ship was sinking. In the ensuing confusion, Mrs. Panula became separated from some of her boys. Once they managed to make their way to the deck, Mrs. Panula broke down and was crying, saying one of her children (nine-year-old Emma) had drowned in Finland and asked if they all were to drown here. The neighbour's daughter managed to get into a lifeboat, but the entire Panula family was lost in the sinking.

Mr. Panula expressed his anger over the loss of his family in a bizarre obituary published in the *New York News* on May 4, 1912 (in which he got the ages of three of his children wrong):

> I hereby announce with deep sorrow that, as victims of capitalism, in the shipwreck of the *Titanic*, I lost my wife, Maria Emilia, age 40...and my children Ernesti Arvid, age 17, Arnold, age 15, Juho Niilo, age 8, Urho Aabram, age 3, Eino Wiljami, age 1. Together with them was drowned Sanna Riihivouri, age 20..., who came along as my children's nanny.

Sidney Goodwin

Despite the mtDNA identification, doubts lingered about the identification of the Unknown Child as Eino Panula. And it was a pair of tiny shoes that finally solved the mystery. When the remains of victims were landed at Halifax, policemen helped guard the bodies, their clothing, and personal items. Authorities ordered all articles of clothing burned to prevent them from being scavenged by souvenir hunters. Clarence Northover was one of these policemen and was ordered to burn the clothing. He followed orders, except for one item. He could not bring himself to destroy a fourteen-centimetre (five-and-a-half-inch)-long pair of well-worn brown leather shoes, hoping a relative might eventually claim

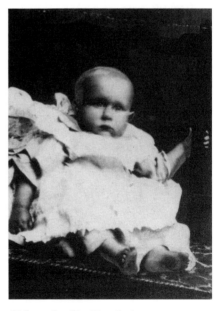

Sidney Leslie Goodwin.

them. That did not happen, so he put them in his desk drawer, where they remained until he retired in 1918, when he took them home. Nearly a century later, in 2005, Northover's grandson donated the shoes to the Maritime Museum of the Atlantic. Museum staff quickly realized the shoes were too big for Eino, who was only thirteen months old.

Dr. Parr and his research team, assisted by the United States Armed Forces DNA Identification Laboratory, studied the teeth again, this time focussing on another section of the DNA sample. In 2007, they discovered a different marker, which indicated with 98.87 percent accuracy the Unknown Child was Sidney Goodwin. The nineteen-month-old boy had been travelling with his father, mother, and five much-older siblings. The family was emigrating from England to Niagara Falls, New York, where Mr. Goodwin had a brother and two sisters. The entire family perished in the sinking; only Sidney's body was recovered.

In August 2008, members of the Goodwin family travelled to Halifax and conducted a memorial service at the gravesite of the Unknown Child, now identified as Sidney Goodwin. A cousin read the names of all the children who perished in the disaster, continuing the tradition that the headstone represents all the lost children of *Titanic*.

As a final act, Sidney's name, his dates of birth and death, and his body number have been added to a new polished granite stone at the foot of the Unknown Child's memorial.

The Unknown Child—unknown no longer.

PART 3 – GONE, BUT NOT FORGOTTEN

I saw that ship sink. I never closed my eyes. I didn't sleep at all. I saw it, I heard it, and nobody could possibly forget it…. It seemed as if once everybody had gone, drowned, finished, the whole world was standing still. There was nothing, just this deathly, terrible silence in the dark night with the stars overhead.

—Eva Hart, 7 on *Titanic*

CHAPTER 8

GROWING UP A SURVIVOR (1912–1961)

I saw it slide down into the ocean to its horrible finish. The
moment it sank left a memory of something that haunts me
till this day. It was the eerie sound of the people groaning and
screaming frantically for help, as they were hurtled into the
icy water. Almost all died from the cold water. The sounds
lasted for about 45 minutes and then faded away.

—Louis Garrett, 12 on *Titanic*

The Canadian Oxford Dictionary gives two related yet slightly different meanings of the word "survivor." The first definition is someone "who remains alive after an event in which others die." In that sense,
the seventy-three children who left *Carpathia* in New York were survivors, having just lived through what is perhaps the most famous marine
disaster in history. The second definition of "survivor" is "someone who
has a knack for overcoming difficulties or surviving afflictions unscathed."

Consider the negative experiences these children encountered in the
immediate aftermath of the rescue. Some of them lost a father or siblings.
In 1912, loss of a father usually meant loss of the primary breadwinner
in the family, which frequently meant a reduced standard of living. Some
mothers remarried quickly, which required adjustment to a stepfather.
While a few children were reunited with fathers who had preceded them
across the Atlantic, other families were forced to return to their homeland. Although the very young on board were frequently unaware of the
danger through which they had just lived, as they grew up, many heard
stories of the sinking and witnessed the impact it had on others in their
family. For some families the subject was taboo, too painful to be even
mentioned. The ultimate question, then, is: what was it like to grow up
as a *Titanic* survivor?

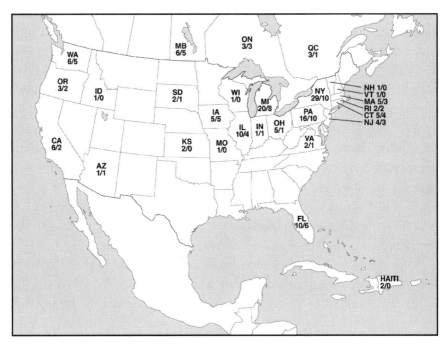

Intended North American destinations for children aboard Titanic *(expected number/number arrived).*

Trauma often leaves markers: the stress resulting from negative experiences in childhood can lead to increases in ailments such as heart disease and cancer. Did these children die younger than average? Trauma can also impact the ability to form close personal relationships. Did these survivors marry and have children of their own? As adults, did they eschew publicity or did they embrace their celebrity as *Titanic* survivors? The answers, unfortunately, are not clear-cut, even for siblings within the same family.

First Survivor Deaths

Sadly, having survived one of the greatest sea disasters of all time, some of the seventy-three children who escaped from *Titanic* never had the opportunity to grow up. Five of them did not even see out the decade and were dead by 1915. The first, second, and fourth survivors to die were Lebanese children. Maria Nackid died of spinal meningitis on July 30, just three and a half months after the disaster. She was in the hospital in her new hometown of Waterbury, Connecticut, and was only sixteen months old. Her mother was so devastated by Maria's death that she never visited her daughter's unmarked grave. Almost a century later, a service was held at the site to finally unveil a memorial stone in her memory.

Exactly one month after Maria died, the first of the three Baclini sisters passed away, when three-year-old Eugenie succumbed to tubercular meningitis. She was being cared for in New York's Bellevue Hospital at the time. Eugenie was buried in an unmarked grave in the pauper's section of Calvary Cemetery, Queens. Five months after Eugenie died, a brother, David, was born on January 28, 1913. He is believed to be the first child conceived by a *Titanic* survivor after the sinking.

Viljo Hämäläinen was the first male child survivor to die. The fourteen-month-old and his mom were among the lucky survivors. Viljo had been reunited with his dad in Detroit and he and his mom were returning from a trip to Finland, travelling second class. His luck, unfortunately, did not last. Not quite two years later, the three-year-old died of endocarditis on March 18, 1914, and was buried four days later in Detroit's Gethsemane Cemetery.

The same day Viljo was being buried, luck also ran out for another young *Titanic* survivor in the same city. Four-year-old Mary Joseph had returned to Detroit after a lengthy visit to Lebanon with her mother and brother, Michael, who was just a few days shy of his seventh birthday. Although all three survived, the children were hospitalized with measles after their arrival in New York before they were allowed to travel to join their father. That March Sunday, Mary's parents and brother attended church and left Mary alone and asleep in her crib in the family apartment above a grocery store. A fire in a small stove kept the room warm. At some point, Michael Tonie, the grocer who lived directly below the Josephs, heard a child's screams and rushed up to the apartment.

Tonie kicked open a bedroom door and was greeted by smoke and flames. Somehow, Mary's night clothes had caught fire, and she was standing in the middle of the room, shrieking in pain. Tonie beat the flames out with his bare hands, scooped up the child, and ran down to his grocery, where he telephoned for an ambulance. Mary was taken to

St. Mary's Hospital. When her family arrived home, a waiting policeman directed them to the hospital. While her anxious parents kept watch at her bedside, Mary died at 1:00 P.M. The next day the *Detroit Times* reported (in language common to the era), "The burned, quivering little piece of suffering humanity moaned and cried and could not talk before death ended her suffering." As the Josephs were too poor to afford a family plot, Mary was buried in a single unmarked grave in the pauper's section of Detroit's Mount Olivet Cemetery.

The deaths of these young children were not unusual for the time. In the United States in 1910 (the closest year to the sinking for which child mortality figures are available), there were 207 deaths of children under five for every one thousand live births—more than 20 percent. The comparable figure for 2020 is 0.7 percent.

Douglas Spedden

Coincidentally, the last two children who died before the age of twenty both passed away in Maine. Once safely back in Tuxedo Park, life returned to normal for Douglas Spedden and his parents. Mr. Spedden's name appeared regularly in the yachting news in the New York papers, while Mrs. Spedden continued to write in her journal and take copious photographs. Young Douglas still dressed up his toy bear, Polar, in elaborate seasonal costumes. For Christmas 1913, Mrs. Spedden wrote *My Story*, a charming children's tale for Douglas, told from the perspective of Polar. The bear recounts the story of his beginnings at the Steiff Toy Factory in Germany, immigration to a New York toy store, and adoption by Douglas. Polar also describes his many travels with Douglas and his parents, including their *Titanic* voyage.

Polar recalls the sinking, when Douglas carried him into a lifeboat, which drifted for a few hours. When *Carpathia* arrives, Douglas somehow leaves Polar behind, until a sailor notices him and reunites him with his delighted owner. The story ends on a rather melancholy note as Polar recounts spending long days alone as his "master" was now in school. For Douglas's mom, however, life did not quite return to pre-*Titanic* days. She noted in her journal: "All the values of life changed, and the daily incidents, which once seemed of such importance to us, dwindled into mere trivialities."

In 1915, when they returned to their summer colony in Winter Harbor, Maine, the fortune that seemed to shine so brightly on this privileged family came to a sudden end. On August 6, nine-year-old Douglas chased a ball into the road in front of their home and was hit by a car driven by a local young man. He sustained a concussion, lingered for two days, briefly regained consciousness, and died on August 8. According to the *Bar Harbor Times*, "It is the first automobile fatality in that vicinity." Young Douglas's body was taken to New York for burial in the family plot in Brooklyn's Green-Wood Cemetery.

Douglas's sudden death only three years after he survived the most famous marine disaster of the century brought a sadly ironic close to the narrative of the Spedden family. But the Speddens' story lives on today through the story of Polar, Douglas's much-travelled teddy bear. (For more about Polar, see page 208.)

Trevor Allison

Trevor Allison, the eleven-month-old baby brother of thirty-four-month-old Loraine—the only child in first class to be lost on *Titanic*—also lost his mother and father in the sinking. Along with André Mallet, he was one of two Canadian children to survive. Trevor escaped in the arms of his nursemaid and was brought up in Canada by his aunt and uncle. In the summer of 1929, Trevor journeyed to Massachusetts to visit his grandfather. During the visit, he became ill with food poisoning after eating a spoiled beef-tongue sandwich but dismissed it and refused to seek medical attention. He then took a train to Portland, Maine, to visit other relatives already vacationing there. In Maine his condition worsened. On August 7, a doctor was called, but Trevor stubbornly refused to be examined. He passed away that night, wailing in his bed. He was only eighteen. Relatives returned his body to Ontario for burial in the Maple Ridge Cemetery near Chesterville. His remains lie beside those of the father he never knew. Mr. Allison's body (No. 135) was the only one retrieved of the three family members who perished in the disaster.

ANASTASIA OF THE ATLANTIC

Like the Spedden's, the Allison family story does not end there. In 1940, a suburban Detroit woman named Helen Loraine Kramer bizarrely claimed on radio she was Loraine Allison. Kramer maintained that, in the last terror-filled minutes before *Titanic* went down, her father had placed her in the safekeeping of James Hyde, who escaped in a lifeboat. Kramer also stated Hyde brought her up in England before she moved to the United States. When she requested Hyde's assistance to obtain her birth certificate, he told her who she really was shortly before his death. Hyde also strangely alleged he was Thomas Andrews, *Titanic*'s designer and builder, in disguise. Supposedly, the White Star Line's chairman, J. Bruce Ismay, paid Andrews to disappear so he could not testify about Ismay's ordering *Titanic*'s excessive speed in the ice field. In fact, Andrews went down with his creation. Kramer became known as "Anastasia of the *Titanic*," a reference to the infamous imposter who claimed to be Grand Duchess Anastasia of Russia and the only survivor of the assassination of the czar's immediate family. She wanted part of Mr. Allison's three-million-dollar estate (C$81,011,612), which went to his brother, as Allison died intestate. The Allisons rejected her claim, and eventually she gave up on it, although she always maintained she was Loraine Allison.

Kramer died in 1992, but her granddaughter, Florida resident Debrina Woods, resurrected her claim in April 2012, on the eve of the disaster's centennial. Woods said she had discovered a treasure trove of letters and legal documents in an old suitcase of her grandmother's, which had not been opened in seventy-five years. Woods created an online forum, in which she continuously promised to obtain and release DNA findings and subject the documents to professional scrutiny to support her case. She started to sell mouse pads and mugs and mentioned book and movie deals, as well as public lectures (for which admission would be charged). A long discussion thread followed, with few supporting her and most expressing total disbelief. When asked online to provide DNA results

more...

...cont'd from previous page

and documentation, Woods always had varying reasons to delay their delivery.

Finally, the Loraine Allison Identification Project, established at Laurentian University in Sudbury, Ontario, in 2012, forensically compared DNA from Kramer's descendants with DNA from the Allisons. In December 2013, it announced the results: there was no genetic link. Despite the evidence, Woods claimed there was "a conspiracy to suppress and discredit us at the 11th hour," just before her various deals came to fruition. She also stated she had her own DNA evidence. As recently as 2023, Woods still claimed "amazing new support evidence has just come to light." She also stated the "heavily biased" identification project was "grossly misinformed" and "solely organized and meant to intimidate and suppress us from telling this story, by the descendants of those whose grandparents are implicated in extremely sinister and criminal actions." Woods promised her book, *The Last* Titanic *Mystery: The TRUE Story of the Helen Loraine Allison Saga*, would reveal the truth and be published "soon."

Growing Up, But Not Growing Old

Fifteen-year-old Adele Kiamie was travelling with the Baclini family (mother and three daughters) and shared a cabin with them. After being treated in a hospital for shock and exposure, Adele's dad took her and (temporarily) the Baclinis to his home. Eventually, Adele's mom and other siblings joined them, and they lived in the Bronx. Adele married a fellow Lebanese immigrant, and they had a daughter in 1919 and a son in 1921. She later developed skin cancer, which led to her death in February 1924, at twenty-seven.

Five-month-old Assed Thomas escaped with his sixteen-year-old mother, Thelma. After hospitalization in New York for shock and exposure, mother and son were reunited with Assed's father in Wilkes-Barre, Pennsylvania. Assed contracted pneumonia and was undergoing treatment in the White Haven Sanitorium when he died of the disease in June 1931 at nineteen years of age. By the time he passed away, Assed had acquired six sisters and three brothers.

Four-year-old English girl Joan Wells, along with her mom and younger brother, was met in New York by her father and uncle, who took them to Akron, Ohio, where the two men worked. After graduation from high school at fifteen, Joan worked as a stenographer before beginning employment at the B. F. Goodrich Company as a private secretary in 1925. As an adult, Joan was not a well person and by 1933 had two major operations. Her surgery required two blood transfusions, one of which was from her fiancé, teacher William Lachman. In early July 1933, William left for a fishing trip to the wilds of Canada, when Joan was still unwell. On July 10, she received a letter from him but was too sick to read it. Joan died later that day in hospital from a combination of sepsis, pelvic cellulitis, and peritonitis, with her family at her side. After a delay, in the hope William could attend the funeral, she was buried before he could return. Joan was the first English child survivor to die. She was twenty-five years old.

Virginia Emanuel (6) and her nurse were met by Virginia's maternal grandparents in New York and taken to their Manhattan home. Shortly afterward, her mom took a brief break from her acting and singing career to visit Virginia before she returned to London. In the US, Virginia moved through a succession of schools and lived with relatives. She rejoined her mother in Europe in 1921. The two visited Brussels and Paris before returning to Elise's Park Lane residence in London. Virginia, now a student, returned to the US in 1924 to live with her grandmother (this time travelling first class). Somewhat bizarrely, on her travel documents, her mother is stated as her next of kin, but described as her sister, while her grandmother is listed as her mother.

Sometime during this period, Virginia's mother had moved to Paris, proclaimed herself a writer, and moved in high-society circles. Virginia joined her mom in France and had a son with Lucien Rosengart, a wealthy French engineer and automobile manufacturer, in 1932. It is not clear if they were married at the time. Four years later, Virginia died, aged thirty, and was buried in a substantial mausoleum in the Cimetière du Père-Lachaise, the largest and most famous burial ground in Paris. Her mother lived until 1959.

The second of the three Baclini sisters, Helen, survived the sinking when she was thirty-three months old. She lived with her family in Brooklyn, where she worked as a department store buyer. In 1935, Helen married a German immigrant and had a daughter the next year. In October 1938, she underwent surgery for breast cancer, but it was unsuccessful. Helen died at home in April 1939, aged twenty-nine. She was buried in St. John Cemetery, Queens, where her parents were interred.

Four-year-old Marion Becker escaped the sinking with her mom, brother Richard, and sister Ruth, all of whom were travelling second class. The father, a Lutheran pastor, joined his family in the United States from India in December. In 1929, Marion contracted tuberculosis and spent a year in a sanitorium in Springfield, Ohio, after which she could only work intermittently. Marion never married and, in 1940, the thirty-three-year-old was living in Denver, Colorado, with another woman, twenty-seven-year-old Alta Johnson. In the census, Alta was listed as the head of the household, while Marion is shown as the partner. It is unknown whether they were more than just housemates, but if they were, it might have been the reason for a subsequent falling-out between Marion and her mother. Some time later, Marion moved to Glendale, Los Angeles County. After a year spent confined to her bed, her condition worsened. She was admitted to Los Angeles County General Hospital in February 1944, where she continued to deteriorate. Marion died of tuberculosis in the hospital on February 15, aged thirty-six. Although she was buried in the family plot in Princeton, Illinois, her mother refused to attend her daughter's funeral. She outlived Marion by seventeen years.

Eight-year-old John Davies Jr. from Cornwall and his widowed mom survived the sinking, but his older stepbrother was lost. They settled in Michigan's Upper Peninsula, where his mother remarried in 1921. John later married, had a son and a daughter, and moved to Detroit in 1951, where he worked as a drugstore clerk. John was also a member of the Fraternal Order of Eagles, a charitable service organization. In November 1951, the couple divorced and, a few days later, on December 16, the forty-eight-year-old took his own life by a deliberate barbiturate overdose, likely because of the divorce. He was the first of two child survivors to die by suicide.

As the Navratil brothers, Michel Jr. and Edmond, were the only children to survive without a parent or a guardian, no one knew their real identity, and they were dubbed the *"Titanic* Orphans" by the press. Newspapers picked up their story, and their photograph was published in North America and Europe. Their mother, Marcelle, saw the photograph and was brought to America, sailing from Cherbourg on *Oceanic*, courtesy of the White Star Line. It was during that voyage that *Oceanic* came across *Titanic*'s Collapsible A containing three badly decomposed bodies on May 13. They were among the last of *Titanic*'s victims to be retrieved. In New York, Marcelle was reunited with her sons, and three days later, returned to France with them aboard *Oceanic*, again with free second-class passage from the White Star Line.

The Navratil brothers, Michel Jr. and Edmond, were reunited with their mother in New York after she recognized them in a newspaper photograph.

At sea, the boys became the centre of attention and were photographed frequently. Once home in France, Marcelle tried to return their lives to some degree of normality. It worked, and within a year, the boys' experience faded from public memory. Edmond, who was only twenty-five months at the time of the disaster, was the first of the "*Titanic* Orphans*"* to die. He graduated from L'Ecole des Beaux Arts and was initially employed as an interior decorator before he became an architect and builder in Lourdes, France. Edmond married in 1934 and raised a family with his wife. During the Second World War, he served in the French Army but was captured in northern France and became a prisoner of war. Edmond later escaped from a POW camp, but his time as a prisoner adversely affected his health. He died prematurely in July 1953, aged forty-three, the first of the four French child survivors to pass away. His mother outlived him and died in 1974.

After recuperation in New York's St. Vincent's Hospital, nine-year-old Mary Thomas accompanied her mother and younger brother George to join their father in Dowagiac, Michigan, where he had purchased a farm in February 1912. Mr. Thomas was initially told his family perished in the disaster, so it came as quite a shock when he received a telegram from his wife on April 20, which asked him to pick them up at the train station. The family was reunited two days later and moved to Indiana before they returned to Michigan permanently. Mary married a fellow Lebanese immigrant in 1919 and had six children. She passed away at her home in Flint in August 1953 from cirrhosis of the liver at fifty years of age.

English-born United States resident Phyllis Quick was only thirty-two months when she survived the *Titanic* disaster, along with her mom and older sister, Winnie. They went by train from New York to Detroit, along with Mr. Quick, a plasterer, who had met them when *Carpathia* docked. Mrs. Quick never received any reimbursement for her $3,190 (C$1,346,700) claim against the White Star Line for the loss of belongings that went down with *Titanic*. The only funds the family received were $100 (C$4,243) from one of the relief committees. This may have influenced Mrs. Quick's decision to accept an offer from a vaudeville producer to tell her story to paying audiences. Eight times a day, Mrs. Quick, Winnie, and Phyllis appeared on stage at the Palace Theatre, where Mrs.

Quick recounted the story of her family's experiences aboard *Titanic*. She stood on a pedestal and wore the same skirt she had on the ship and held her listeners' attention, although the first time she appeared, she "wanted to run back." Once she became used to speaking in public, she toured Grand Rapids and Battle Creek before she quit because she was "tired of hearing [her]self talk." As an adult, Phyllis worked for a telephone company in Detroit until her marriage to William Murphy. Their union produced four children. On March 15, 1954, Phyllis died by suicide at her home, apparently due to marital problems. She was the second and last child survivor to end her life, as well as the seventh of eight survivors to do so. Unusually for a woman, Phyllis killed herself with a shot to the head. She was forty-four.

Mr. Hirvonen met his wife and daughter, Hildur (26 months), in New York and took them to the family's home in Monessen, Pennsylvania, where he had a manufacturing job. Hildur lived there until April 1914, when the family returned to Finland, and stayed there until some time in 1915. Next, the family took up residence in Syracuse, New York, where Hildur completed her schooling, which included graduation from a business college. She never married and continued to live with her parents until she died of cancer in April 1956, aged forty-six.

After surviving the sinking, nine-year-old Willie Coutts, his mother, and three-year-old brother, Neville, settled in Brooklyn, where his father had earlier secured employment. The family later moved to Pennsylvania. Willie married and had two daughters. He worked as a professional musician and taught music. Willie was later a manager for a loan company and was held up at gunpoint six times. He was hospitalized with low blood pressure and a heart condition in April 1956, while his wife passed away that August. On Christmas Day 1957, Willie was discovered dead in a street in Steubenville, Ohio, with his car parked nearby. He had died of a stroke at age fifty-five.

CHAPTER 9

FIFTY TO SEVENTY·FIVE YEARS LATER
(1962–1987)

Fifty Years Later

Fifty years after *Titanic* sank, coincidentally there were fifty child survivors still living. First-class passenger fourteen-year-old Lucile Carter survived the sinking along with her father, mother, brother, and one of three servants. According to one story, the survival of her father—in another lifeboat that reached *Carpathia* before her mother—so incensed Mrs. Carter that she divorced her husband in June 1914, citing "cruel and barbarous treatment and indignities to the person." Another version has it that Mrs. Carter divorced Mr. Carter to avoid the ostracism directed against him as an adult male survivor. Meanwhile, Lucile continued to enjoy the wealthy lifestyle to which she was accustomed. When the First World War broke out, mother and daughter were in Paris, but soon crossed to Britain. In London, before they returned home, her mother married iron and steel heir George Brooke Jr., who was also Philadelphia's "most popular cotillion [a formal social dance of four couples] leader." Lucile's extravagant coming out party at her mother's home in Newport, Rhode Island, in August 1916, made the *New York Times*. A tall woman, who stood at 179 centimetres (five-foot-ten), Lucile married an iron-company executive in October 1922 and had three children.

Her *Titanic* experience did not turn Lucile against ocean travel, and she made several more voyages, although she never liked to talk about *Titanic*. Her husband died in 1944, when he crashed his automobile into the stone wall of a cemetery (perhaps asleep at the wheel), and six years later, her eldest daughter died. Eventually, Lucile went to live with her surviving daughter in South Carolina. She passed away there of heart failure, in October 1962, one day before her sixty-fifth birthday and was buried in Pennsylvania.

Four-year-old Marguerite Sandström, her mother, and twenty-month-old sister, Beatrice, were returning from a visit to Sweden to their home in San Francisco, where Mrs. Sandström and her husband had been living since 1908. Their residence in the US was short; the entire family moved back to Sweden in the fall of 1912. Little is known of Marguerite's later life, other than she married and lived in the small town of Bankeryd. In 1962, Marguerite and her mom related their *Titanic* experiences for an interview on Swedish television. Marguerite died the next year, aged fifty-five.

Constance West, who survived the sinking when she was four, was the first of the three West sisters to die. As their father did not survive, their mother decided to forsake a new life in the United States and return the family to Truro in Cornwall, England, aboard *Celtic*. A baby sister, Edwyna, was born that September. The education of Constance and Barbara up to the age of twelve was sponsored by the Worshipful Company of Drapers, and they attended the company's boarding school in Purley, Surrey. After schooling, Constance became a teacher and was active in the Girl Guides. She never married and later contracted multiple sclerosis. Her last years were spent in a nursing home in Penzance, Cornwall, where she died in September 1963, aged fifty-six.

Soon after Charlotte Collyer and her daughter, Marjorie (8), arrived in the US, they returned to England rather than settle in Idaho as fruit farmers without Mr. Collyer. Mrs. Collyer remarried in 1914, this time to the owner of The Fox and Pelican pub in Surrey. When Charlotte died of tuberculosis in 1916, followed by her husband in 1919, Marjorie went to live with her gamekeeper uncle and his family on a nearby farm. Although it is believed that her time there was an unhappy one, she remained with the uncle until her marriage to a mechanic in 1927. They were wed in the same church as her parents.

The newly married couple may have had a child who died in infancy, although this is unconfirmed. When her husband died in 1943, Marjorie did not remarry and remained in the house she had shared with him, while she worked as a doctor's receptionist. Walter Lord corresponded with her for his seminal 1956 book, *A Night to Remember*, and Marjorie was a guest at one of the London screenings of the film that followed its publication, along with other survivors. In her later years, she had to

Charlotte Collyer and her daughter, Marjorie.

move into a nursing home in Hampshire and died there of a stroke in February 1965, aged sixty-one.

After their arrival in New York, Harold Johnson, his mother, and younger sister, Eleanor, were met by Mr. Johnson and took a train to St. Charles, Illinois. In 1913, a brother was born, followed by the father's death in 1917. Their mom remarried the next year and, although her new husband died less than a month later, the union produced a half-brother for Harold and Eleanor. Mrs. Johnson married again in 1920, to a man who already had four children. This union resulted in a half-sister for Harold and Eleanor and brought the family total to nine children. After high school, Harold worked for the International Harvester Company as a tinsmith in Melrose Park, Illinois, and lived nearby. He married and had a son and a daughter. During the 1950s, Harold, Eleanor, and their mother were guests at the screening of two *Titanic* films. In an interview afterward, Harold stated with some resentment he recalled getting into a lifeboat, but they had been kept "from the upper decks as long as possible while the crew tried to save the first-class passengers." He retired in 1967 and lived in Wayne, Illinois. Harold did not live long enough to enjoy retirement as he died in April of the next year of acute pancreatitis, aged sixty, just eight months before his mother's passing.

While recovering at St. Vincent's Hospital in New York, Karen Abelseth (16) wrote a letter to her dad back in Norway, "We are at a hospital. Here everything is so sad. They are only speaking English...It isn't easy making sense of what I am writing today, because I have got a terrible headache." Once she was well enough to travel, Karen crossed the country by train to Los Angeles, where her sisters had immigrated earlier. Two years later she married and raised five children. Most of her life was spent as a homemaker. The *Titanic* story was not spoken of much in their home, but in 1958, she was pictured in the *Los Angeles Times* with William MacQuitty, the producer of the movie *A Night to Remember*. Karen died there in July 1969, when she was seventy-three. She left behind not only her five children but nineteen grandchildren and eleven great-grandchildren.

After recuperation in New York, fourteen-year-old Amelia Garrett and her twelve-year-old brother, Louis (some sources state they were each two years younger), were met by their older brother, who ran a grocery, fruit, and confection store on Main Street in Liverpool, Nova Scotia. On April 24, he took his younger siblings by steamer from New York to Yarmouth and then up the coast to Liverpool. Amelia and Louis lived above the store until they were able to travel again. They went to Jacksonville, Florida, where they joined their mother and other siblings. By July, their father was well enough to join them from France, where he had been denied boarding because of an eye infection. He also had enough money to travel, having received $240 (C$10,180) to replace the money lost by his children in the sinking. When she was sixteen, Amelia married a fellow Lebanese immigrant in December 1914, and together they had three sons and four daughters. After her husband died in 1942, Amelia never remarried and carried on his grocery and property rental business.

Amelia often spoke to students and newspapers about her experience. In 1953, she attended a special screening of the film *Titanic* shown in her honour. Amelia never wanted to return to Lebanon, however, because she felt she was extremely lucky to have survived the *Titanic* sinking and did not wish to tempt fate. When Amelia's eldest son Albert died suddenly in 1968, her youngest daughter believed Amelia grieved herself to death, asking why she had lived through her son's death and not died on *Titanic*. Amelia passed away in March 1970, aged sixty-nine (or seventy-one).

A year after the *Titanic* disaster, Manca Karun, who was four when the liner went down, returned to Milje, Slovenia, with her family. While her four siblings later immigrated to the US, Manca remained in Slovenia, where she was often interviewed about her *Titanic* experience on the anniversary of the disaster. She married and had four children. Although Manca never moved to the United States, she occasionally visited her relatives there. She died in September 1971, when she was sixty-four years old.

Sixty Years Later

By 1972, sixty years after *Titanic* sank, more than half of the original child survivors were still alive: forty-two out of seventy-three. Joan Wells's brother, twenty-eight-month-old Ralph, spent the rest of his life in Akron, Ohio, where he worked as a shipping and receiving clerk at a machine parts manufacturer. Like John Davies Jr, he joined the Fraternal Order of Eagles, where he rose to a leadership position. Ralph married a Scottish immigrant in 1950. She had two children from a previous marriage, but they had no children of their own. Ralph died suddenly of a stroke in September 1972, aged sixty-two.

After the death of her husband in the sinking, Juliette Laroche decided to return to France rather than carry on with the family's plan to immigrate to Haiti. Accordingly, Mrs. Laroche, Simonne, and her younger sister, Louise, sailed on the French liner *Chicago* in May. The family lived with Mrs. Laroche's father in Villejuif, a commune in the southern suburbs of Paris, where he ran a small wine business. On December 17, a brother was born and named Joseph Lemercier Laroche Jr. As the business could not support all of them, Mrs. Laroche's father urged her to sue the White Star Line. After several years of litigation, she received 150,000 francs (C$602,206) in 1918. This was enough to start a small business in a room of the house, dyeing cloth and making crafts, which supported the family. In 1920, Mr. Laroche's mother sailed from Haiti to meet her daughter-in-law and grandchildren for the first time. The visit did not go well, however, as the elder Mrs. Laroche treated them like foreigners instead of family. She returned to Haiti, and the family never saw her again. On the death of her father, Mrs. Laroche inherited his house in Villejuif. Simonne never married. She looked after her mom, who became paralyzed on her right side. Simonne died of cancer in Paris in August 1973, aged sixty-four. Her mother lived another six years and died when she was ninety-one.

The last of two Canadian-born children to die was André Mallet, a twenty-two-month-old baby travelling to his home city of Montreal with his parents. After arrival in Montreal via New York, his now-widowed mother quickly sold their house and returned to her birthplace, Paris, with her son. She remarried there in 1918. Most of André's life is unknown, but he died in Paris in September 1973 at sixty-three and was buried in Conches-en-Ouche Cemetery in Normandy. Coincidentally, thirteen Canadian soldiers from the First World War are buried in the same cemetery. André's mother died a year later.

By the third quarter of the twentieth century, *Titanic*'s child survivors were senior citizens. The years 1974 and 1975 saw the most deaths: four in 1974 and six in 1975; almost 14 percent of all child survivor deaths. Half of them were aged seventy-seven to eighty. A sixteen-year-old bride at the time of the sinking, Thelma Thomas ran a produce store and raised her family as a single parent after her husband died in 1956. On the sixtieth anniversary of the sinking in 1972, a local radio reporter interviewed Thelma about her experience. She related the story of being separated from her son, Assed, during the sinking and only being reunited in New York's St. Vincent's Hospital, when she recognized the coloured blanket in which she had wrapped him. The next day, the reporter happened to see survivor Edwina Troutt, then eighty-eight years old, being interviewed on NBC's *Today Show*. Edwina described being handed a baby wrapped in a coloured blanket as the ship went down. The reporter promptly contacted NBC and explained the connection. The television network arranged a telephone link, and the two women "met" for the first time in sixty years. They continued to correspond afterward. Although Thelma freely related her story to reporters every April, the experience appeared to drain her—and she never went near water again. Thelma died in a nursing home in January 1974, after a brief stay, aged seventy-eight.

Within a few years of her rescue, Georgette Madill worked for the Red Cross and travelled extensively. She was in Japan and China in 1917 and in Siberia in 1919. After the First World War, she journeyed around Europe in the 1920s. Some of her travels were with her mom, and the two crossed the Atlantic several times. Although from St. Louis, Georgette spent much of her life in England and was married in London in October 1931 to a Maltese marquess. The couple lived in wealthy London areas, such as Chelsea and Westminster, and remained childless. During the

Many of Titanic's *children were treated at St. Vincent's Hospital in New York.*

Second World War, her husband was a captain in the Intelligence Corps and was made a Member of the Most Excellent Order of the British Empire (MBE) in 1944 for his service. Georgette died in February 1974, aged seventy-seven, predeceasing her husband by eighteen years.

Laura Cribb was another sixteen-year-old who survived *Titanic*, but her dad was lost. On arrival in New York, she spent time in St. Vincent's Hospital until relatives found her and took her to Newark, New Jersey, which had been her destination. While there, Laura was ill for several weeks before she was able to return to England in June to her mother and siblings. In the immediate aftermath of the sinking (as well as several years later), she gave contradictory accounts of the disaster. Laura remained in Dorset for a couple of years and worked as a sales clerk in a department store before she went to live with other relatives in Toronto. In October 1916, she returned to England aboard a wartime-camouflaged RMS *Baltic*, where she met her future husband, an American mechanic and electrician. By the time the liner docked, they were engaged and then married in November.

After initially settling in London, the couple moved to Albany, New York, in December 1918. Her husband continued to work as an electrician, and the couple moved several times, both within New York state and then to Arizona and finally to Carlsbad, New Mexico, in 1948. Along the way, the couple had two sons and three daughters. Shortly after their arrival in Carlsbad, Laura's *Titanic* experience became known, and for the next twenty-seven years, she enjoyed celebrity status locally and gave several interviews. She did, however, turn down an offer to attend the premiere of *A Night to Remember* in New York, claiming it would be too emotional for her. When her husband died in 1961, Laura moved into a retirement home but continued her work with several volunteer organizations, as well as her church. She died of a stroke in April 1974, aged seventy-eight.

The survival of four-year-old Washington Dodge Jr. and his parents was headline news in their hometown of San Francisco. In a congratulatory telegram to Dr. Dodge, Mayor James Rolph Jr. sent the wishes of the whole city: "I have just received news of the safety of yourself, Mrs. Dodge and little son. The people of San Francisco thank Got [*sic*] over your safety, and through me extend to you all affectionate greetings, and shall be glad to welcome you home."

The headlines seven years later were not so upbeat when Washington's father shot himself in an elevator and died nine days later. Mrs. Dodge took Washington and his half-sister from a previous marriage to live in New York. Washington became a stockbroker and was married twice, in 1932 and 1941. Between 1929 and 1933, Washington was the financial editor of *Time Magazine* and went on to work in public relations and business publications. As an investment adviser, he became vice-president of stockbrokers Clark Dodge & Company. Washington travelled extensively. In 1958, he attended a special screening of *A Night to Remember* with several other *Titanic* survivors. Washington died of a heart attack in his office in December 1974, aged sixty-seven, and his remains were cremated.

After Arthur Olsen (9) lost his dad, the same young woman who took him into her care in the lifeboat saw him safely ashore in New York. There he was taken to a nursery before meeting his stepmother for the first time on April 19. She remarried and had two children before Arthur left home. His brush with death at sea did not seem to cause any lasting fear of the water. Arthur joined the US Navy in July 1922 and served for four years. After the navy, he worked on passenger liners, first as a bell-boy and then as an assistant steward. He later moved to a variety of other jobs in different cities and was married along the way. The marriage was both childless and cheerless, and the couple divorced in 1946. Arthur moved to St. Petersburg, Florida, the next year, where he worked as a house painter. He died there in January 1975, aged seventy-one.

On arrival in New York, Meyer Moore (7) and his mom were looked after by the Hebrew Immigrant Aid Society. Rather than going immediately to their stated destination of Chicago, due to immigration difficulties, they instead spent two years in Canada (to which they had attempted to emigrate from Romania, then a part of Russia, in 1911), before settling in the Windy City. In the US, Meyer married in 1937, had three sons, and settled in El Paso, Texas, where he worked as a wholesaler of dry goods and later ran a shoe store. He died in April 1975, aged seventy, on the sixty-third anniversary of the sinking.

When *Carpathia* docked in New York, sixteen-year-old Irish immigrant Nora O'Leary was met at the pier by her older sister. Nora worked as a maid before she returned to Ireland in 1921. The voyage did not bother her, "It never cost me a thought." Nora arrived in Ireland during the final months of the Irish War of Independence (1919–1921), also known as the Anglo-Irish War, which created the Irish Free State and left Northern Ireland as a part of the United Kingdom. In April 1922, she married a farmer and a veteran of that bitterly fought conflict. Together they had four daughters and a son. For the rest of her life, Nora lived in the rural County Cork village she had left in 1912. In later life she was reluctant to discuss *Titanic*. Nora became a widow in 1968 and died in May 1975, aged seventy-nine. She was buried just in front of the grave of Daniel Buckley, the twenty-one-year-old who had led her and five other young Irish men and women to the United States aboard *Titanic*.

In the United States, the Borek family settled in Clearfield, Pennsylvania, where the senior Borek ran a grocery store. William and George had two more brothers born in 1916 and 1918. Their mother contracted tuberculosis shortly afterward and entered a sanitarium. She desperately wanted to see her mom and returned to Lebanon in the early 1920s, where she died, leaving her four boys motherless. The family moved to Wilkes-Barre, but they were very poor, and life was a struggle for them. William married the daughter of a Lebanese immigrant, and together they raised three daughters. The family settled in Observatory, Pennsylvania, just north of Pittsburgh, where William ran his own business. Although he recalled the sinking, he never wanted to be interviewed about it or discuss it. He died in August 1975, aged sixty-eight.

George Borek outlived his younger brother by four years. He remained in Wilkes-Barre all his life, where he worked as a used-car dealer. He married a recent Lebanese immigrant in 1930, but the couple did not have children. Unlike his brother, George talked about his *Titanic* experience to his relatives. He retired in 1950 and died in hospital in October 1979 of an aneurysm, when he was seventy-four.

Twenty-one-month-old Richard Becker, whose sister Marion died in 1944, was the reason the family was travelling from India to the United States. Richard, who had been born and raised in India, needed medical attention. He later became a singer before he qualified as a social worker. Richard lived in Jacksonville, Illinois, in the late 1930s and early 1940s, where he married in 1938 and had a son. When his first wife died in 1942, he remarried and had two daughters. The family settled in

Minnesota, where Richard was a regional director for the American Red Cross. He later relocated to Peoria, Illinois, and was a safety supervisor for the Caterpillar Tractor Company. Richard died of kidney disease, aged sixty-five, in September 1975, the year after his second wife died. He was buried in Peoria.

Mary Lines (16) and her mom managed to make it to her brother's graduation from Dartmouth College. She later returned to her Paris home and, during the First World War, served as a nurse's aide in a French hospital for four years. Mary married an attorney and fellow American in Paris in 1919 and settled in Topsfield, Massachusetts, in 1920, where they had a daughter and two sons. Mary and her husband were very active in local civic and charitable organizations, with Mary particularly devoted to Girl Scouts. She was also a member of the Herb Society of America for thirty years, during which time she assisted in the translation of the *Natural History of the Lavenders* from French to English and in the publication of *Herbs of Greece*. In 1964, she received the Society's Medal of Honor. Mary did not speak about her *Titanic* experience until her mother died in 1942, after which she recounted her story to the local press on many occasions. She did, however, turn down an invitation to the New York premiere of *A Night to Remember*, saying she did not want to relive the experience. Mary died of a cerebral hemorrhage in November 1975, aged eighty.

After Madeline Mellenger (13) and her mom arrived in New York, they continued on to Bennington, Vermont, where Mrs. Mellenger had planned to work as a housekeeper. Now, however, they were there to pay their respects to the widow of the superintendent at the Colgate estate, who had been lost on *Titanic*. In August, the pair returned to England on *Oceanic*. A photograph of Madeline taken on board shows a slightly frowning, very proper young lady, dressed in a sailor-themed suit and holding an *Oceanic* life ring. A postcard of the image, signed by Madeline and *Titanic*'s Third Officer Herbert Pitman, sold at auction in England in 2009 for £1,260 (C$3,695). Madeline and her mom returned to North America in October 1913 and settled in Welland, Ontario, where Mrs. Mellenger had a brother. Madeline married a banker in 1921, settled in The Beaches area of east Toronto, and had four sons. Madeline was not reluctant to share her *Titanic* memories. In 1939, she and her mom attended a *Titanic* reunion at Toronto's Royal York Hotel with two other survivors. During the 1950s, Walter Lord interviewed Madeline for *A Night to Remember*, and she attended the first Titanic Historical Society convention in 1973. She died in May 1976, aged seventy-seven.

Willie Coutts's younger brother, Neville, lived twenty years longer than he did. After his schooling, Neville became a steelworker in Pennsylvania. He married in July 1941, but he and his wife did not have any children. Neville later became a stocks and bonds salesman in New York and looked after his mother in her last years. In 1958, he attended the New York premiere of *A Night to Remember* with other invited survivors. Neville retired to Florida, where he died in March 1977, aged sixty-eight.

Sixteen-year-old Ellen Corr, one of the few teens to travel alone, was reunited with two older sisters in New York and was later joined by another sister from Ireland. Ellen worked as a domestic and called herself Helen. Seven years after the disaster, Helen made her only trip back to Ireland. In 1922, she married a fellow Irish immigrant and lived in the Bronx. The couple had no children and her husband died in 1929, when a van hit the bicycle he was riding. Helen never remarried. She was a waitress at the Royal Restaurant, later becoming a head waitress. During the 1940s and 1950s, she sponsored five other Irish immigrants to the US. Like many survivors, Helen did not like to talk about *Titanic* and would only briefly state how she was saved. She died in a nursing home in March 1980, aged eighty-four; the last of the Irish passengers to pass away. On the centennial of the sinking, her niece presented a penny carried by Helen on *Titanic* to County Longford Heritage and Archives Services in Ireland.

Louis Garrett outlived his older sister by a little more than a decade. He attended school just long enough to learn English and married a fellow Lebanese immigrant who was his brother's sister-in-law in February 1926. Their first son arrived in April of the next year but lived only a few hours. A second son followed in 1929. Louis operated a grocery store in Jacksonville and became a devout Jehovah's Witness after he fell out with his Greek Orthodox faith in the early 1930s. He became very active in his new religion's door-to-door ministry and remained so until he died.

Louis had promised himself that he would never go on a ship again but returned to his homeland in 1949—by airplane. The flight route took him almost over the spot where *Titanic* sank, bringing tears to his eyes as he remembered that fateful night. After his wife died of complications from diabetes in 1951, Louis married three more times. One wife died, and he divorced the other two. In May 1981, Louis required prostate surgery and visited his son in Tucker, Georgia, to have the operation. While in the hospital, he died of a heart attack, aged seventy-nine (or eighty-one because of confusion about his date of birth). His remains were returned to Jacksonville for burial.

On arrival in New York, fourteen-year-old Johan Svensson was met by an uncle, who set him on his way to join his father and elder sister in Garfield, South Dakota. Shortly after his arrival, the *Dakota Republican* in Vermillion wrote, "Despite the harrowing experiences he underwent, and the exposure he endured after seeking refuge in the lifeboat, he is now in good physical condition. He is a lad of promise, and will in time make a good American citizen."

Johan worked on the family farm, changed his name to John Johnson, and was eventually joined by the rest of his family from Sweden (except for his mother, who died in 1914). John, who was known as "Titanic Johnson," later moved to Michigan, where he met his future wife, whom he married in Ohio in 1929. Their marriage was childless, and they later divorced. John finally settled in Long Beach, California, where he worked as a ship welder for a marine construction company and married again. He had one daughter. In 1961, John made his only visit to his homeland, which must have been a frightening experience, as he suffered from nightmares about *Titanic* all his life. He died on Independence Day in 1981, aged eighty-three.

Seventy Years Later

Seventy years after *Titanic* sank, there were twenty-four survivors still living who were children on April 15, 1912. English boy Frankie Goldsmith, nine years old at the time, was one of them. Frankie and his mother went from New York via Niagara Falls to Detroit, where they had relatives.

Besides the train tickets, all the White Star Line provided them was fifteen dollars (C$635). Mother and son lived near the newly opened Navin Field, home of the Detroit Tigers. Because of his age, Frankie did not understand his dad was dead. For years, he thought "another ship must have picked him up and one day he will come walking right through the door and say, 'Hello, Frankie.'" Frankie started to work at fourteen but returned to school for two years on a part-time basis and later worked delivering milk. When he was eighteen and after his return from a two-month trip to England, he met his future wife, who was only fifteen at the time. They married in 1926 and had three sons. Frank worked in advertising until the Great Depression, when he lost his job. He and his wife moved in with his mom for the next three and a half years.

Frank found work with the Detroit Creamery Company, where he worked for another thirteen years. The couple bought their first house with money his mother loaned them; part of the $2,400 (C$101,635) she received from the Women's Central Relief Association of New York. In 1942, Frank started work as a civilian in a United States Army Air Forces photographic unit. The next year he was sent to Denver, Colorado. After the war, Frank and his wife started a photographic and art supply store in Mansfield, Ohio. It was only in the 1960s that Frank started to talk about *Titanic* and attended several conventions in the 1970s. He retired in 1973, having had a stroke in 1970 and suffering from painful arthritis. The couple moved to Orlando, Florida, in 1979, where Frank had a fatal stroke in January 1982, aged seventy-nine. A few months later, on April 15, exactly seventy years after the disaster, in accordance with his wishes, a Coast Guard Ice Patrol aircraft scattered his ashes over the assumed site of *Titanic*'s sinking (the actual location was not discovered until 1985). Frankie was finally reunited with his father. Frank never brought his children to a baseball game at Navin Field, where the roar of the crowd evoked painful memories of the sounds of the people in the water when *Titanic* sank. Nine years after his death, the Titanic Historical Society published Frank's story, *Echoes in the Night: Memories of a Titanic Survivor*. It was written by one of his sons and based on his father's notes and diary. It is a rare account of the memories of a third-class passenger.

Maria was the last of the Baclini sisters to die and the only one to have lived what could be considered a full life. She worked as a department store manager before her marriage to a man of Lebanese descent in 1934. They lived in Brooklyn and had a daughter born in 1937. Maria died in June 1982, aged seventy-five, and was buried in the same cemetery in Queens as her sister, Eugenie.

Three-year-old Felix Asplund was rescued along with his mother and older sister, Lillian, while his father and three older siblings died in the sinking. His father's body (No. 142) was recovered by *Mackay-Bennett* and shipped to Worcester, Massachusetts, where the family had lived before their four-year visit to Sweden. The three surviving members of the family initially lived with relatives in Worcester. According to a report in a local paper:

> Lillian and Felix are rapidly recovering from the effects of their sad experience. The girl realizes to some extent what had happened, but little baby Felix, three years old cries for his papa. A gloom is cast over the Asplund family and mention of the tragedy is made only in a whisper.

Because the Asplunds lost all their belongings on *Titanic*, the city of Worcester organized a fundraising for them, which collected almost $2,000 (C$84,550). The money was invested in a trust, with funds dispensed as needed. In 1951, the family moved to nearby Shrewsbury, where Felix worked as a draftsman at an engineering firm and remained a lifelong bachelor. He died of pneumonia at his home in March 1983, aged seventy-three, and was buried in Worcester's Old Swedish Cemetery.

In 1919, nineteen-year-old William Carter II accompanied his new stepfather (since his mother's 1914 divorce) to Europe aboard the Cunard luxury liner *Mauretania*. In Europe, he studied in England, France, Switzerland, and Italy. After his schooling, William followed his new father into banking. He married in May 1925, a union that produced a son in 1926 and a daughter in 1930. They lived in the affluent Philadelphia suburb of Bryn Mawr. William continued to travel across the Atlantic on many of the most popular ships of the time, such as *Aquitania*, *Île de France*, and *Homeric*; the latter was a White Star Line vessel. William later divorced and married a Boston native. He disliked talking about his

Titanic experience and would not speak to media outlets about it. Even though William had not suffered the loss of a family member, he apparently continued to be emotional over the loss of his Airedale terrier. William outlived his sister, Lucile (who died in 1962), and passed away in January 1985, aged eighty-four. He was the last *Titanic* child survivor to die before the wreck was discovered. William was buried in the Carter family mausoleum in West Laurel Hill Cemetery in nearby Bala Cynwyd.

Jack Ryerson

After the disaster, Jack Ryerson's mom devoted herself to charity work— and travel. He accompanied her on some of her early trips, attended Yale and, after graduation in 1921, worked briefly in banking in Chicago before turning his attention to his passion—golf. In 1930, he purchased the Otsego Golf Club near Cooperstown, New York. The town, which would become the location of the National Baseball Home of Fame and Museum in 1939, was also close to Ringwood, the Ryersons' summer home. During his golf career, Jack played with many of the game's greats:

The Ryersons' summer home was close to Cooperstown, New York.

Bobby Jones, Julius Boros, Gene Littler, and Babe Zaharias. His goal was to play more courses than anyone else and, by 1954, he made it into the Ripley's Believe It or Not newspaper column with more than 1,015 different courses. By 1971, he had increased this total to some 1,400 links, but never reached the world record of 3,200.

Like many other survivors, Jack was reluctant to talk about *Titanic*, although he visited the film set of the 1953 movie *Titanic* as an invited guest and related his experiences to the actors. Shortly afterward, he contributed to Walter Lord's research for 1956's *A Night to Remember*. Jack did not get married until 1953, when he was fifty-four, and eventually settled in Palm Beach, Florida, with his wife, where they had previously been winter residents. As he grew older, Jack became increasingly close-mouthed to the media about *Titanic*, but was willing to discuss it one on one. He was eventually diagnosed with Alzheimer's disease and by 1985 had lost most of his cognitive powers and was admitted to a nursing home. Jack died of the disease in the facility in January 1986, aged eighty-seven, while eating his lunch. According to his wife, he "simply closed his eyes and stopped breathing. It was very peaceful." He died unaware the wreck of *Titanic* had been discovered just five months earlier. His remains were returned to Cooperstown for burial in the family plot in Lakewood Cemetery beside his mother and siblings. Jack was the last of *Titanic*'s first-class survivors to die.

On arrival in New York, Jessie Leitch opted to return to England with her six-year-old cousin, Nana Harper, as Nana's pastor father had been lost in the sinking. In London, an aunt and uncle raised the young survivor. In 1921, Nana participated in the opening ceremony of Glasgow's Harper Memorial Baptist Church, dedicated to her father's memory. She worked at a London Bible college, where she met her future husband, whom she married in 1934. They had a son and a daughter. Nana returned to Scotland about 1936, where her husband was pastor at several churches before ending up in Glasgow. When he retired in 1984, the two moved to Lanarkshire. Nan (as she was known in her later years) had few memories of the disaster but remained in contact with other *Titanic* survivors, especially Eva Hart, with whom she had played aboard *Titanic*. Nan died at home on April 10, 1986, aged eighty, exactly seventy-four years after *Titanic* departed Southampton.

Marshall Drew (8) and his aunt (whose husband was lost in the sinking) were met in New York by his widowed father, who took them to Southold on Long Island. When Marshall's dad died of tuberculosis in 1917, his aunt remarried, and Marshall later went to live with her parents. Marshall was a talented artist; he graduated from New York's Pratt Institute in 1928 and attended Columbia University. Marshall married in 1930 and had a daughter. He taught fine arts at Grover Cleveland High School in Queens for thirty-six years until his retirement. In retirement, he moved to Westerly, Rhode Island, and spent his summers on Long Island. Marshall continued to teach art and was an accomplished wildlife photographer and origami practitioner. The goateed, white-haired Marshall could often be seen tearing down a road in his red sports car, red beret perched on his head at a jaunty angle, on his way to some art show or photography exhibit. Marshall was happy to share his *Titanic* experiences, especially with young people, gave numerous detailed interviews, and attended the premiere of *Raise the Titanic* in Boston in 1980. One of his favourite stories was that he was not on the initial survivors' list because, when it was being compiled aboard *Carpathia*, he was somewhere eating doughnuts and drinking hot chocolate. To Marshall, his art was far more important than his *Titanic* experience. He once said, "Teaching I did on purpose. The *Titanic* was purely accidental." Marshall died in June 1986, aged eighty-two. Although his headstone carries a depiction of *Titanic* and notes "Survivor R.M.S Titanic," above is the inscription "Teacher – Artist – Friend."

Few people get to participate in more than one world-famous event in their lifetime, yet Sibley Richards was involved in three. One was the *Titanic* disaster, which he survived when he was only ten months old. The others occurred during the Second World War: a sea battle and a surrender. After settling in Akron, Ohio, the Richards family returned to Cornwall in 1914, where Sibley completed his education. He was employed as a fish worker, married in 1938, and had one son. Sibley joined the Royal Navy during the Second World War and served on HMS *Duke of York*, a battleship, during its lengthy and ultimately successful engagement with the German battleship *Scharnhorst* off Norway's North Cape on December 26, 1943.

Survivors from the German battleship Scharnhorst *aboard the battle-ship HMS* Duke of York, *in which Sibley Richards served.*

In 1945, *Duke of York* did not participate in operations against Japan due to required repairs, but it did reach Japan in time for the formal surrender ceremony. It was anchored in Tokyo Bay on September 2, when the official documents were signed aboard the USS *Missouri*. In his later life, Sibley was reportedly estranged from his older brother William for unknown reasons. In 1980, he joined other *Titanic* survivors in London for the premiere of the movie *Raise the Titanic*. He died in December 1987, aged seventy-six.

Little is known of the later life of Erna Andersson, who was sixteen when she survived the *Titanic* disaster. After her arrival in New York, she worked as a maid and a housekeeper. In 1923 and living on East 80th Street, she declared her intention to become an American citizen and in 1926 filed a petition for naturalization. On both documents she declared she was not married. Yet other information suggests that she had married in January 1921, and a falsehood such as this would have voided her application if discovered. Nevertheless, she took the Oath of Allegiance in May 1926. She began using Anna as her first name in 1940. Although she was known to be alive in 1944 and her husband died in 1968, Erna's trail runs cold. She is the only one of *Titanic*'s seventy-three child survivors whose fate remains unknown.

CHAPTER 10

THE LAST SURVIVORS (1988-2009)

Rowing away looking at Titanic, it was a beautiful sight outlined against the starry sky, every port hole and saloon blazing with light. It was impossible to think anything could be wrong with such an enormous ship were it not for the tilt downward towards the bow.

—Ruth Becker, 12 on *Titanic*

As of 1988, there were nineteen child survivors of *Titanic* still living. By 2009—twenty-one years later—there were none.

William Richards

Like his younger brother, Sibley, William Richards participated in another major event besides the *Titanic* sinking, which he survived when he was three. William returned to Cornwall with Sibley and the rest of his family in 1914, completed his schooling, and married in 1929. They had three children. During the Second World War, William joined the Royal Navy, where he participated in another momentous twentieth-century event: the evacuation of the British Army from Dunkirk from late May to early June 1940.

After the war, William worked as general manager for a smoked salmon factory until his retirement. He and his wife later divorced, and William lived with another woman. After a move, he called his new house *Carpathia*. Although William had few memories of the disaster, he was often interviewed about it by local media. He died in January 1988 following a heart attack, aged seventy-eight.

Ruth Becker

The death of Marion in 1944 and Richard in 1975 left the eldest of the Becker children, Ruth (twelve years old on *Titanic*), as the longest-lived and the only one of the three siblings with memories of the disaster. She attended school in Wooster, Ohio, and after graduation from the College of Wooster, became a teacher. In 1924, she married a former classmate, who ran a dry-cleaning business. The couple settled in Manhattan, Kansas, and had three children. Ruth taught high school for eighteen years and did not even tell her children about *Titanic*. After more than twenty years of marriage, Ruth and her husband divorced. She moved to Michigan and returned to teaching until her retirement. It was not until after she moved to Santa Barbara, California, in 1971, that she began to speak about her *Titanic* experience. Ruth became one of the most famous survivors of the sinking, was interviewed on several occasions for newspapers and television documentaries, became friends with *Titanic* historians and other survivors, and attended a few Titanic Historical Society conventions.

At a Titanic Historical Society meeting in 1982, Ruth told the audience she saw the ship split into two parts. To illustrate what happened, she held up two fingers on each hand and separated them, to indicate two funnels went one way and two—the other. After her comments, the Society's treasurer took the microphone from her and told her and the audience she was mistaken; it was the falling of the front funnel she had witnessed. While other survivors had mentioned the split, Charles Lightoller, the most senior officer to survive, said the liner sank intact. In addition, teacher Lawrence Beesley, who was in the same lifeboat as Ruth and wrote an early account of the disaster, did not mention any break. When the wreck was discovered in 1985 in two large sections about six hundred metres (656 yards) apart, Ruth was finally vindicated.

At the same time, Ruth became an outspoken opponent of individuals and companies disturbing the site for commercial purposes. She believed the wreck should remain untouched and preserved as a memorial and graveyard but did not object to artifacts being recovered for museum displays. When she died in July 1990 at ninety years of age, in accordance with her wishes, her ashes were scattered over the spot where *Titanic* went down in the Atlantic Ocean. Very sadly, the cause of her death was listed as malnutrition.

Until 1985 most people believed that Titanic *sank in one piece, as depicted in this image, instead of two.*

Michael Joseph

Mary Joseph's older brother, Michael, outlived his unfortunate sister by several decades, although not without his share of heartache. In 1915, a baby brother was born but only lived for five months. His mom died of tuberculosis later that year when she was twenty-six. While attending grades 1 to 8, the nuns at Saints Peter & Paul School in Detroit nicknamed him "Ty," in memory of his miraculous escape from *Titanic*. In 1926, Michael's dad died of a heart attack, aged forty-two. At eighteen, Michael was left without parents or siblings. An aunt and uncle looked after him, and he eventually got a job as a truck driver for a beer and soft drinks company. Michael moved to nearby Warren, Michigan, married a woman of Lebanese descent in 1937, and had four children. He retired in 1967 after twenty-four years with the soft drinks company. In May 1991, Michael died of heart failure in hospital, aged eighty-four. Although he seldom spoke of his *Titanic* experience, he always maintained he was saved by a guardian angel who grabbed his hand and rushed him into a lifeboat as the liner sank. Above his grave in Resurrection Cemetery stands a two-metre (seven-foot) tombstone containing an etched picture of *Titanic*.

Frank Aks

Frank Aks was only ten months old when he escaped from *Titanic* with his mom, although they were in different lifeboats. After the reunion with Mr. Aks, a tailor in Norfolk, Virginia, Mrs. Aks bore two siblings for Frank, a girl and a boy. Mrs. Aks intended to name her daughter Sara Carpathia, but the nuns at the hospital were confused, and Sara Titanic Aks was put on her birth certificate. Frank's father later switched jobs and worked as a car salesman before he managed his own garage. This likely influenced Frank's career path, as he never completed high school and began work as an auto mechanic. Frank married a woman whom he had met when he was eighteen. The couple was married twice—once by a justice of the peace and once by a rabbi. They had two daughters.

Frank later moved into car sales and ended up owning a salvage company. He was active in his temple, the Masons, the Shriners, and his Jewish community centre. During the 1950s, Frank and his mom were guests at showings of the films *Titanic* and *A Night to Remember*. In his last twenty years, Frank amassed a large collection of *Titanic* memorabilia, which was on display at the nearby Mariner's Museum in Newport News until 1996. He joined the Titanic Historical Society and attended several of its conventions. Frank died of a heart attack in July 1991, aged eighty.

George Thomas

George Thomas, Mary's eight-year-old brother, married in 1926 and had three children. For several years, the family continued to live with George's parents in Flint, Michigan. After the couple divorced, in 1936 George wed a woman who had been previously married. They had a son together. George purchased a grocery store from his uncle and ran it with his father and brothers. He sold the store—by now a supermarket— to his brothers in the 1940s. He then bought a smaller store but retired from the grocery business in 1948. George next became a real estate investor before finally retiring in 1970. In later life, he often recounted his experience of the sinking. George was a Mason and a Shriner and became a member of the Titanic Historical Society. He attended its 1982 convention in Philadelphia. George's wife died on October 31, 1991, and George followed her shortly afterward on December 9, dying of a stroke. At eighty-seven, he was the last Lebanese survivor to pass away. In 2008, George's son published *Grandma Survived the Titanic*, the story of his family's *Titanic* experience and their later life.

Eighty Years Later

Bert Dean

By 1992, there were just twelve child survivors still living. When *Titanic* foundered, Bert Dean was twenty-three months old, while his sister Millvina was only two months old. After arriving in New York with his now-widowed mother and little sister and with no visible means of support, the family immediately returned to Britain on board the RMS *Adriatic*. Initially, the family lived with grandparents on their farm in the New Forest, near Southampton. His mother received £40 (C$9,980) from an emergency relief fund, along with a pension of twenty-three shillings (C$287) a week for care of the children until they turned eighteen. Bert received some of his education at King Edward VI School in Southampton, paid for from compensation, and later took a job at Husband's Shipyard near Southampton.

Bert married, was keen about the disaster, gave several interviews, and was often a guest at *Titanic* conventions, along with his sister. Like Millvina, he had no memory of the disaster, but often noted he "lived it over and over again as my mother told me." On September 3, 1985, a special commemorative envelope with an image of *Titanic* was produced in Britain to recognize the discovery of the wreck. The White Star Memories Company sold copies signed by Bert for £49.99 (C$330). He died in his sleep of pneumonia while in hospital on April 14, 1992, on the eightieth anniversary of *Titanic* hitting the iceberg, aged eighty-one. His ashes were scattered in St. Mary the Virgin churchyard in a Southampton suburb. Bert was the last surviving male third-class passenger.

Alden Caldwell (about six years old) with his younger brother, Raymond.

Alden Caldwell

Like Frank Aks, Alden Caldwell was only ten months old when he escaped from *Titanic*. He was well-educated and had a master's degree in chemical engineering, which led to thirty-three years at the Lehigh Portland Cement Company in Allentown, Pennsylvania, as a chemical engineer. Alden never married and, due to being born in Siam, spent much of his life trying to prove his American citizenship so he could eventually receive social security benefits. In 1977, he retired to a winter home in Florida, while spending his summers at a cottage in Wisconsin. These locations were perfect for his two pastimes: golf and fishing.

When Alden's father died in 1977 at ninety-one, Frank Aks attended his funeral and met Alden for the first time. Up till then, Frank had thought he was the youngest survivor from *Titanic*, but when they compared birthdates, it turned out Alden was three days younger. Frank eventually met the youngest survivor, Millvina Dean, at a survivors' reunion, to which Alden had turned down an invitation. Memories of Alden differ.

Some of his nearest neighbours had never met him. Opinions varied from an unfriendly recluse to a kind and pleasant person. All agree on his unmistakeable appearance in his last years, marked by an unkempt long white beard. He died in December 1992 at eighty-one years of age.

Louise Kink-Heilmann

After spending four days in St. Vincent's Hospital in New York, Louise Kink-Heilmann (4) and her parents travelled to their new home on a rented farm outside Milwaukee, Wisconsin. The money for the train trip had been sent by a great uncle, as her father lost everything in the sinking. After Louise's parents divorced in 1919, she remained with her mom when her father returned to Switzerland. She had to leave school at an early age and get a job to help her mother run the farm. Louise married in 1932 and had three daughters and a son. Shortly after the birth of the fourth child, the couple divorced.

As she grew older, Louise became involved in various *Titanic*-related activities. When the wreck was discovered in 1985, she testified before a congressional committee to urge permanent protection of the site as a memorial. She attended several *Titanic* reunions in the late 1980s, and in 1990, was a guest of honour at an Ellis Island plaque unveiling, which commemorated immigrants who were lost on their way to the United States. The next year, Louise joined Halifax's mayor for unveiling ceremonies at the Fairview Lawn Cemetery for six newly identified victims whose names had been added to their headstones. Louise worked into her eighties while battling tuberculosis, arthritis, and breast cancer. She even attended *Titanic* commemorative ceremonies in Massachusetts and New Jersey in the months before she died. Louise passed away in August 1992 of lung cancer, aged eighty-four, and was buried beside her mother in Milwaukee. In addition to her four children, she left seventeen grandchildren and fourteen great-grandchildren.

Bertha Watt

Bertha Watt and her mom went to Portland, Oregon, where Mr. Watt had established residence the year before. After attending Jefferson High School and Oregon Agricultural College, Bertha became a bookkeeper and married a Canadian dentist in 1923. The couple settled in Vancouver, where Bertha became a Canadian citizen. They had three sons and a daughter; all the boys became dentists. Bertha's *Titanic* experience did not dissuade her from sailing, and the couple owned a fourteen-metre (forty-five-foot) yacht. They also owned an ocean-front cottage, accessible only by boat. Bertha's husband died in 1971, while their daughter and a grandson were killed by a drunk driver in 1978. Bertha generally avoided being associated with *Titanic*, although she attended the first Titanic Historical Society convention held in 1973 and granted interviews from time to time. In a 1975 interview for the *Vancouver Province*, she noted:

> I never dwelt on it—perhaps because of the mother I had. I consider myself darned lucky. I've had a very busy life raising a family and we were active in different organizations, the Yacht Club among them. I don't remember having fear of the water since.

Bertha died in March 1993 in a nursing home at ninety-three years of age, the last Canadian survivor.

Beatrice Sandström

Beatrice Sandström was twenty months old when she survived the sinking of *Titanic* with her mom and her older sister, Marguerite. When the entire family moved back to Sweden later that year, Mr. Sandström bought a small shop. At school, few of Beatrice's classmates believed she was a *Titanic* survivor, especially as she did not remember anything about the voyage, but only what others had told her. One phrase she repeated as a child may have been related to the sinking, however— "Look, the moon is falling down." Family members interpreted this as her memory of *Titanic*'s distress rockets being fired. A colour interview of her *Titanic* experience for Swedish television was spliced into an earlier 1962 black-and-white interview with her mother and sister. Although she did not speak English, in 1988, Beatrice attended the twenty-fifth anniversary celebration of the Titanic Historical Society in Boston. Later, she also attended the Titanic International Society convention in New York, where she signed autographs and met fellow survivors. As an adult, Beatrice ran a bakery until her death in September 1995, aged eighty-five. She was the last Swedish survivor to die.

Eva Hart

Like other families who had lost their breadwinners, Eva Hart and her mom returned to Britain shortly after their arrival in New York. Instead of settling in Canada, they settled in Chadwell Heath in East London. Her mother remarried, while Eva—like Johan Svensson (John Johnson)—continued to be troubled by nightmares of her *Titanic* experience. To take her mind off the tragedy, Eva learned to play the piano and developed her singing voice. After her schooling, she taught music to young children. Her mom died in 1928 when Eva was twenty-three. Once her mother passed away, Eva faced her fears directly. On a lengthy sea voyage to Singapore and Australia to visit relatives, she locked herself in her stateroom for two days until the nightmares passed. Eva returned home two years later.

Eva remained single and worked at a car dealership and a department store before becoming a Justice of the Peace and a welfare officer. She

The Eva Hart pub in in Chadwell Heath, East London, England.

was made an MBE in 1974 for her good works. Although she initially tried to supress all memories of *Titanic*, Eva went on to become one of the most outspoken of the survivors. She blamed the White Star Line for failing to provide enough lifeboats for everyone on board *Titanic*, noting that to die because there were insufficient lifeboats was "ridiculous." She also criticized any attempts at salvaging items from the wreck site. "That's my father's grave," she once said and described the salvers as "fortune hunters, vultures, pirates, and grave robbers."

Eva became active in various *Titanic*-related events and enjoyed her newfound status as a *Titanic* celebrity, especially once many survivors began to die. Eva was not a fan of Millvina Dean, whom she considered an imposter as Millvina was only two months old when *Titanic* sank and had no memories of the disaster. She would get angry whenever Millvina's name was mentioned. Eva went to the United States in 1982 for a Titanic Historical Society convention on the seventieth anniversary of the disaster and returned for three more in 1987, 1988, and 1992. In 1994, she collaborated in writing her autobiography, titled *Shadow of the Titanic—A Survivor's Story*. In April 1995, on the eighty-third anniversary of the disaster, Eva and fellow survivor Edith Brown officially opened the Titanic Memorial Garden at the National Maritime Museum in Greenwich, outside London, and unveiled a plaque in memory of those lost. Eva developed osteoporosis and cancer and spent her later years in a London hospice. She died on February 14, 1996, aged ninety-one. In her honour, two years later the J D Wetherspoon chain opened a pub in a converted police station in Chadwell Heath, which they named the Eva Hart.

Edith Brown

After staying in New York for several days and despite Mr. Brown's death, South African Edith Brown and her mom made their way to their intended destination of Seattle, Washington. Following a turn for the worse in her mother's health, Edith and her mom soon returned to the comfort of Cape Town. Surprisingly, after their harrowing experience on *Titanic*, a doctor advised a cruise, and mother and daughter sailed to Australia. On their return, they moved to Johannesburg, where Mrs. Brown started a clothing business. Much to Edith's displeasure, her mother began a relationship with a much-younger man, whom she later married. Relations between Edith and her stepfather were not good, causing her to leave home and live with friends.

In 1917 Edith married, and in 1920 moved to Southampton, England, with her husband and their newborn son. Although Edith was an only child, in England, another nine children followed between 1921 and 1938. Her husband was an engineer draftsman and was posted to South Africa during the war. Edith and the children followed, but the entire family moved back to Southampton in 1948. The city still showed the effects of German bombing, and the family had to live in a Nissen hut into the 1950s. Although they moved into a house later in 1950s, they immigrated to Australia in the mid-1960s and lived there for a few years before again returning to Southampton.

After her husband died in 1977, Edith began to be asked to talk about her *Titanic* experience on a regular basis. She was a guest of honour at the screening of *A Night to Remember* in London in 1958, where she met fellow survivors, including Millvina Dean, with whom she became friends. Edith attended several *Titanic* conventions in England and the United States and was often interviewed by the media. She criticized salvaging of the wreck, remarking it was wrong to disturb anything that had been "down there so long." Her disapproval, however, did not extend to any personal items that might be recovered and, in 1993, she received her dad's pocket watch that an expedition had retrieved. In August 1996, at age ninety-nine, Edith sailed aboard the cruise ship *Island Breeze* to the spot where *Titanic* went down, along with Michel Navratil (and Eleanor Johnson on another ship). The main purpose of the voyage was to watch the attempted recovery of a twenty-tonne (eighteen-ton) section of *Titanic*'s hull, known as "the big piece," on video monitors. In an emotional ceremony during the voyage, Edith dropped flowers into the ocean in memory of her father and other victims. After the two "spectator" ships left the area, the recovery operation had to be aborted, but the piece was eventually recovered in August 1998. Meanwhile, Edith had died in her Southampton retirement home in January 1997, aged one hundred, following a chest infection. In 2009, her son wrote a biography of his mother, titled *Titanic: The Edith Brown Story*.

TITANIC CENTENARIANS

Edith Brown was one of just five *Titanic* survivors—and the only one who was a child at the time—to live to one hundred. The *Titanic* centenarians are:

- Mary (Davis) Wilburn: May 18, 1883–July 29, 1987 (104)
- Marjorie (Newell) Robb: February 12, 1889–June 11, 1992 (103)
- Ellen (Shine) Callaghan: December 30, 1891–March 5, 1993 (101)
- Edith (Brown) Haisman: October 27, 1896–January 20, 1997 (100)
- Edwina (Troutt) MacKenzie: July 8, 1884–December 3, 1984 (100)

First-class saloon steward Fred Ray was the longest-lived male on board and passed away at ninety-seven. Englishman Jack Odell, who lived to be ninety-five, was the longest-lived male child passenger. Jack was not a survivor of the sinking per se, as he and his family were only on the Southampton-Queenstown portion of the voyage. Norwegian Olaus Abelseth was the longest-lived male passenger who survived the disaster. He died at ninety-four.

Eleanor Johnson

Harold Johnson's younger sister, twenty-month-old Eleanor, was far too young to have any recollection of the sinking, but maintained in her later years she did have an early-life memory of the event. She claimed to recall being held at a great height, cradled in her mom's arms, with other hands reaching up toward her from below and everybody "yelling and crying and screaming." As an adult, Eleanor worked in a watch factory in Elgin, Illinois, where she met her future husband, who eventually became an engineer at International Harvester. Eleanor later worked as a telephone operator until she retired in 1962. The couple had a son, born in 1944.

Eleanor, Harold, and their mother were guests at screenings of *Titanic* in 1953 and *A Night to Remember* in 1958. When Eleanor's husband died in September 1981, she continued to live on her own. She was interviewed by the media on several occasions and attended Titanic Historical Society conventions in 1987 and 1988. In 1996, Eleanor sailed on a special cruise to a spot over the wreck site on *Royal Majesty*, along with survivors Edith Brown and Michel Navratil, who were aboard *Island Breeze*. She saw James Cameron's 1997 *Titanic* three times and was the only survivor the director met. Eleanor said that Cameron told her that she "reminded him of Rose" and she later told a reporter, "When you see Rose, think of me." Eleanor said the movie was so realistic it was difficult to watch and she "did a lot of crying." After the movie's release, she became very much in demand for media interviews and by *Titanic* aficionados simply wanting to talk with her, so much so she had to have her telephone number unlisted. Eleanor was admitted to hospital in April 1998 complaining of back problems and was subsequently moved to a rehabilitation centre. While there, she caught pneumonia and died the next month, aged eighty-seven.

Louise Laroche

Like her sister Simonne, Parisienne Louise Laroche never married. She worked as a clerk in the justice department. When she passed away in January 1998 at eighty-seven, Louise was the last child survivor to die in the twentieth century. Her passing left only five child survivors still living. The final five child survivors, surprisingly, lived into the twenty-first century.

Michel Navratil

Edmond Navratil's older brother, Michel, never completely overcame his sibling's early death and would not permit his brother's health to be discussed in his presence. Michel was a scholar and went to university, where he married a fellow philosophy student in 1933. He received his Doctor of Philosophy degree in 1952 and was a philosophy professor at the University of Montpellier until his retirement in 1969. The next year, his wife died. Their children followed their parents' scholarly pursuits. Their son became a medical doctor, while one daughter became a psychoanalyst and the other a French-German translator and music critic. The translator/critic daughter, Elisabeth Navratil, wrote a book for young adults in 1982 about Michel and Edmond, titled *Les Enfants du Titanic* (English edition: *Survivors: A True-Life Titanic Story*), which uses a combination of fact and fiction to tell the boys' account.

In April 1987, on the seventy-fifth anniversary of the sinking, Michel returned to the United States for the first time, when he attended a Titanic Historical Society convention in Wilmington, Delaware, accompanied by his son. He was one of eight child survivors present. Michel returned via New York, where he met and spent time with Margaret Hays Easton Starbuck, the daughter of Margaret Hays, who looked after the boys before their mother picked them up. In 1988, he met several fellow survivors at another convention, this time in Boston. Michel and other survivors captivated the audience with their first-person memories of *Titanic*. That same year, Alden Caldwell died, making Michel the last surviving male *Titanic* survivor.

In 1996, when he was eighty-eight, Michel sailed to the site of the wreck aboard *Island Breeze* during an ocean expedition mounted by RMS Titanic Inc., along with survivors Edith Brown and Eleanor Johnson (who visited the site on another ship, *Royal Majesty*). But first, Michel and Edith journeyed to Halifax, where he visited his dad's grave for the first time on August 27. Michel Sr.'s body was one of the first recovered by *Mackay-Bennett* and assigned No. 15. Besides a pistol found in a pocket, his second-class ticket identified him by the pseudonym under which he had been travelling: Louis M. Hoffman. Based on this name, authorities assumed Michel was Jewish and buried him in the Jewish Baron de Hirsch Cemetery. Even after his identity became known, and it was discovered he was Catholic, his remains were left in the Baron de Hirsch Cemetery at his estranged widow's request. Of the ten victims buried in this cemetery, only one other has been identified. Like Michel, he was also misidentified as Jewish due to his name. In fact, first-class saloon steward Fred Wormald of Southampton was Anglican.

Michel passed away quietly in his sleep on January 29, 2001, aged ninety-two. He was the last French and the last male survivor of the tragedy. Michel always maintained that an early brush with death and the loss of his father affected his thinking for the rest of his life. His philosophical bent may also have contributed to his outlook on life. "I died at four," he claimed. "Since then I have been a fare-dodger of life. A gleaner of time."

Winnie Quick

At her new home in Detroit, Phyllis Quick's elder sister, Winnie, did not like school and quit when she completed grade eight. She worked at several jobs: in a candy factory and as a sales clerk in a few stores. In 1916 and 1918, new baby sisters were born, bringing the family's total to four girls. The same year her third sister was born, by now fourteen-year-old Winnie met a nineteen-year-old Belgian immigrant at a house party and decided she liked him very much. When she told the fellow immigrant of her affection for him, he told her he would see her again when she was older. Winnie and her husband, a master carpenter, were married in 1923.

Their first child was born in 1924 and, eventually, they had three sons and two daughters. When her husband retired in 1966, the couple was finally able to take the trips they had always wanted to and visited every state but Hawaii. Although an inveterate traveller, Winnie never returned to Britain, limiting their travels to anywhere "a tent and a station wagon could take us." She remained uneasy near deep water and large ships but did make an overnight ferry crossing between Michigan and Wisconsin. Awakened by a slightly alarming noise in the night that reminded her of *Titanic*, Winnie silently left their cabin and went out on deck. Her husband found her there, standing at a railing and peering into the darkness, attempting to overcome her fear. Winnie was predeceased by her father, mother, sister, husband, and two of her sons. She remained one of the more elusive *Titanic* survivors. Although Winnie answered letters and media requests for interviews, she would not attend *Titanic* conventions or survivor reunions, preferring the safety of her home in Warren, Michigan. In 1995, Winnie moved into a retirement home in nearby East Lansing. When she passed away in the hospital on Independence Day in 2002 at ninety-eight, her death left only three remaining *Titanic* survivors.

Lillian Asplund

If little is known of Felix Asplund's life, the same is not true of his sister, Lillian, who became the last survivor with memories of the sinking. She lived in Worcester, Massachusetts, until 1951, when she moved to nearby Shrewsbury. Like her brother, Lillian never married and worked in various secretarial jobs, including at the State Mutual Insurance Co. She retired early to look after her mom, who lived until she was ninety-one and died on the fifty-second anniversary of the sinking in 1964. Although Lillian remembered the voyage, she shunned publicity and rarely discussed the disaster, even if offered money to do so. When asked why, she reportedly replied, "Why do I want money from the *Titanic*? Look what I lost. A father and three brothers."

Beginning in 2003, however, Lillian granted a series of interviews that extended over three Easter weekends in 2003, 2004, and 2005 to a *Washington Post* reporter. She died at her home on May 6, 2006, at ninety-nine, the last American survivor of the sinking. The last living memories of *Titanic* also died with her. Fittingly for someone whose hobby was growing roses, her white metal casket was decorated with inlaid pink roses. She is buried in Worcester's Old Swedish Cemetery, beside her father (Body No. 142), mother, and brother. After Lillian's death, 364 items, including letters, postcards, documents, and other memorabilia related to the disaster, were found in a shoe box in her dresser drawer. They included her ticket for *Titanic*, which sold at a British auction in 2008 for £33,000 (C$96,100). Her dad's gold pocket watch, stopped at 2:19 A.M., one minute before *Titanic*'s plunge, sold for £31,000 (C$90,275) at the same time.

Barbara West

Constance West's younger sister, Barbara, went on to attend high school in Truro, Cornwall. This was followed by teacher training at St. Luke's College, Exeter, where she specialized in physical education and geography. Barbara became a governess for a Cornish family and moved with them to Spain. In 1936, she returned to Britain at the outbreak of the Spanish Civil War and became a teacher at Guildford High School, Surrey. The next year, Barbara married a rugby player, and the couple continued to live in Surrey. They did not have any children, and her husband died at age fifty in 1951, following a heart attack.

Barbara married again in 1952; both were avid rugby fans. She returned to Cornwall shortly afterward and taught in her old high school in Truro. Barbara then became deputy head of physical education at a Plymstock school, where she remained until her retirement in 1972. During her teaching career, Barbara was noted as a kind, devoted teacher, with a liking for bright-red lipstick, who encouraged attention to grooming—as well as correct speech and grammar. In retirement, Barbara and her husband returned to Truro and attended the cathedral where her father, who had been a chorister there, was commemorated. She also conducted cathedral tours and did volunteer work. Barbara became a widow for a second time in 1990. Like Lillian Asplund, she was reluctant to talk about *Titanic* and rejected all media requests for interviews, especially at the time of the release of James Cameron's *Titanic* in 1997. She did, however, keep marginally in touch with the British Titanic Society.

During her final years, Barbara lived in a nursing home in Camborne, Cornwall. She died there on October 16, 2007, aged ninety-six, the second last *Titanic* survivor and the last second-class passenger. To avoid unwanted media attention, her death was not announced until after her funeral, in accordance with her wishes. Barbara's remains were cremated and scattered in a garden of rest at Penmount Crematorium in Truro, where there is now a memorial plaque in her honour.

Millvina Dean

Bert Dean's younger sister, Millvina, first became a *Titanic* celebrity during her family's return voyage to Britain. Fellow passengers crowded around the baby, hoping to have their photograph taken with her. As the *Daily Mirror* (London) noted in its May 12 edition, "She was the pet of the voyage and so keen was the rivalry between women to nurse this loveable mite of humanity that one of the officers decreed that first- and second-class passengers might hold her in turn for no more than ten minutes." Perhaps overlooked in the excitement was the irony that Millvina and her family had been third-class passengers on *Titanic*. Like her brother, Millvina was raised and educated from relief funds and attended The Gregg School in Southampton, until she left at sixteen. Initially, Millvina was unaware she had been on *Titanic* and only discovered it when she was eight, at the time her mother was going to remarry.

For most of her life, Millvina led a quiet existence. She never married and lived at home for many years. During the Second World War, she worked for the Ordnance Survey drawing maps. Later, Millvina was employed by a local Southampton engineering firm in their purchasing department. Her private life changed dramatically in 1985, with the discovery of the wreck of *Titanic* by a joint Franco-American search team under Jean-Louis Michel and Robert Ballard. As she noted, "Nobody knew about me and the *Titanic*...but then they found the wreck, and after they found the wreck, they found me." Suddenly, Millvina became a celebrity. She was in great demand to attend conventions and exhibitions, appear in documentaries, be interviewed by newspapers and on radio and television programmes, and sign autographs. "The telephone rang all day long," she once complained to an author. "I think I spoke to every radio station in England. Everybody wanted interviews. Then I wished I had never been on the *Titanic*, it became too much at times."

The fact that Millvina—like Bert—had no memories of *Titanic* and any account she gave was second hand, based on stories her mom had told her and newspaper and magazine articles, did not deter her many fans or the media. In 1997, she was a guest of the Titanic Historical Society aboard *Queen Elizabeth 2* for a voyage to New York. From there, she flew to Wichita, Kansas, to see the house in which she would have grown up had her father not died in the sinking. She did, however, refuse to see James Cameron's *Titanic*, recalling the nightmares she experienced after viewing *A Night to Remember* in 1958.

Millvina suffered from health problems in later life. She broke her hip in her early eighties, had cataracts (which required her to wear thick glasses), and developed a blood infection from another hip operation in her nineties. In 2006, she went into the Woodlands Ridge Nursing Home, by now requiring oxygen. Millvina made headlines two years later when it was announced she planned to sell some of her *Titanic* memorabilia to pay the £3,000 (C$9,475) monthly fees at Woodlands. When the items did not fetch as much as she had hoped for, a fund was established to cover her nursing home costs. James Cameron, Leonardo DiCaprio, Kate Winslet, and several others contributed to it. Millvina died of pneumonia after a brief illness on May 31, 2009, at ninety-seven. After cremation, her ashes were scattered from a small launch off *Titanic*'s former berth at the Southampton docks. Fittingly, the youngest child to survive the sinking of *Titanic* was also the last to die.

***

Perhaps the most remarkable fact about *Titanic*'s child survivors is how generally unremarkable their post-disaster lives were. Many of them did not publicly acknowledge the fact they were on *Titanic*, even to their families, until later in life. In many cases, this occurred in the 1950s, with the publicity surrounding Walter Lord's book, *A Night to Remember*, and the films *Titanic* and *A Night to Remember*. Any fame child survivors garnered was usually in relation to the fact they had survived. In later life, many of them were highly sought after to attend conventions organized by *Titanic* enthusiasts—even if the survivor had been a young child or baby at the time and had no recollection of the disaster. Some who had memories of that dreadful night recorded their experiences in books, but none of them came anywhere near to achieving bestseller status. For almost all the survivors, however, the fact they had come through the most famous marine disaster in history did not seem to affect them. Usually, their lives consisted of simply getting on with the humdrum of daily existence: education, employment, marriage, children, and the other minutiae of everyday life.

CHAPTER 11

UNBORN ABOARD & ORPHANS ASHORE

My poor grandmother never knew her father, and that was
something that troubled her until the day she died.

—Beverly Farmer, granddaughter of Ellen Phillips

The Unborn Aboard

All human beings begin life afloat in warm amniotic fluid designed
to protect them from injury and heat loss. Where their mothers go,
they go. At least seventeen unborn babies were aboard *Titanic*, afloat not
only within their mothers' wombs but also upon the North Atlantic. For
three women, their unborn perished with them when they died in the
sinking. Four pregnant women survived the sinking, but subsequently
miscarried or gave birth to children who died soon thereafter. Ten more
women gave birth to children who grew to adulthood; these are, in a
sense, the youngest *Titanic* survivors. Their stories are told here.

The stories of those women whose pregnancies are known, from that
of one of the wealthiest women in the world to the poorest Irish immigrant in steerage, reflect hope and joy, fear and uncertainty, happiness
and sorrow. Indeed, the same emotions that women around the world
may experience when they realize they are pregnant. Most pregnant
women, however, do not have the additional trauma of surviving a disaster and, for some, losing a spouse. Their children, while never having
had the chance to run along the decks of *Titanic*, nevertheless grew up in
families forever marked by the tragedy.

Alfhild Backström

The first *Titanic* baby to be born post-sinking was Alfhild Backström,
born in Finland on June 29, 1912. Her parents had been childhood friends.

Although each had lived previously in the United States, it was not until they returned to Finland that they married in 1911. But Mr. Backström, a carpenter by trade, had been offered a job in construction management back in the US and, with a baby on the way, decided to accept the opportunity. Joining them on the journey were Mrs. Backström's two brothers and a young woman from their hometown, Erna Andersson (16). All three men were lost in the sinking. Alone, six months pregnant, and widowed, Mrs. Backström returned to Finland, courtesy of the White Star Line. Back in her hometown, she gave birth to a daughter, Alfhild. It appears that Mrs. Backström never remarried, as her obituary in 1947 notes, "Thankful memories kept by daughter, son in law...Alfhild and Yrjo Forso." Alfhild, the first *Titanic* baby, died in 1973, aged sixty-one.

John Jacob Astor VI

The second *Titanic* baby born post-tragedy was also the most anticipated. Among the eight women on board who were newlyweds or on their honeymoon, Madeleine Astor received the most publicity. In the summer of 1910, the athletic teenager from Brooklyn had caught the eye of the recently divorced Colonel John Jacob Astor IV while she was playing tennis in Bar Harbor, Maine. He was the forty-six-year-old scion of the enormously wealthy and socially prominent Astor family of New York. She was a tall, blonde seventeen-year-old, only a year younger than Astor's son, Vincent. Their marriage a year later at Beechwood, the Astor mansion in Newport, Rhode Island, scandalized New York society. To avoid rejection by that society, the newlyweds departed for an extended honeymoon in Egypt and Europe, hoping that the furor over their marriage would abate with time. Madeleine's pregnancy and morning sickness, however, brought an abrupt end to their travels abroad. The five-month-pregnant Madeleine and Colonel Astor boarded *Titanic* in Cherbourg, the wealthiest of the wealthy in first class. Accompanying them were Madeleine's nurse, a maid, a manservant, and their pet Airedale, Kitty.

Their journey, covered extensively by the press, is one of the most well-known stories of the sinking. Astor saw his young bride safely into Lifeboat 4, asked if he could accompany her because of her "delicate condition," and then, despite his enormous wealth and power, took the refusal stoically and went down with the ship. From the moment of her arrival in New York to the funeral of her husband (Body No. 124 had been recovered and sent by a special train from Halifax) to the reading of the will, the young widow and her "*Titanic* Baby" were the focus of intense speculation. Indeed, although the will provided her with an income from a five-million-dollar (C$211,463,325) trust fund, there was a shocking stipulation—she would remain eligible for it only if she did not remarry. Moreover, her unborn child would receive a three-million-dollar (C$126,877,995) trust fund, far less than the $150 million (C$6,343,899,750) that elder son Vincent would inherit when he turned twenty-one that November.

John Jacob Astor VI, nicknamed Jakey, was born on August 14, 1912, into a life of enormous wealth. (John Jacob Astor V was born into another branch of the family tree). The baby spent the following summer in Bar Harbor with his still-mourning mother. When she petitioned the court to increase the allowance for her son's upkeep, the press was not kind. By the summer of 1915, Madeleine, now out of mourning, had begun seeing a friend from her childhood. When they married the next summer, Jakey gained a stepfather and Madeleine gave up her trust fund.

John Jacob Astor VI grew up in Newport, where he attended St. George's School. Like his father before him, he went to Harvard, but unlike his father, who was a successful businessman, Jakey became a member of the class known as the idle rich. Shortly after he

Madeleine Astor and her baby, John Jacob Astor VI.

received his inheritance in 1933, he went through a broken engagement, followed by a hasty marriage, the first of four. Jack (as he was now known; also having given up the Roman numerals after his name) and his marriages and divorces, like those of his mother, were the subject of extensive press coverage. The same New York society that had disapproved of the newlywed Madeleine now rejected her son, and in 1954, his name was removed from the all-important Social Register. Jack had always resented his half-brother Vincent who, he believed, had unfairly received more than his share of the Astor estate. When Vincent died in 1959, Jack sought, unsuccessfully, to have his father's will overturned. He died in Miami in 1992 at the age of seventy-nine. An interesting postscript to his unhappy domestic life: in 2012, one hundred years after the loss of the father he never knew, Jack's grandson Gregory Astor portrayed Colonel Astor in a production of *Titanic the Musical.*

Mrs. W. K. Dick (formerly Madeleine Astor) and Jakey.

Other 1912 babies

The fall of 1912 saw the birth of five more *Titanic* babies. Irish citizens and newlyweds Hannah and Thomas O'Brien boarded at Queenstown planning to join Mr. O'Brien's sisters in Chicago. He died in the sinking. After arrival in New York, twenty-seven-year-old Hannah decided not to return to Ireland or go on to Chicago. She gave birth on September 3, 1912, to her daughter, Marion, in Brooklyn, New York. She prevailed in a dispute with her husband's family over claims for compensation for his loss by producing proof of her marriage. In a letter to her sister-in-law, she wrote bitterly, "You needn't worry about me. My baby and myself will be alright. I knew ye were all trying to get some money." She stayed in Brooklyn, married another Irish expatriate, and had a son in 1918. Shortly thereafter, she died during the influenza pandemic, leaving Marion to be raised by her stepfather. When Marion grew up, she worked as a telephone operator, married an Irish immigrant, had three children, and lived most of her life in Albany, New York. She died in 1994 at the age of eighty-one in Tennessee, where she had been living with her daughter. Once again, however, an ending can also be a beginning. In 2005, Irish writer Martina Devlin discovered her connection to Marion's father, Thomas O'Brien: he was her great-uncle. Subsequent research within her family fleshed out the details, and she used some of this as the basis for her 2007 novel *Ship of Dreams*, a fictional tale of several people in a *Titanic* lifeboat.

Upon the loss of her husband, Edwy, in the sinking, pregnant Ada West returned to England with her daughters Constance and Barbara. On September 14, 1912, Edwyna West was born and named after the father she never knew. Like her two older sisters, she grew up and was educated in Cornwall. In 1941, she married a young second lieutenant in the army. Their married life took them to the Bahamas, where her husband became the Permanent Secretary for the Ministry of Agriculture, Fisheries and Local Government. Edwyna returned to England and died in Plymouth in 1969.

Only eighteen years old, first-class passengers Mary and Daniel Marvin of New York married in January 1912 and departed on a grand European honeymoon. Four months later, they boarded *Titanic* for their return to New York. Like two-thirds of the men in first class, Daniel died in the sinking, but Mary survived, and seven months later in October, Mary Margaret "Peggy" Marvin was born in New York. By Christmas 1913, Mary had remarried to a friend of her late husband, who adopted Peggy in 1916. Like her mother, Peggy married at eighteen and had a child in 1931. She died in October 1993 in Stockbridge, Massachusetts, aged eighty-one.

Italian immigrants Argene and Sebastiano del Carlo boarded *Titanic* in Cherbourg as second-class passengers bound for a new life in the United States. Argene escaped the sinking ship; Sebastiano's body (No. 295) was recovered by *Mackay-Bennett* and his remains sent to Boston from Halifax by train. Argene, who had found shelter with nuns in New York, travelled to Boston and then accompanied her husband's body back to Italy aboard *Cretic* in May. On November 14, 1912, their daughter was born in Tuscany. Perhaps with a nod to her miraculous survival, she named her daughter Maria Salvata del Carlo, the middle name translating to "saved." Argene remarried after seventeen years, and Maria gained two half-siblings.

According to her sister, Maria did not have an easy life. She married and had two sons, but her husband died young. Maria's house was destroyed by bombing during the Second World War. She lived in relative obscurity until 1998, when the movie *Titanic* was released in Italy. Suddenly, at the age of eighty-six, she became famous as a *Titanic* baby. Maria's story appeared in newspaper articles, she was interviewed for television, and people sought her autograph. Italian newspapers called her "l'ultima superstite italiana"—the last Italian survivor. When Maria died in Tuscany in October 2008 at the age of ninety-five, she was the oldest of the unborn aboard *Titanic*. According to her wishes, she was buried next to the father she never knew in the Altopascio cemetery.

Another young woman from first class who was wed, pregnant, widowed, and became a mother within months was eighteen-year-old Eloise Smith. The daughter of a West Virginia congressman, the debutante Eloise met twenty-four-year-old Lucian Philip Smith, whose family was involved in the coal business in West Virginia. Married in February 1912, they departed on a grand around-the-world honeymoon. Perhaps because of her pregnancy, they ended their honeymoon prematurely and boarded *Titanic* in Cherbourg. The night of the sinking, Lucian left his card game, roused his wife, placed her in Lifeboat 6, and went down with the ship. Her affidavit critical of the ship was read to the Senate inquiry by her father. On November 29, 1912, Lucian Philip Smith II was born in Cincinnati, Ohio. Madeleine Astor telegraphed her congratulations.

A little over two years later, Eloise married fellow *Titanic* survivor Robert Daniel, whom she had first met onboard *Carpathia*. It appeared that young Lucian would have a typical upper-class American childhood, but this storybook ending was not to be. The couple

Eloise Smith and her son Lucian.

divorced in 1923. Eloise remarried in 1924, was widowed again in 1929, remarried, and divorced once more. Despite the marital strife, Lucian grew up the centre of his mother's attention. On his twenty-first birthday, she wrote to him about his birth: "You were so adorable and such a gift from God to assuage all my grief." His mother died at forty-six, when he was twenty-eight years old. According to Lucian's obituary, he had his own realty business in Pennsylvania, served in the Second World War, married, had two daughters, joined the Elks and the Veterans of Foreign Wars, and retired to Venice, Florida, where he died in 1971, at fifty-eight.

The Last *Titanic* Babies

As the calendar turned over to 1913, the last three *Titanic* babies were born. At the time, the discovery of a pregnancy in an unmarried woman was often regarded as scandalous. Because nineteen-year-old

Englishwoman Kate Phillips was running away with her married thirty-eight-year-old lover and employer, Henry Morley, the couple were in second class under the assumed names of Mr. and Mrs. Marshall. Henry, senior partner in an English confectionery firm, was lost in the sinking, but Kate survived and returned to England to give birth to Ellen on January 11, 1913. Because this birth occurred almost nine months exactly after the sinking, Kate may have been unaware that she was pregnant on board. While in New York, however, the realization that her hoped-for escape to a fresh start in the US was impossible with her condition had implications for the rest of her unhappy life. Kate's parents raised Ellen for the first nine years of her life, and she had minimal contact with her mother. When Kate remarried in 1918 and had another daughter in 1919, she brought her first daughter to live with them in London. Ellen described years of abuse by her mother, whom she suspected had a mental illness, although she recalled her stepfather was very kind.

Ellen only became aware of her heritage when her aunts revealed her dad's name to her when she was ten or eleven. Although she was curious, she never attempted to make contact with his family. She married in 1935, had a son, lost custody of her son in a divorce, and in 1944 married again. Estranged from her mother, Ellen was not immediately made aware of her death in 1964 at age seventy-one. In her later years, she sought recognition as Henry Morley's daughter. The British Titanic Society did officially recognize her as a descendant of a *Titanic* survivor, but it was not until 2020 that DNA testing of the Phillips and Morley families confirmed that status. That acknowledgment came too late for Ellen, however, who had died in 2005 at the age of ninety-two. Her last request was to have her ashes scattered off the North Cornwall coast, hundreds of kilometres away from her father's resting place, but at least part of the same ocean.

The Laroche family's plan to move to Haiti, Mr. Laroche's birthplace, ended with his death. A pregnant Mrs. Laroche and her two daughters returned to France where they lived with her father in Villejuif. On January 17, 1912, she gave birth to Joseph Philippe Lemercier Laroche, named after his dead father. The next few years were difficult financially, until after the First World War, when Mrs. Laroche was able to secure

The second-class promenade area of the boat deck. The middle female in the group of three may be Ada Doling.

compensation from the White Star Line. Unlike his older sisters who never left home or married, Joseph grew up, married a co-worker at Électricité de France, and had three children. He died in 1987.

Because determining gestation dates is not an exact science, the last pregnant woman may have been Englishwoman Ada Doling, thirty-four. Accompanied by her sister-in-law, Mrs. Doling was travelling to New York to visit her mother, who had moved there some years previously. After her rescue, Mrs. Doling returned to England on May 11, where she was reunited with her husband. On January 30, 1913, she gave birth to a baby girl, Ida, her fifth and last child—and possibly the last baby in utero on *Titanic*. Given the passage of nine months and fifteen days since the sinking, it is plausible that she was already pregnant while on board, and the baby was overdue. Alternatively, the birth might have been the result of the presumably joyful reunion of husband and wife, and the baby was premature. Ida died in 1981, aged sixty-nine.

Orphans Ashore

"What are we waiting for Mummy? Why are we waiting
such a long time?"
"We are waiting for news of father dear."
—*Daily Mail* (London), April 18, 1912

Southampton is unique among cities for the disaster which befell its citizens in April 1912. Unlike Halifax in 1917 or New York in 2001 or New Orleans in 2005, the city itself remained unscathed: no explosion in the harbour rained down debris, no hijacked airplanes collapsed skyscrapers, no breached levees wiped out whole sections of the city. Instead, the residents of Southampton suffered from a tragedy that occurred 2,900 kilometres (1,800 miles) away in the Atlantic Ocean. Nevertheless, the impact upon Southampton was dramatic, for almost 700 of the 900 crew aboard *Titanic* listed Southampton as their last address. Of the 695 crew members lost, 549 called Southampton home. Some of those Sotonians had lived in various Southampton neighbourhoods for generations, while others had arrived since the relocation of the White Star Line in 1907. Still others had arrived just prior to signing on *Titanic*. For many coming to find work, the Sailors' Home on Oxford Road offered a temporary place to stay and was listed as the address of twenty-six crew members.

The loss of *Titanic* was a cruel blow to this port city since only one week earlier, those who had signed on to *Titanic* were considered the lucky ones. Because most crew members were not permanent employees but employed on a per-voyage basis, the spring of 1912 had been particularly tough. The coal strike, which had been going on since February, meant fewer ships were leaving port, which meant less work for the people in town, which meant more hungry families. By some accounts, at least 17,000 men were out of work. Because the White Star Line wanted the maiden voyage of *Titanic* to go off as planned, coal was transferred from other ships. The ship would sail and it needed crew. While most of the senior officers had already been assigned in Belfast, it fell to Southampton to provide firemen, engineers, stewards, kitchen staff, and other crew members needed to keep the ship steaming across the Atlantic and to take care of the passengers. In addition to the anticipation of desperately needed pay, the crew and their families also enjoyed a bit of bragging rights; after all, would not they be serving on the grandest ship ever to set sail from Southampton?

When wives and children waved goodbye to family members on April 10, they believed their loved ones would return within the month. After the six-day crossing to New York and time for loading and provisioning, the ship would turn around and sail back to Southampton via Plymouth and Cherbourg. Bedroom steward Fred Simmons's last letter to his wife, posted from Queenstown, was full of love and optimism, "How are you going on I hope you and the baby are keeping well." He closed with, "love to all at home and heaps of it and kisses for you and Teddy."

The first reports of *Titanic*'s sinking on Monday, April 15, brought hopeful news. From neighbourhoods across Southampton—the docklands areas of Northam and Chapel, where the firemen, greasers, and trimmers lived, and the not-quite-as-poor areas of Freemantle and Shirley, where the stewards lived—family members streamed to the White Star Line offices on Canute Road. In their quest for information about the fate of their loved ones, they were met by frustrating silence. Some sought news from the recently formed Seafarers' Union, to which many crew belonged. The agonizing wait for information stretched on for days, and it was not until Friday, April 19, that the first lists of survivors were posted outside the White Star Offices. Hope gave way to despair as more youngsters, like William Hawkesworth, were told, "Your father will not be coming home anymore, children."

Southampton plunged into mourning. Charles Morgan, who was a child at the time, recalled, "A great hush descended on the town...because I don't think that there was hardly a single street in Southampton who hadn't lost somebody on that ship." Blinds were drawn, flags flew at half mast, and newspapers of the day described a city of widows and streets of sorrow. Around the world, there was an outpouring not only of grief but also of money to assist both survivors and families of victims. In England, local and national fundraising efforts eventually coalesced into the Titanic Relief Fund (amassing £414,000—C$22,261,865). In Southampton, this fund was initially under the purview of Lord Mayor Henry Bowyer and his wife. By the end of 1912, a more formal relief fund committee had been set up with members drawn from the upper echelons of Southampton society.

In early twentieth-century England, many believed that poverty was somehow a moral failing. *Titanic* widows were at least spared that shame, as their loved ones were elevated to heroic status. At St. Augustine's Church in Northam, where so many of the deceased lived, Rev. H. M. Ellis told the widows in his sermon that they "would be able to teach their children that their fathers died as Christian Englishmen should die, that England would always remember them with thankful pride, and that England was today the better for what they did." It was only later that stories began to emerge that, other than the few crewmen enlisted to row the lifeboats, crew members were treated similarly to male passengers. They did not volunteer to stay on board; some were ordered to stay below deck, while others were denied access to lifeboats.

But the grieving families needed more than sympathy. Many families were in dire financial straits. Upon *Titanic*'s sinking, all crew members, dead or alive, had their pay stopped immediately. When the owed wages were finally rendered to their families, the amount might have been less the cost of the uniforms in which they had died. In neighbourhoods across Southampton, there was rent to be paid, children to be fed, and no money to do either. It took time, of course, to put into place the rules and methods of disbursing relief funds. In the interim, some sought relief under the Workmen's Compensation Act. Others received support from the Seafarers' Union. Churches, the Salvation Army, schools, and charitable organizations stepped into the breach. An article in the Salvation Army's *The War Cry* of April 27, 1912, noted, "Everything is being done by our comrades to minimize the suffering on the part of the women and children." According to the descendants of Emily Bessant, wife of fireman William Bessant and mother of five, some widows resorted to taking in washing to make ends meet.

While there was general agreement that the dependent families deserved compensation, there was less agreement about how much, for how long, and how it would be distributed. Even though the wives of seafaring husbands were quite used to managing a household and its finances during their husbands' long absences, it was determined that the money needed to be carefully allocated over time, so that it would last until the final dependant died. In addition to preservation of the capital, the fund was to sustain, but not improve, the living standard of recipients. For families already living in poverty, this stipulation basically ensured they would continue to live in poverty. Upward mobility was not the goal. Finally, funds were to be used to steer dependent children toward gainful employment. For many children, this took the form of paying school and apprenticeship fees.

Relief amounts followed a formula based on the occupation of the deceased crew member and awarded half the wages formerly earned by each worker to their widow, with an additional stipend for each child. At the top, Class A covered officers and engineers, whose widows would receive £2 (C$500) weekly and 7 shillings and 6 pence (C$93.50) for each child. At the bottom of the seven classes, Class G covered firemen, scullions, and lower-class stewards, whose widows would receive weekly support payments of 12 shillings and 6 pence (C$126), with an additional 2 shillings and 6 pence (C$31.15) for each child. Payments would cease when the girls reached eighteen and the boys turned sixteen. If widows remarried, their allowance would end. Moreover, if families received other forms of compensation, their awards could be reduced.

For *Titanic* dependants, the committee rejected lump sum payouts and felt the need to have someone watch over the families. Thus, they created the position of Lady Visitor, who for £100 (C$25,000) per year and expenses, would monitor the families, visit their homes, and assess not only their needs but also their fitness to continue to receive funds. Indeed, she would have her work cut out for her, as it was calculated that the fund would be required to assist 239 widows, 533 children under sixteen, 42 children over sixteen, and 213 other dependants, such as parents and siblings. Miss Ethel Newman, thirty-six, a Southampton resident, filled this role until her death in 1940. Children who grew up in Southampton recall her bicycling down the streets of their neighbourhoods, accompanied by her dog on her way to home visits. They also recalled her visits as rather benign affairs; she was just someone who came by their homes on a regular basis. Nevertheless, the Relief Fund Committee minutes detail several incidents of relief being suspended for undesirable behaviour, such as drinking: "It was reported that Mrs. B had again been before the magistrates on a charge of drunkenness and it was reluctantly decided to suspend her allowance for a period of 3 months. March 8 1918."

So not only were the widows not to be entrusted with lump sum pay-outs of the money that had been donated to sustain their families, they were also required to meet certain standards of behaviour. An article in the *English Historical Review* maintains these patriarchal attitudes "con-signed many of the relatives of victims to poverty-stricken lives, despite the massive funds collected in their names."

What, then, became of the over five hundred children who were left fatherless in Southampton? While the stories of these children could eas-ily fill a book, a few examples will highlight what it was like to live in the city of widows.

At Northam Girls' School, where 120 out of 250 pupils lost their father, the headmistress's entries in the daily log reflect the direness of their situation:

> *April 15:* A great many girls are absent this afternoon owing to the sad news regarding the '*Titanic*', fathers and brothers are on the vessel and some of the little ones have been in tears all afternoon.
> *April 17:* So many of the crew belonged to Northam & it is pathetic to witness the children's grief.
> *May 18:* The acute distress among the people is daily becoming more evident. 24 free meals given today and the shoeless and hungry children are many.

The *Southampton Pictorial* in May 1912 recorded the dubious—and decidedly insensitive—"prize" awarded to nine-year-old student Amy Willsher, daughter of assistant butcher William Willsher. As the young-est child at the Northam Girls' School to lose a father, she received a doll which had been donated by the children of the Fourth Avenue Girls' School in London. Amy had three younger siblings at home; her mom gave birth to another son in July.

Among the forty-four headstones of *Titanic* victims in Southampton Old Cemetery are those of Arthur May, sixty, and his twenty-three-year-old son, also called Arthur (their bodies were never recovered). According to the elder May's widow, "It was the first time that Arthur and his father had been at sea together." The loss of both her husband and son had "left eleven of us." She had eight other children and her son's wife had just given birth to their first child in February.

While most of the families were left to grieve without a body to bury, Emily Wormald received notice that her husband's body (No. 144) had been recovered by *Mackay-Bennett* and taken to Halifax. Thus began an odyssey, which can best be described as an unfortunate comedy of errors, for the family. To begin with, first-class saloon steward Frederick Wormald had been misclassified in Halifax as a Jewish man because of his Hebrew-sounding name and was buried in the Baron de Hirsch Cemetery. In August, the White Star Line arranged for Emily and her six children to sail to New York aboard *Olympic* and from there make their way to Halifax to visit his grave. All did not go according to plan when immigration officials at Ellis Island refused the family entry on the grounds of "no visible means of support" and sent them back to England. Their trials did not end there. Arriving in Southampton on September 15 after a six-week absence, the family found that their landlord had rented their home out and removed their belongings, which kindly neighbours had retrieved. The Wormalds secured new accommodation the next day and received assistance from the Titanic Relief Fund.

Others among the crew left behind pregnant wives. Florence, the wife of Harry Jones, a roast cook, gave birth to a son in October 1912. That child would never know his father. Eleanor, wife of trimmer Arthur Morgan, was also pregnant but died during childbirth in September. The orphaned child was fortunate in that Eleanor's mother took in her grandchild, saving him from the orphanage. Greaser Frederick Woodford, whose body (No. 163) was recovered and buried in Halifax, left behind a wife and two daughters in Southampton. When both his younger daughter and his wife died shortly thereafter, the elder daughter was taken in by her aunt. The Titanic Relief Fund allowed for relatives like this to also receive support, which surely helped keep more children out of orphanages and workhouses.

Other children, who were orphaned or in families where there may have been simply too many mouths to feed, were not so fortunate, and in some cases *Titanic* relief funds were paid directly to orphanages, such as Dr. Barnardo Homes. From the minutes of the Relief Fund Committee on November 27, 1913: "Allowance discontinued as dependant is an inmate of the Southampton Workhouse." Other families were split up, and some children sent overseas.

While the crew was predominantly male, twenty-three females served aboard *Titanic*. Of the three female crew members who died, two lived in Southampton and left behind children. Sotonian Cissie Wallis was a thirty-six-year-old hospital matron aboard *Titanic*. Widowed only the year prior, she needed her £3 (C$750) monthly wages to support her four children. Her orphaned children were taken in by family members and received aid from the Titanic Relief Fund as Class G dependants. As adults, her two daughters immigrated to Canada in the 1920s. Her younger son died in 1929, while the older son went on to serve in the Royal Navy during the Second World War.

Although married, Irish-born Kate Walsh used her maiden name when signing on to *Titanic* as a steward. The forty-two-year-old lived with her eight-year-old daughter in Southampton, apparently estranged from her husband, who lived with two older children in London. After her mother's death, the daughter received support from the Titanic Relief Fund, which ended in 1922 with a grant for an apprenticeship. She went on to become a teacher and later moved to Ireland, where she married, had four children, and was reluctant to ever speak about the tragedy that killed her mom.

Socially, the most prominent widow in Southampton was Eleanor, wife of Captain E. J. Smith and mother of their fourteen-year-old daughter, Helen. The captain and his family had relocated to Southampton from Liverpool in 1907 and lived in a red-brick house on Winn Road, far removed from the docklands where the firemen and trimmers lived. Soon after the sinking, she expressed her solidarity with the people of Southampton in a notice posted outside the White Star Line offices:

> To my poor fellow sufferers—my heart overflows with grief for you all and is laden with sorrow that you are weighed down with this terrible burden that has been thrust upon us. May God be with us and comfort us all. Yours in sympathy, Eleanor Smith

As the wife of the captain, of course, Eleanor did not have the same financial worries as the families of his crew; the White Star Line's pension and insurance provided her with a £1,168 (C$291,306) annual income. Although both American and English inquiries found fault with some of Captain Smith's decisions, in England he was generally regarded as a hero who went down with his ship in true English fashion. His daughter, Helen Melville Smith, who had just turned fourteen when her father died, led a life dogged by tragedy. Mel, as she was known, lost her husband in a hunting accident in 1930. The next year her mother died in London when struck by a taxi outside her home. Both of Mel's twins predeceased her: her son was killed in action in 1944 and her daughter died of polio in 1947. When she met the actor playing Captain Smith in the movie *A Night to Remember* in 1956, she remarked to the press that he bore a striking resemblance to her father. Mel died in 1973 at seventy-five and is buried in Brookwood Cemetery, along with her mother and two *Titanic* survivors.

Despite the rules of disbursement, despite the strict oversight, despite the paltry amounts that kept some families in poverty, the fund did have a significant impact. A hundred years later, a local Southampton historian noted, "You can never replace the loss of a husband but many of the widows and children suddenly found they had a dependable income for the first time in their lives." As Edward Simmons, who was only five months old when his steward father went down on *Titanic*, recounted, "When I left school at 14 and mother didn't want me to go to sea obviously... anyhow Miss Newman the visitor from the disaster fund suggested I should be apprenticed to an upholsterer...they paid my apprenticeship fees and bought my tools." Sadly, despite the loss of their fathers at sea, many young men saw no other alternative but to follow in their footsteps. From the minutes of December 22, 1913: "That the special grant of 5/- [5 shillings and zero pence] (C$62.35) a week be discontinued as the surviving son is now earning on the *Olympic.*"

The five youngest crew members who died (four from Southampton), boys of fourteen, fifteen, and sixteen, left no orphaned children. Although they earned wages, because of their youth, they still received special supervision on board. At the end, however, no one took responsibility for their safety. Last seen smoking on the deck of the sinking ship, not one of these young crewmen survived. Their loss was sorely grieved by their families, who in many cases relied upon their wages. Arthur Barratt's death notice in the *Hampshire Independent* on May 1, 1912, reads: "Barratt, Arthur. Dearly beloved son of Arthur and Margaret Barratt, 164 Northumberland Road, Aged 15 years." His family received support from the Titanic Relief Fund.

The Harris family mourned the loss of two sons, the younger Clifford and the older Charles. Their death notice in the *Hampshire Advertiser* on April 27, 1912, notes: "Harris—On the 15th inst, at sea on s.s. Titanic, Charles William, aged 19, and Clifford Henry, aged 16, the sons of Wallace and Christina Harris, of Chapel Road, Southampton."

Beyond his family, the death of Frederick Hopkins (14) was mourned by many in the community because he had been an exemplary Boy Scout. His scoutmaster, Mr. J. Mew, wrote of him, "He was a thorough scout in every sense, always ready to serve and lend a helping hand." He continued, seemingly without realizing the irony of his praise, "He was very fond of swimming and gained several certificates at life-saving and swimming classes, and took great interest in teaching and helping the younger boys to swim." His parents also received support from the Titanic Relief Fund. Among the crew on *Titanic*, the restaurant staff suffered especially high losses. Only three survived and assistant waiter Paolo Crovella (16) was not one of them.

Two years after the sinking of *Titanic*, England entered the First World War, bringing even more tragedy to Southampton. It became sadly normal to be fatherless. Edward Simmons, who was brought up on the Titanic Relief Fund, reflected, "When I was growing up there were so many other orphans around about my age whose fathers had been killed in the war. When we were growing up there weren't a lot of young men about, very few...I mean it was just normal for quite a lot of people not to have a father."

CHAPTER 12

TITANIC IN POPULAR MEMORY

I don't remember anything of the actual event. But I have
lived it over and over again as my mother told me, as I read
books and magazines about the events.

—Bert Dean, 23 months on *Titanic*

What is the deadliest peacetime disaster in maritime history?
With little hesitation, most would respond *"Titanic."* The correct
response, however, is the 1987 sinking of the MV *Doña Paz*, a passenger
ferry in the Philippines, after a collision with an oil tanker. Estimates put
the death toll over four thousand. Only twenty-six people survived. And
yet, that more recent disaster, sometimes referred to as Asia's *Titanic*,
has never reached the same iconic status. A seemingly endless stream
of books, articles, websites, online discussion groups, theme parks, television programmes, and movies attests to the continuing interest in
Titanic. Curiously, among *Titanic* enthusiasts, children are among the
most well-informed.

Many theories about the lasting popularity of the *Titanic* story centre
on universal themes: Edwardian hubris at declaring the ship unsinkable,
humans versus nature, heroes and villains, sin and redemption, class dif-
ferences, and unnecessary errors that led to the tragedy. Certainly, the
advent of wireless telegraphy provided quicker access as the story sped
around the globe. Newspapers of the day sought the most sensational
survivor stories to sell their papers and were not above inventing details
of the sinking. Moreover, because the disaster was not limited to one
social class or to one country, *Titanic* stories had wide appeal. From villages in Lebanon to farms in Ireland, from shipbuilders in Belfast to widows in Southampton, from manor houses in England to wealthy enclaves
in the United States, from New York (which received the survivors) to

Halifax (which received the bodies), reports reached across the Western world and beyond. The story has also endured across time; more than a century later, *Titanic* can still grab the headlines. The rise in public fascination with *Titanic* can often be linked to a defining event: the initial sinking, the mid-century book and movie releases, the discovery of the wreck and the subsequent movie blockbuster, and, in the twenty-first century, the centennial of the sinking. Each wave of interest amplifies the previous wave while, at the same time, introducing the story to the next generation. The waves continue to roll on today.

The First Wave – *Titanic* Memorials (beginning in 1912)

As maritime historian John Maxtone-Graham noted, *Titanic*'s loss "precipitated an orgy of remembrance." In the immediate aftermath of the disaster, both personal and group memorials were erected: headstones, monuments, fountains, plaques, stained glass windows, statues, and gardens. In the United Kingdom, memorials were erected not only to individual crew members but also to whole groups: engineers, musicians, wireless operators, postal workers, restaurant staff. Visiting these memorials left an indelible impression on many children. As noted in the Southampton City Heritage Oral History, "Another memory is going with him (my father) to stand by the memorial to the men and women who lost their lives in the disaster."

For the most part, however, children were not the subject of public memorials. Occasionally, a child was involved in a dedication, as was the case in 1914 when teenager Helen "Mel" Smith, daughter of *Titanic*'s captain, dedicated her father's memorial in Lichfield. Sometimes a memorial was designed to actually benefit children. In Dalbeattie, Scotland, in addition to creating a memorial tablet honouring First Officer William Murdoch, the town also established the Murdoch Memorial Prize to be awarded annually to a pupil not exceeding the age of fourteen years who "attends the school where Lieutenant Murdoch was educated." (That prize is still awarded today, and the trust fund received an infusion of £5,000 (C$19,210) in 1998 when 20th Century Fox attempted to make amends for its unflattering portrayal of Murdoch in the movie *Titanic*.)

Belfast, Ireland, the birthplace of *Titanic*, mourned not only the loss of life but also the loss of the great ship itself. The first name listed on their memorial statue is that of Thomas Andrews, managing director of the Harland and Wolff shipyard and *Titanic*'s designer who was on board as head of the guarantee group. Only half an hour away, his hometown of Comber dedicated the Thomas Andrews Memorial Hall in 1915. The imposing structure served as a community centre for many years and later became part of the eponymous Andrews Memorial Primary School.

The Titanic Memorial in Washington, DC, is one of the few memorials that specifically mentions children. Although often called the Women's Titanic Memorial, it is, in fact, dedicated, "To the Brave Men Who Perished in the Wreck...They Gave Their Lives that Women and Children Might Be Saved." The name stems from the fact that it was championed, funded, and designed by women. The Women's Titanic Memorial Association sought one-dollar donations from American women, sponsored fundraising events, and with the help of prominent women like First Ladies Mrs. Grover Cleveland and Mrs. William Taft, by 1914 had raised enough funds to sponsor a design competition, open only to women.

The Titanic Memorial in Washington, DC.

Gertrude Vanderbilt's design of a semi-naked man with outstretched arms was chosen, and the sculpture was dedicated in 1931 (some have described the figure as Christ-like, while contemporary visitors note that the pose is not unlike that of Rose in the 1997 *Titanic* movie). Now located in a quiet waterfront park in southwest Washington, the four-metre (thirteen-foot)-tall statue rests on a square base and is one of the lesser-known monuments in DC. Each year after midnight on April 15, the Men's Titanic Society gathers at its base to lay a wreath and raise a champagne toast.

As the city that saw the recovery operation for *Titanic*'s victims and as the final resting place for 150 of them, by default Halifax has the largest number of *Titanic* memorials in the world—the headstones of those individuals. They are in three cemeteries: 121 in non-denominational Fairview Lawn, 19 in Roman Catholic Mount Olivet, and 10 in Jewish Baron de Hirsch. The White Star Line covered expenses for burials at all three cemeteries and paid for the upkeep of the graves until 1930, when it established a C$7,500 (C$133,233) fund with the Royal Trust Company for future care.

A stonemason from the Halifax Marble Works used polished black granite for standard headstones: small black rectangles with sloping tops. On these tops, all headstones bear the inscription "Died April 15, 1912," followed by the body number. Where the name was known, it was placed above this inscription. If an individual's identity was discovered later, the name is inscribed on the front of the stone.

Relatives were also able to pay to have a more traditional headstone of their choice placed on a grave with the inscription they wanted. The headstone of twenty-four-year-old coal trimmer Everett Edward Elliott is one of these, and it bears a very moving quotation. In the aftermath of the disaster, several newspapers carried stories about members of the crew who survived, while women and children were lost. Elliot's family wanted to correct this misapprehension and ensure the public knew he had died bravely while doing his duty.

One of the larger standard headstones is for a passenger: Alma Pålsson (spelled Paulson on the stone, the anglicized version of the name her husband had chosen). Besides noting her age and husband's name, it also lists the names and ages of her four children: "Torburg Danria aged 8, Paul Folke aged 6, Stina Viola aged 4, and Gosta Leonard aged 2."

Nearby, one of the traditional headstones holds a special place in the hearts of Haligonians and those who visit the cemetery. It is that of the Unknown Child, for many years thought to be Alma Pålsson's youngest child, Gösta, then Finnish boy Eino Panula in 2002, and finally confirmed as English boy Sidney Goodwin in 2007.

There is also a parent buried in each of Baron de Hirsch and Mount Olivet cemeteries, who had their children with them on *Titanic*. Michel Navratil lies in Baron de Hirsch, mistakenly assumed to be Jewish because of his assumed name, Louis M. Hoffman, while Margaret Rice is buried at Mount Olivet.

The *Titanic* story was also memorialized beyond monuments of brass and stone, often by the survivors themselves. Survivor Charlotte Collyer (mother of Marjorie, 8) received $300 (C$12,710) for her account "How I Was Saved From the Titanic" for the *Semi-Monthly Magazine Section*, which was inserted in several American newspapers in May 1912. For a little over $7 (C$296) per show, Jane Quick, accompanied by her daughters, Winnie and Phyllis, gave presentations to vaudeville audiences in Detroit and other Michigan cities about their *Titanic* experience.

Notable British writers such as Sir Arthur Conan Doyle, Joseph Conrad, and George Bernard Shaw offered their conflicting opinions on the causes of the disaster. Thomas Hardy composed and delivered his poem "The Convergence of the Twain" for a Titanic Relief Fund event in London in 1912. Moved by the tragedy, amateur poets also felt the need to memorialize the disaster in verse. The *New York Times* received so much mediocre poetry submitted by readers that, by the end of April, they published an editorial "Only Poets Should Write Verse," asking submissions to stop because "a poem worth printing requires that the author should have more than paper, pencil, and a strong feeling that the disaster was a terrible one." Certainly not in that category is the lengthy 1935 narrative poem "The Titanic" by award-winning Canadian poet E. J. Pratt. The poem, which tells the *Titanic* story from launching to sinking, contains this poignant description:

> A boy of ten,
> Ranking himself within the class of men,
> Though given a seat, made up his mind to waive
> The privilege of his youth and size, and piled

The inches on his stature as he gave
Place to a Magyar woman and her child.

With changing tastes in art, literature, and music, it is natural that some memorials did not stand the test of time. Although more than one hundred songs about *Titanic* were published in 1912 and 1913, most, like "My Sweetheart Went Down with the Ship," did not endure. Strangely enough, it is a song loved by children which has lasted across the decades. Believed to date from 1915, the American folk song "The Titanic" was recorded by folksingers such as Woody Guthrie and Pete Seeger. Its catchy refrain has been sung around the fire at summer camps for generations:

It was sad. It was sad.
It was sad when the great ship went down
(to the bottom of the...)
Husbands and wives,
Little children lost their lives
It was sad when the great ship went down.

The Second Wave – The Night Remembered (beginning in 1953)

By the mid-twentieth century the *Titanic* story had largely faded away. In the intervening years, global attention was on two world wars and a depression. Other than a brief mention in an obituary when a survivor passed away, or newspaper reports of the scandalous behaviour of the likes of John Jacob Astor VI, little attention was paid to *Titanic*—until the 1950s when the *Titanic* story was thrust front and centre again. Many people who were not alive when *Titanic* sank recall their interest in the disaster started at this time.

First came the Oscar-winning movie *Titanic* starring Barbara Stanwyck, Clifton Webb, and Robert Wagner in 1953. Its plot line focuses on fictional characters aboard the ship and a parental kidnapping (shades of the Navratil story?). Next came Walter Lord's non-fiction book *A Night to Remember*, published in 1955, adapted for television in 1956, and made into a movie in 1958 (producer William MacQuitty, who had been born in Belfast, recalled watching the ship's launch as a six-year-old). The dramatic minute-by-minute account in Lord's book gripped

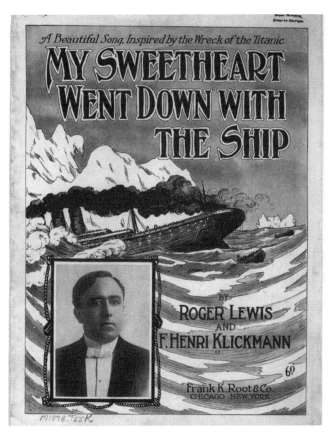

*The cover page for the sheet music to "My Sweetheart
Went Down with the Ship."*

readers; the ensuing film was one of the earliest in the genre known as
disaster movies. Both were critical successes and not only introduced
the *Titanic* story to new generations but also brought survivors into the
spotlight. The same could not be said of the next *Titanic* movie. *Raise the
Titanic* was released in 1980, based on the 1976 book of the same name
by Clive Cussler. While the book was a bestseller, the movie bombed
at the box office, causing its British producer Lew Grade to remark, "It
would have been cheaper to lower the Atlantic."

The Third Wave – Discovery (beginning in 1985)

Except for those few who were passionate about *Titanic*, again the story largely receded from the public consciousness, overtaken by the tremendous cultural upheavals of the 1960s and '70s. Then, early on September 1, 1985, oceanographer Dr. Robert Ballard out of the Woods Hole Oceanographic Institution in Massachusetts and his joint Franco-American team aboard the US Navy vessel *Knorr* sent out the first pic-tures of the *Titanic* debris field taken by the unmanned submersible *Argo*. Subsequent dives in the manned vessel *Alvin* and by the remotely operated vehicle *Jason Junior* produced stunning photos and videos. *Titanic* was in the headlines once again, and this time the wave of inter-est became a tsunami.

Ballard, acutely aware that the site was the grave of 1,500 people, sought only photos and films: "It is a quiet, peaceful place...Forever may it remain that way." His view was not shared by others who wanted to recover artifacts—and possibly gold and jewels rumoured to be on board. Survivors largely favoured leaving the wreck as it was. In a television interview, Eva Hart, who was just seven when she lost her dad, reacted to the discovery: "It is my father's grave and I would rather it were left untouched." Frank Aks, who was only ten months old when the ship sank, expressed a wish to view the ship: "I'd like to see part of it."

Who "owns" the wreck has resulted in years of litigation, which continues to this day. RMS Titanic Inc. was granted salvor-in-possession rights in June 1994, making it the only company allowed to collect artifacts. Over the course of several years and multiple dives, the company collected more than 5,500 artifacts, including a 15.5-tonne (17-ton) section of the hull that was raised out of the ocean in 1998. These artifacts have circled the world in travelling exhibitions, which have attracted over 35 million visitors, and are displayed in two permanent exhibitions in the entertainment centres of Las Vegas and Orlando.

With the discovery of the wreck, many people began to question how to memorialize the site and preserve the remains of the ship. Although it held no jurisdiction over international waters, the United States passed the RMS Titanic Maritime Memorial Act of 1986, which sought to encourage recognition of the wreck as a maritime memorial to those who lost their lives when it sank, to promote the development of an international agreement providing for the protection of the wreck, and to cultivate internationally recognized guidelines for research, exploration and, if appropriate, salvage activities. In addition, in 2012 when the wreck became one hundred years old, it became eligible for protection under UNESCO's Convention on the Protection of Underwater Cultural Heritage. Neither has prevented further exploration, or, as some believe, exploitation.

The Titanic Historical Society, which had assisted Dr. Ballard in researching the location of the wreck, was now emulated by similar societies around the world. Survivors and their descendants were in demand as guests and speakers at meetings and conventions held by the Titanic International Society, British Titanic Society, Belfast Titanic Society, and Titanic Society of Atlantic Canada. In 1986, Walter Lord updated his seminal book *A Night to Remember* with a sequel, *The Night Lives On*, bringing the story forward with twenty more years of knowledge.

Back in Halifax, unveiling ceremonies for six newly inscribed head-stones of recently identified victims were held at Fairview Lawn Cemetery in September 1991. The event was attended by hundreds of Halifax residents and televised. *QE2*'s captain also participated, expressing to the assemblage the Cunard Line's pride in *Carpathia*'s vital role in rescuing the survivors. After seventy years, however, the original gravestones needed maintenance. In the mid-1990s, the remaining money from the Royal Trust Company's maintenance fund was transferred to the city and apportioned out to the three cemeteries. In 1998, new foundations were made to reset the gravestones. Other improvements, such as better signage, whitening of the letters on the stones, and new walkways, have also been made. On July 28, 1999, the Titanic International Society returned to Fairview Lawn Cemetery and presented a ceremony titled "For the Children," remembering the fifty-three children under the age of fourteen who perished in the disaster.

The nineties also saw the return of *Titanic* to the big screen. In 1992, IMAX theatres presented the documentary *Titanica* narrated by Leonard Nimoy, which showed extraordinary video footage of the wreck interspersed with archival photos, commentary from experts, and clips of Frank Goldsmith and Eva Hart. Numerous documentaries for Discovery, History, and National Geographic channels fed an ever-increasing desire by the public to know every detail of the voyage. And it was one of these documentaries that first drew the interest of Canadian-born filmmaker James Cameron.

In December 1997, he introduced yet another generation to the tragedy in his romantic epic *Titanic*. Starring Kate Winslet and Leonardo DiCaprio and with stunning special effects, the film tells the love story of two fictional characters, Rose from first class and Jack from steerage. With extensive research—Cameron even visited the wreckage in a Russian submersible—he faithfully reproduced the look and feel of life aboard the vessel. Celine Dion's plaintive love song "My Heart Will Go On" from the movie soundtrack still evokes powerful emotions a generation later. Many moviegoers were convinced that Rose and Jack were real people, and even today notes and flowers are left on the grave of Body No. 227 in Halifax: coal trimmer J. Dawson.

So entrenched is *Titanic* in popular culture that it has also become a plot device in movies and television. When a character in a movie mentions departure for New York aboard *Titanic*, the audience suspects that character will not return. In a 1973 episode, members of the Bellamy family in the British series *Upstairs, Downstairs* perished on the *Titanic*. Thirty-five years later, the popular British series *Downton Abbey* begins with the news that Lord Grantham's cousin and his cousin's son have been lost on *Titanic*. The animated characters in a 2015 episode of the television series *Family Guy* time travel to *Titanic*. Containing details such as a dinner with Captain Smith, the irreverent show offered this disclaimer: "All history facts in this episode were gathered by quick glances at Wikipedia."

Non-fiction books about *Titanic* cover everything from the menu on the last night to the steel used in the hull. "Patently destructible in life," according to historian John Maxtone-Graham, "the *Titanic* has proved indestructible in memory." An internet search produces thousands of titles, most of which came after the mid-century wave: conspiracy theories, survivor memoirs, social history, iceberg formation, biographies, wireless technology, ship design, photographs and illustrations, and, ironically, even books about why the subject is so popular. Indeed, Walter Lord once noted that a new book about the *Titanic* disaster is published every week. Very few books, however, focus on capturing the stories of the children. For example, Walter Lord's updated book *The Night Lives On* devotes eight pages to the debate about the last song the band played but contains few references to children.

Over the years numerous books of popular fiction have also been set aboard *Titanic*. A huge subset of *Titanic* literature is books for children. Like the adult audience, children never seem to tire of the story. On the centennial of the disaster, Nimbus Publishing of Halifax released *Children of the Titanic* by Christine Welldon. The book covers three fictional children—one from each class—and their experiences aboard the ship from sailing to sinking. Scholastic, the world's largest publisher and distributor of children's books, has a whole library of *Titanic* books, covering grade levels from pre-K to high school. Their book *I Survived the Sinking of the Titanic, 1912* for grades 4 to 5 has recently been updated

POLAR, THE *TITANIC* BEAR

Nine-year-old Douglas Spedden's untimely death just three years after the sinking might have been the end of his story but for a fortuitous discovery. When Leighton Coleman was fourteen years old, he came across a dusty Louis Vuitton steamer trunk in his grandfather's barn on Long Island, New York. Inside were twenty-seven meticulously assembled photo albums, which depicted a close-knit family and their world of leisure and travel. As they looked through the albums together, his grandfather explained the family connection to the amateur photographer, Douglas's mom, Daisy Spedden. Several years later, when Coleman was helping his grandfather clear out the same barn, he rescued the trunk from a load meant for the dump. He was so enthralled by this time capsule of a glamorous age, that his grandfather gave him the trunk and its contents for his twenty-first birthday. In addition to photo albums, the trunk contained the manuscript for *My Story*, written by Daisy. As he delved deeper into the family history, the idea occurred to Coleman that he could bring their story to the world by combining photos, artifacts, and journals with the original manuscript.

The result was the successful children's book *Polar, The Titanic Bear*. Published in 1994 by a Canadian publisher, it went on to sell almost a million copies and was translated into four languages. The multiple award–winning book contains an introduction by Coleman, Daisy's photos, a slightly edited version of her original manuscript, archival photos, and watercolour illustrations by Canadian Laurie McGaw. Critics called the book "a curious but successful hybrid of fact and fiction." Younger children are drawn in by the polar bear's story and charming illustrations, while older children learn a history lesson about the *Titanic* disaster and life in the early years of the twentieth century. *Titanic* fans of all ages delight in the photos and insights into the life of this family of *Titanic* survivors. In the 1990s, FAO Schwarz toy store created a replica of the bear, and Steiff issued collectible reproductions of the original bear, which quickly sold out. It had taken more than eighty years to complete the story of six-year-old *Titanic* survivor Douglas Spedden.

as a graphic novel. Another organization geared toward information for children is National Geographic Kids. In 2012, they published *National Geographic Readers: Titanic* for six- to eight-year-olds. Their website offers numerous resources for children about *Titanic*, including fact sheets and a quiz "Would you have survived the *Titanic*?" (Your chances went up if you were rich, brave, and obeyed orders.) In addition, several versions of *Titanic* colouring books are widely available for kids of all ages.

Children's books, museum field trips (in person and virtual), and travelling exhibitions seek to add an educational focus to their *Titanic* information by providing lesson plans which link to curriculum objectives. In the United Kingdom, for example, Titanic Honour & Glory Ltd. sends presenters dressed as White Star Line engineers into schools to take "each child on a riveting tour of the *Titanic* story," geared to the curriculum.

With the advent of the internet, *Titanic* information became more accessible, and in 1996 Encyclopedia Titanica (encyclopedia-titanica.org) was born. The go-to site for all things *Titanic*, it contains profiles of passengers and crew, a message board for questions and discussions, deck plans, photographs, and links to articles and books. In its "Resources for Teachers" section, it offers lesson plans and suggests teachers "engage your students with the real *Titanic* story by encouraging them to download and print their own *Titanic* tickets based on a real 1912 original." Participants in the discussion forums range from knowledgeable experts to passionate enthusiasts to people looking for information about relatives who were on *Titanic*.

The Current (Fourth) Wave – *Titanic* Tourism (beginning in the 1990s)

Each wave of *Titanic* interest seems to build upon the last until, in the years leading to the twenty-first century, we came full circle to the cities where it all began. As interest grew, so did the desire by many to visit the sites connected with the tragedy and their memorials. In the decade leading up to the centennial of the sinking, cities such as Southampton and Belfast realized that tourists were looking for more than just statues.

A new kind of memorial museum emerged, less centred on artifacts in glass cases and more designed to give visitors, both adults and children, an experience.

Southampton, the site of so many *Titanic* crew memorials, sought to provide more for an increasing number of tourists. Most importantly, the city set out to capture the memories of survivors and families of victims with the Southampton City Council's Oral History Project. Its team of interviewers preserved on audiotape the memories of *Titanic* children Millvina Dean, Edith Brown, Eva Hart, and Eileen Lenox-Conyngham. In 1992, Millvina Dean, Edith Brown, and Eva Hart had presided at the opening of the Titanic Voices Exhibition at the Southampton Maritime Museum. This project became the foundation for a more modern SeaCity Museum that opened in 2012, which houses a permanent *Titanic* exhibit. The city also used the occasion of the centennial to dedicate the Millvina Dean Memorial Garden in honour of the last *Titanic* survivor.

Although Belfast in Northern Ireland had *Titanic* memorials erected soon after the disaster, it took eighty-six years for Cobh (Queenstown), *Titanic*'s last stop, to memorialize the event. In 1998, it unveiled the Titanic Memorial, which bears a bas-relief plaque showing a mother and five children—representing the Rice family—with their baggage on the tender heading out to board *Titanic*. In 2014, the city opened the Titanic Memorial Garden, which contains a glass memorial listing all 123 passengers, including the children, who boarded at Cobh.

Belfast also wanted to provide more than statuary for *Titanic* tourists and, in 2012, Titanic Belfast opened on the former site of the Harland and Wolff shipyard. The spectacular glass building, based on the shape of an iceberg, is exactly the same height as *Titanic*. The museum offers the Titanic Experience, a tour which it claims is "the world's most authentic retelling of the iconic story." On April 15, 2012, the city also added a memorial garden to its existing *Titanic* memorial, which includes five bronze plaques naming 1,512 victims—the first memorial anywhere in the world to record all victims' names on one monument.

Certainly, two commercial museums in the United States, neither with any physical connection to the 1912 voyage and both entirely land-locked, understood this new kind of *Titanic* tourism. *Titanic* Museum Attractions in Branson, Missouri (opened in 2006) and Pigeon Forge, Tennessee (opened in 2010), draw hundreds of thousands of visitors each year. From the outside, the Pigeon Forge museum (just fifteen minutes from Dollywood) is a half-size reconstruction of the front half of *Titanic*. Inside, after visitors receive a boarding ticket with the name of a real passenger or crew member, they can walk up a replica of the Grand Staircase, touch an iceberg, listen to costumed interpreters, eat in the White Star Café, and view almost four hundred artifacts. At the end of the tour, visitors can check to see if their boarding pass belonged to a victim or survivor. (Young children, however, are only issued boarding passes of survivors.) In 2021, art imitated life when the iceberg wall at the museum collapsed, injuring three visitors. Blurring the line between education and entertainment, the attraction's website contains lesson plans, and they invite teachers to "link the *Titanic* experience to your curriculum, reinforce your students' skills, and help them develop proficiencies in areas beyond history."

Since 2018, the museum has displayed a *Titanic* model built out of 65,000 LEGO® bricks by a ten-year-old Icelandic boy. At one and a half metres (five feet) high and eight metres (twenty-six feet) long, the model was transported there after touring several European countries. The impressive result of his eleven-month building project, widely reported in the international press, may have been the impetus for the fall 2021 launch of a LEGO *Titanic* set containing 9,090 pieces. The set comes with a titanic price tag: C$850.

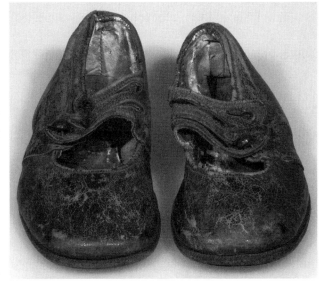

In Springfield, Massachusetts, Titanic Historical Society members raised funds to create the Titanic

This pair of children's shoes helped solve the mystery of the identity of the Unknown Child.

Centennial Memorial in the Oak Grove Cemetery in April 2012. Founder Edward Kamuda, who had been so instrumental in preserving survivor stories, dedicated the black-marble monument surrounded by a garden and walkway. Fittingly, the garden now also contains a memorial to Edward Kamuda, who died in 2014, "Called Home To Titanic."

Halifax continues to be a major draw for both *Titanic* tourists and researchers. The permanent exhibit at the Maritime Museum of the Atlantic, Titanic: The Unsinkable Ship and Halifax, showcases the museum's unique *Titanic* artifact collection. Among its treasures are Sidney Goodwin's shoes (the Unknown Child), Melville Hays's gloves (president of the Grand Trunk Railway), a deck chair, and several pieces of wooden flotsam (known as "wreckwood") gathered and then carved by crews of the recovery ships.

In addition to the cemeteries, several other locations in Halifax connected to *Titanic* still exist today. The Snow & Company Undertakers building, responsible for all burial arrangements, is now the Five Fishermen Restaurant on Argyle Street. An army surplus store on Agricola Street currently occupies the site of the Mayflower Curling Club, which was used as a morgue. Services for *Titanic* victims were conducted at St. Paul's Anglican, St. George's Anglican, All Saints Anglican, Saint Mary's Catholic, and Brunswick Street Methodist (now United) churches.

The Lebanese memorial in Mount Olivet Cemetery, Halifax.

The Nova Scotia Archives on University Avenue holds the original documents concerned with the recovery of *Titanic* bodies, including descriptions, lists of personal belongings, coroner's reports, and correspondence with families. Both the Maritime Museum of the Atlantic and the Public Archives have extensive collections of images associated with *Titanic*. After *Titanic* wreckage was discovered in 1985, the Bedford Institute of Oceanography in Dartmouth conducted research on *Titanic*'s "rusticles" and conducted the first tests of the steel plating. In 2007, Halifax's Queen Elizabeth High School closed and amalgamated with another school to become Citadel High School in a new building. Its final student play before it closed was *Titanic: A New Musical*.

One of the latest *Titanic* tributes in Halifax was unveiled on September 23, 2018. The Maronite Patriarch of Antioch and All the East planted a Lebanese cedar in Mount Olivet Cemetery and unveiled an interpretive plaque in memory of the Lebanese victims aboard *Titanic*. The honorary Lebanese Consuls in Halifax and Vancouver, as well as the International Lebanese Titanic Committee, sponsored the event. Unfortunately, the Lebanese cedar did not survive the harsh local winters and later had to be replaced by a Canadian one.

The ultimate tourist destination, however, lies almost five kilometres (three miles) down on the bottom of the North Atlantic. Founded in 2009, OceanGate Expeditions offered more adventurous tourists the opportunity to become "mission specialists" and participate in dives to the wreck for a fee of C$330,000. They pledged that their expeditions would be "conducted with great respect for those who lost their lives in the tragic sinking of the *Titanic*." They planned "to observe...UNESCO guidelines for the preservation of underwater world heritage sites." In June 2023 their submersible *Titan* met a catastrophic end on a dive to the wreck, and five more deaths, including that of a teenager, are now linked to *Titanic*. The company subsequently suspended operations. Whether others will try to replicate these expeditions remains to be seen, but time is running out. Scientists report that the wreck seems to be deteriorating rapidly, and some predict that by as early as 2030 little more than a rust stain will remain on the ocean floor.

DOOMED TO FAIL?

There were three major flaws in the design of *Titanic* that resulted in its sinking. Two were within human control to correct, but one did not become known until well after the disaster, when pieces of the ship's hull were recovered from the seabed.

Compartments

The first flaw was inherent in the design of the watertight compartments. If any two of the large midship compartments or the first four forward ones flooded, *Titanic* could have remained afloat. Unfortunately, the bulkheads separating the watertight compartments only went as high as D or E Decks, depending on their location. If water poured into the forward part of the hull from a crack or hole, it pulled the bow of the ship down. When water reached the top of a compartment, it spilled over into the next one, resulting in the so-called "ice-cube-tray effect." Although nothing could have stopped this process, if the watertight bulkheads had extended higher, it could have slowed down the progression of the flooding.

Lifeboats

The second flaw concerned *Titanic's* lifeboats. When the ship was launched, the British Board of Trade regulation that governed the number of lifeboats that ships were required to carry was based on tonnage. It had last been updated in 1894, when the largest vessels reached 10,160 tonnes (10,000 tons) and had to have enough lifeboats to carry about 960 people. For *Titanic*, even at some 46,738 tonnes (46,000 tons), this number remained the same, far less than the liner's total capacity of 3,547 passengers and crew. Despite the rules, *Titanic* had sufficient lifeboats to carry 1,178 people; more than 200 over the number legally required. But the liner could have carried far more lifeboats. Each of the ship's new type of Welin davits could hold four lifeboats for a total of sixty-four boats, enough to carry all passengers and crew on the liner's maiden voyage. Unfortunately, at some stage of the building process, White Star Line Chairman J. Bruce Ismay got involved and sent a note to designer Thomas Andrews, reminding him, "I have final say on the design. I'll not have so many little boats, as you call them, cluttering up decks and putting fear into my passengers."

Ismay's veto—in the belief the extra boats would spoil the vessel's elegant lines and scare its passengers—condemned more than fifteen hundred men, women, and children to their unnecessary deaths. Ismay survived.

And there was yet another aspect to *Titanic*'s lifeboats that could have easily been corrected before the ship sailed from Southampton. At no time did *Titanic*'s crew practise lowering and raising all the lifeboats when they were filled to capacity. Under later questioning at the American inquiry into the disaster, Second Officer Lightoller (the most senior officer to survive) testified that before reaching Southampton, "all the boats on the ship were swung out." But he then reluctantly admitted, only "about six" actually went into the water, while the remainder were only lowered "part of the way, as far as I thought necessary." Lightoller maintained that the purpose of this exercise was to test the gear: "The lifeboats we know to be all right."

Unfortunately, this was simply not the case. Harland and Wolff had tested the lifeboats, each carrying seventy men, in Belfast on March 25. Based on this, the company knew the boats could be lowered safely with their full complement of sixty-five people and not collapse. But this was never fully explained to the officers and crew. It resulted in most of the lifeboats being lowered after the collision with far fewer people than they could hold. This was due to fears of the lifeboats splitting in two as they were lowered away or the mechanism being unable to carry the load and dumping everyone into the ocean.

There was a final lifeboat test carried out on *Titanic*. Before the ship could leave England, it had to be inspected and cleared by Board of Trade officials as an emigrant vessel under the Merchant Shipping Act. Assistant Immigration Officer Captain Maurice Clarke and his small team conducted their inspections on April 4, 9, and 10. For one of the tests, Clarke ordered starboard Lifeboats 11 and 13 be lowered. Fifth Officer Lowe and Sixth Officer Moody supervised the demonstration, with eight crewmen in each boat. Clarke also checked *Titanic's* distress signals and coal supply, while others inspected the ship's water, water distilling apparatus, and provisions.

Before Clarke gave his approval on the day of sailing, he demanded ten more lifeboats, a fact that only came to light in 2012, when his private papers were put up for auction. In them, he noted the ship's owners threatened to have him moved elsewhere if he persisted in his demands as they wanted *Titanic* to leave on time. Clarke bowed under this threat and signed the Report of Survey of an Emigrant Ship, which allowed *Titanic* to depart Southampton. If his recommendations had been followed, at least another 650 people could have been saved.

Within the overall enormity of *Titanic's* sinking, there were also at least seven major omissions directly associated with the ship's lifeboats besides an insufficient number. Captain Smith cancelled the mandated lifeboat drill for Sunday, the day *Titanic* hit the iceberg, so he could hold a church service instead; filling the lifeboats did not start early enough or with any degree of urgency; far too many crew members were unfamiliar with the operation of the lifeboats; only three of the twenty lifeboats were filled to capacity; Second Officer Lightoller generally would not allow men or older boys into the lifeboats he controlled; a number of third-class passengers were held below for too long before they were allowed on the boat deck; and, once lowered away and, despite orders to do so, only one lifeboat returned in time to pick up additional people, either directly from the ship or among those struggling in the freezing water.

Steel

The third and final flaw concerned the quality of the steel used in *Titanic's* hull—although nothing could have been done about it. It was not recognized at the time, but the liner's hull steel was too brittle in the low temperatures the ship encountered in the North Atlantic's "Iceberg Alley." In 1996 and 1997, University of Missouri–Rolla professor emeritus of metallurgy Dr. H. P. Leighly and two graduate students conducted tests on about ninety kilograms (198 pounds) of hull and bulkhead steel from the wreckage. They discovered that the *Titanic* steel was not as impact resistant as and about ten times more brittle than the modern steel at freezing temperatures. The investigation revealed *Titanic*'s steel had high sulphur, oxygen, and phosphorus content, which causes steel to be more brittle. Chemical analysis also showed a low level of manganese, another characteristic of brittle steel. The steel used in *Titanic*'s hull was, however, "the best available at the time."

Aside from the design features that led to the loss of *Titanic* and hundreds of its passengers and crew, there was also an intangible factor. The hubris of the time—the excessive pride of the Edwardians in themselves and their accomplishments—certainly bore some responsibility for the disaster. As a result of recent remarkable technological changes in society, personified by modern industrialization and mass production, human beings fervently believed they were the masters of their world and had subjugated nature and the elements. It was a Golden Age of technology and innovation, and *Titanic* was an unquestionable example of the age.

Perhaps nothing signified this attitude in the nautical world more than a statement made by Captain Smith in 1907, speaking about the maiden voyage of *Adriatic*, another White Star Line ship. "I cannot imagine any condition," he said, "which would cause a ship to founder. I cannot conceive," he went on, "of any vital disaster happening to this vessel. Modern shipbuilding has gone beyond that."

Did Smith recall any of these earlier statements as he stood on the massive ship he commanded as it slowly went down by the head and sank beneath the waves, taking him and hundreds of others with it?

WHEN DOES CHILDHOOD END?

When fifteen-year-old catch boy Sam Scott fell seven metres to his death while working on *Titanic* in the Harland and Wolff shipyard, was he actually a child?

What about fourteen-year-old Frederick Hopkins, who was not only a beloved member of the 20th Southampton Boy Scout Troop but also a plate steward aboard *Titanic*?

Consider also sixteen-year-old Thelma Thomas and her five-month-old son Assed on their way from Lebanon to join her husband of two years in Wilkes-Barre, Pennsylvania, travelling under the protective watch of her brother-in-law. Was she a girl or a woman?

When thirteen-year-old Jack Ryerson was initially denied a spot with his mother in a lifeboat by Second Officer Charles Lightoller, his father Arthur Ryerson said, "Of course that boy goes with his mother—he is only thirteen." Did he qualify for priority evacuation under the "women and children first" standard?

What these four brief scenarios have in common, of course, is that they revolve around the issue of who aboard *Titanic* should be considered a child. Perhaps the simplest classification was established by the White Star Line and its ticket agents. For them, anyone twelve and under was considered a child. Under this definition there were 109 children aboard and none of the thirteen- to sixteen-year-olds mentioned previously was deemed a child. From our twenty-first-century perspective, most would agree with Arthur Ryerson that his thirteen-year-old son, "the boy," belonged in the lifeboat with his mother.

In real life, of course, there is no clear-cut line of demarcation: a child one day and an adult the next. Indeed, it was only in 1904 that American psychologist G. Stanley Hall proposed a new term to describe this transition from child to adult, and a whole new category was added to the lexicon: adolescence.

Mill workers, Rock Hill, SC, May 1912.

For the purposes of this book and using a combination of today's standards and the situation in 1912, adolescents as old as sixteen have been included. Even though many minors by the age of sixteen had acquired some latitude in terms of work, school, and marriage, most were still in transition to adulthood at that time and had not yet attained that full status under the law. Although some of the 160 aboard who were sixteen and under were employed or married, the vast majority were not travelling alone, but were part of a family unit or group from their hometown or region. They were not yet fully independent. Especially in steerage or third class, they were frequently en route to join a relative—parent, sibling, aunt, or uncle—who had migrated before them. They were not heading into a great unknown, but had relatives and homes and jobs waiting for them. The teenagers among them were in transition not only from childhood to adulthood, but also from one country and/or culture to another.

Adding adolescents to the passengers and crew under consideration broadened the scope of this book and brought many more stories to light. Additionally, these adolescents were of an age when their memories of the event were more vivid, and their stories add depth and richness to this book. Other *Titanic* historians have reached a similar conclusion, and discussions of the children aboard often include teenagers. Encyclopedia Titanica, the online trove of all things *Titanic*, uses fourteen as the marker and, according to its definition, there were 128 children on board. Some *Titanic* historians have used different cut-off points: sixteen, seventeen, and eighteen being the most common.

Despite the millions of pages devoted to *Titanic* in books, articles, newspapers, official inquiry reports, and websites, surprisingly no definitive lists of *Titanic* passengers, crew, survivors, and the lost exist. From the White Star Line passenger list to *Carpathia's* list of survivors, from the subsequent inquiries to the newspapers of the day, from the bodies catalogued by recovery ships to appendices in thousands of books about the disaster, there are many discrepancies.

Several factors add further complications to the identification of just who was on the ship, who survived, who was buried at sea, and who rests unknown in a grave in Halifax, Nova Scotia. Some passengers travelled under assumed names—a situation which was highlighted in the story of the Navratil boys, dubbed by the press of the day as the "*Titanic* Orphans." Some aboard the ship gave false information about their age, perhaps wanting to appear older to qualify for work. Problematically, birthdates and ages recorded on official records such as birth certificates, passenger lists, census records, immigration records, and social security applications were often inconsistent with newspaper reports and personal memories.

For example, Anna Thomas recalled in later years that her children George and Mary were eight and twelve respectively when they immigrated. George's marriage records, however, list his birth year as 1908, making him only four on *Titanic*. In a newspaper article on the fiftieth anniversary of the sinking, he claimed to have no recollection of the event since he was only four and his sister six. Another newspaper article lists their ages as seven and nine.

Similarly, the Garrett siblings, Amelia and Louis, are generally thought to be two years apart in age, but in various documents those ages vary from twelve and ten to fourteen and twelve. Amelia's descendants say they were twelve and ten; Louis's descendants believe the latter. Both their gravestones in Florida list 1900 as their birth year. Not only is their birth year in question, so is their exact date of birth. Both chose April 15 as their birthday, the anniversary of the sinking, because according to Louis, by surviving he had been born again. The Thomases and the Garretts highlight another problem—documentation of names, especially the spelling of the non-English names of immigrants. Birth names were often anglicized, sometimes by the official recording their names and at other times by the immigrants themselves. Lebanese names, especially, underwent significant changes.

The 160 children and youth covered in this book range in age from two months to sixteen years. They came from twenty different countries of origin and four continents. Some were returning from family vacations abroad, but the majority were leaving their homeland to start a new life across the Atlantic.

By class, there were 9 children in first class (5 males, 4 females), 28 in second class (13 males, 15 females), and 114 in third class (64 males, 50 females). Additionally, there were 4 children travelling cross-channel (3 males, 1 female), who were not on board when *Titanic* went down, but had disembarked in Cherbourg or Queenstown. Another 5 male teenagers were *Titanic* crew members.

The standard of "women and children first" appears to have applied only to first and second classes. Tragically, seventy-five third-class children were lost, a shocking survival rate of only 34 percent. All five of the youngest crew members were also lost. In total, eighty-three children who were sixteen and younger died in the sinking, an overall youth survival rate of 47 percent.

The Appendix lists all 160 children with demographic data. Given the documentation challenges previously mentioned, as well as the passage of time, there will undoubtedly be some inaccuracies in the list.

THE CHILDREN OF *TITANIC*

S orted by class; victims' names are in boldface text; names are listed in alphabetical order; ages of children under three years are shown in months (m).

First Class: 9 children from 7 families

NAME: **Loraine Allison**   SEX: Female   AGE: 34m
NATIONALITY: Canadian   BODY NUMBER: Not recovered
DESTINATION/TRAVELLING PARTY/REASON FOR VOYAGE:
Loraine and Trevor Allison were returning to Montreal with their parents after parents' business trip to England and a vacation in Scotland. Their party included four servants. Only Trevor and his nursemaid survived; Loraine was the only child lost in first class.

NAME: **Trevor Allison**   SEX: Male   AGE: 11m
NATIONALITY: Canadian   LIFEBOAT NUMBER: 11
YEAR/AGE OF DEATH: 1929/18
CAUSE OF DEATH/BURIAL: Food poisoning/Chesterville, ON

NAME: **Lucile Carter**   SEX: Female   AGE: 14
NATIONALITY: American   LIFEBOAT NUMBER: 4
DESTINATION/TRAVELLING PARTY/REASON FOR VOYAGE:
William and Lucile Carter were returning to the US with their parents after a year-long stay in England. Their party included three servants and two dogs. The family and one servant survived.
YEAR/AGE OF DEATH: 1962/64
CAUSE OF DEATH/BURIAL: Heart failure/Valley Forge, PA

NAME: **William Carter II**   SEX: Male   AGE: 11
NATIONALITY: American   LIFEBOAT NUMBER: 4
YEAR/AGE OF DEATH: 1985/84
CAUSE OF DEATH/BURIAL: Heart attack/Bala Cynwyd, PA

NAME: **Washington Dodge Jr.**   SEX: Male   AGE: 4
NATIONALITY: American   LIFEBOAT NUMBER: 5
DESTINATION/TRAVELLING PARTY/REASON FOR VOYAGE:
Washington Dodge Jr. was returning to San Francisco with parents after a trip to France, where his father was being treated for a medical condition. All survived.
YEAR/AGE OF DEATH: 1974/67
CAUSE OF DEATH/BURIAL: Heart attack/North Bergen, NJ, cremated

---

NAME: **Mary Lines**   SEX: Female   AGE: 16
NATIONALITY: American   LIFEBOAT NUMBER: 9
DESTINATION/TRAVELLING PARTY/REASON FOR VOYAGE:
Mary was travelling with mother from their home in Paris to attend Mary's brother's graduation from Dartmouth College in New Hampshire.
YEAR/AGE OF DEATH: 1975/80
CAUSE OF DEATH/BURIAL: Stroke/Topsfield, MA

NAME: **Georgette Madill**   SEX: Female   AGE: 16
NATIONALITY: American   LIFEBOAT NUMBER: 2
DESTINATION/TRAVELLING PARTY/REASON FOR VOYAGE:
Georgette was returning to St. Louis, MO, after a European vacation with mother. Their party included a niece and a maid. All survived.
YEAR/AGE OF DEATH: 1974/77
CAUSE OF DEATH/BURIAL: Stroke/Clevedon, Somerset, England

NAME: **John (Jack) Ryerson**   SEX: Male   AGE: 13
NATIONALITY: American   LIFEBOAT NUMBER: 4
DESTINATION/TRAVELLING PARTY/REASON FOR VOYAGE:
Jack was returning to the US with parents, two older sisters, a governess, and a maid because the Ryersons' elder son Arthur Jr. had been killed in an automobile accident near Philadelphia. All survived except Mr. Ryerson.
YEAR/AGE OF DEATH: 1986/87
CAUSE OF DEATH/BURIAL: Alzheimer's/Cooperstown, NY

NAME: **Douglas Spedden**   SEX: Male   AGE: 6
NATIONALITY: American   LIFEBOAT NUMBER: 3
DESTINATION/TRAVELLING PARTY/REASON FOR VOYAGE:
Douglas was returning home to Tuxedo Park, NY, with parents, a nursemaid, and a servant after a lengthy trip to Europe and North Africa. All survived.
YEAR/AGE OF DEATH: 1915/9
CAUSE OF DEATH/BURIAL: Automobile accident/Brooklyn, NY

	Male	Female	Total
First Class	5	4	9
Lost	0	1	1
Saved	5	3	8
Percentage saved	100%	75%	**89%**

Second Class: 28 children from 20 families

NAME: **Ruth Becker**   SEX: Female   AGE: 12
NATIONALITY: American   LIFEBOAT NUMBER: 13
DESTINATION/TRAVELLING PARTY/REASON FOR VOYAGE:
The three Becker children were travelling to Benton Harbor, MI, with mother to seek treatment in the US for youngest son Richard's illness. All survived, although Ruth was in another lifeboat.
YEAR/AGE OF DEATH: 1990/90
CAUSE OF DEATH/BURIAL: Malnutrition/Cremated, ashes scattered over *Titanic* site

NAME: **Marion Becker**   SEX: Female   AGE: 4
NATIONALITY: American   LIFEBOAT NUMBER: 11
YEAR/AGE OF DEATH: 1944/36
CAUSE OF DEATH/BURIAL:Tuberculosis/Princeton, IL

NAME: **Richard Becker**   SEX: Male   AGE: 21m
NATIONALITY: American   LIFEBOAT NUMBER: 11
YEAR/AGE OF DEATH: 1975/65
CAUSE OF DEATH/BURIAL: Kidney disease/Peoria, IL

NAME: **Edith Brown**   SEX: Female   AGE: 15
NATIONALITY: South African   LIFEBOAT NUMBER: 14
DESTINATION/TRAVELLING PARTY/REASON FOR VOYAGE:
Edith was immigrating with parents to Seattle, WA, where her mother's sister lived. Edith and her mother survived.
YEAR/AGE OF DEATH: 1997/100
CAUSE OF DEATH/BURIAL: Chest infection/Southampton, England

NAME: **Alden Caldwell**   SEX: Male   AGE: 10m
NATIONALITY: Siamese-American   LIFEBOAT NUMBER: 13
DESTINATION/TRAVELLING PARTY/REASON FOR VOYAGE:
Baby Alden was returning home to Biggsville, IL, with parents after living in
Bangkok, Siam. All survived.
YEAR/AGE OF DEATH: 1992/81
CAUSE OF DEATH/BURIAL: Unknown/Clearwater, FL, cremated

NAME: **Marjorie Collyer**   SEX: Female   AGE: 8
NATIONALITY: English   LIFEBOAT NUMBER: 14
DESTINATION/TRAVELLING PARTY/REASON FOR VOYAGE:
Marjorie was immigrating with parents to Payette, ID, where her father planned
to buy a farm near friends who had previously settled there. Marjorie and her
mother survived and returned to England.
YEAR/AGE OF DEATH: 1965/61
CAUSE OF DEATH/BURIAL: Stroke/Hampshire, England, cremated

NAME: **John Davies Jr.**   SEX: Male   AGE: 8
NATIONALITY: English   LIFEBOAT NUMBER: 14
DESTINATION/TRAVELLING PARTY/REASON FOR VOYAGE:
John left home in Cornwall with mother and stepbrother to join his brother and
his wife in Michigan. Stepbrother was lost.
YEAR/AGE OF DEATH: 1951/48
CAUSE OF DEATH/BURIAL: Suicide/Houghton, MI

NAME: **Marshall Drew**   SEX: Male   AGE: 8
NATIONALITY: American   LIFEBOAT NUMBER: 10
DESTINATION/TRAVELLING PARTY/REASON FOR VOYAGE:
Marshall was returning to Southold, NY, from a trip to England with his aunt and
uncle, who were his surrogate parents. Marshall and his aunt survived, but his
uncle was lost. Marshall was reunited with his father upon arrival in New York.
YEAR/AGE OF DEATH: 1986/82
CAUSE OF DEATH/BURIAL: Unknown/Westerly, RI

NAME: **Viljo Hämäläinen**   SEX: Male   AGE: 14m
NATIONALITY: American   LIFEBOAT NUMBER: 4
DESTINATION/TRAVELLING PARTY/REASON FOR VOYAGE:
Viljo was returning to Detroit, MI, from Finland with his mother and Martta
Hiltunen, who was to be their housekeeper. Viljo and his mother survived, but
Martta did not.
YEAR/AGE OF DEATH: 1914/3
CAUSE OF DEATH/BURIAL: Endocarditis/Detroit, MI

NAME: **Annie (Nana) Harper**   SEX: Female   AGE: 6
NATIONALITY: Scottish   LIFEBOAT NUMBER: 11
DESTINATION/TRAVELLING PARTY/REASON FOR VOYAGE:
Nana was travelling with father and cousin to Chicago where her pastor father
was to preach a series of revivals. Nana and cousin Jessie survived and returned
to England.
YEAR/AGE OF DEATH: 1986/80
CAUSE OF DEATH/BURIAL: Unknown/Dumfries, Scotland

NAME: **Eva Hart**   SEX: Female   AGE: 7
NATIONALITY: English   LIFEBOAT NUMBER: 14
DESTINATION/TRAVELLING PARTY/REASON FOR VOYAGE:
Eva was immigrating with parents to Winnipeg, MB, where her father planned to
open a drug store. Eva and her mother survived.
YEAR/AGE OF DEATH: 1996/91
CAUSE OF DEATH/BURIAL: Cancer/London, England, cremated.

NAME: **Simonne Laroche**   SEX: Female   AGE: 3
NATIONALITY: French-Haitian   LIFEBOAT NUMBER: 14
DESTINATION/TRAVELLING PARTY/REASON FOR VOYAGE:
The Laroche sisters were immigrating with parents to their father's home in
Haiti. As a Black man, Joseph Laroche hoped there would be more opportuni-
ties in his native land. Pregnant Mrs. Laroche and her daughters survived and
returned to France.
YEAR/AGE OF DEATH: 1973/64
CAUSE OF DEATH/BURIAL: Cancer/Villejuif, France

NAME: **Louise Laroche**   Sex: Female   Age: 21m
NATIONALITY: French-Haitian   LIFEBOAT NUMBER: 14
YEAR/AGE OF DEATH: 1998/87
CAUSE OF DEATH/BURIAL: Unknown/Villejuif, France

NAME: **André Mallet**   Sex: Male   Age: 22m
NATIONALITY: French-Canadian   LIFEBOAT NUMBER: 10
DESTINATION/TRAVELLING PARTY/REASON FOR VOYAGE:
Toddler André was returning home to Montreal with parents after a two-month visit to their families in Paris. Travelling with them was a young friend of the family. Both men were lost; André and his mother returned to France permanently.
YEAR/AGE OF DEATH: 1973/63
CAUSE OF DEATH/BURIAL: Unknown/Normandy, France

NAME: **Madeline Mellenger**   Sex: Female   Age: 13
NATIONALITY: English   LIFEBOAT NUMBER: 14
DESTINATION/TRAVELLING PARTY/REASON FOR VOYAGE:
Madeline and her mother Elizabeth were en route to Bennington, VT, where her mother was to be a housekeeper at the summer estate of the wealthy Colgate family. Both survived but returned to England until 1915, then immigrated to Canada.
YEAR/AGE OF DEATH: 1976/77
CAUSE OF DEATH/BURIAL: Unknown/Welland, ON

NAME: **Thomas Mudd****   Sex: Male   Age: 16
NATIONALITY: English   LIFEBOAT NUMBER: Not recovered
DESTINATION/TRAVELLING PARTY/REASON FOR VOYAGE:
Thomas left his job as a bookkeeper in Huntingfield, England, to join his two older brothers who had immigrated to Pennsylvania. One of the few young people travelling alone, he was lost.

NAME: **Michel Navratil Jr.**   Sex: Male   Age: 3
NATIONALITY: French   LIFEBOAT NUMBER: D
DESTINATION/TRAVELLING PARTY/REASON FOR VOYAGE:
Michel and Edmond had been taken from their mother by their father and were being spirited away to the US. Their father, travelling under the name of Hoffman, was lost. The French-speaking toddlers, nicknamed the "*Titanic* Orphans," were reunited with their mother in New York and returned to France.
YEAR/AGE OF DEATH: 2001/92
CAUSE OF DEATH/BURIAL: Unknown

NAME: **Edmond Navratil** SEX: Male   AGE: 25m
NATIONALITY: French LIFEBOAT NUMBER: D
YEAR/AGE OF DEATH: 1953/43
CAUSE OF DEATH/BURIAL: Unknown/Lourdes, France

NAME: **Winnifred (Winnie) Quick**   SEX: Female   AGE: 8
NATIONALITY: English-American   LIFEBOAT NUMBER: 11
DESTINATION/TRAVELLING PARTY/REASON FOR VOYAGE:
The Quick sisters were returning to Detroit with mother after a visit to family in England. All survived.
YEAR/AGE OF DEATH: 2002/98
CAUSE OF DEATH/BURIAL: Unknown/Detroit, MI

NAME: **Phyllis Quick** SEX: Female   AGE: 32m
NATIONALITY: English-American   LIFEBOAT NUMBER: 11
YEAR/AGE OF DEATH: 1954/44
CAUSE OF DEATH/BURIAL: Suicide/Detroit, MI

NAME: **William Richards** SEX: Male   AGE: 3
NATIONALITY: English LIFEBOAT NUMBER: 4
DESTINATION/TRAVELLING PARTY/REASON FOR VOYAGE:
The two Richards boys and their mother, Emily, were joining their father and his brother-in-law in Akron, OH. Also travelling with them were uncle and his wife, a grandmother, and a great aunt. Uncle was lost. The family stayed in Ohio only two years; then returned to Cornwall.
YEAR/AGE OF DEATH: 1988/78
CAUSE OF DEATH/BURIAL: Heart attack/Cornwall, England

NAME: **Sibley Richards** SEX: Male   AGE: 10m
NATIONALITY: English LIFEBOAT NUMBER: 4
YEAR/AGE OF DEATH: 1987/76
CAUSE OF DEATH/BURIAL: Unknown/Cornwall, England

NAME: **George Sweet**** SEX: Male   AGE: 14
NATIONALITY: English BODY NUMBER: Not recovered
DESTINATION/TRAVELLING PARTY/REASON FOR VOYAGE:
George was immigrating to Bernardsville, NJ, with employer and his family. Lost one day short of his 15th birthday.

NAME: **Robertha (Bertha) Watt**   SEX: Female   AGE: 12
NATIONALITY: Scottish   LIFEBOAT NUMBER: 9
DESTINATION/TRAVELLING PARTY/REASON FOR VOYAGE:
Bertha was immigrating with mother to Portland, OR, where her father had
moved in 1911. Both survived.
YEAR/AGE OF DEATH: 1993/93
CAUSE OF DEATH/BURIAL: Unknown/Vancouver, BC

NAME: **Joan Wells**   SEX: Female   AGE: 4
NATIONALITY: English   LIFEBOAT NUMBER: 14
DESTINATION/TRAVELLING PARTY/REASON FOR VOYAGE:
Joan and Ralph Wells and their mother were joining father in Akron, OH, where
he had emigrated two years prior. All survived.
YEAR/AGE OF DEATH: 1933/25
CAUSE OF DEATH/BURIAL: Sepsis/Akron, OH

NAME: **Ralph Wells**   SEX: Male   AGE: 28m
NATIONALITY: English   LIFEBOAT NUMBER: 14
YEAR/AGE OF DEATH: 1972/62
CAUSE OF DEATH/BURIAL: Stroke/Akron, OH

NAME: **Constance West**   SEX: Female   AGE: 4
NATIONALITY: English   LIFEBOAT NUMBER: 10
DESTINATION/TRAVELLING PARTY/REASON FOR VOYAGE:
Constance and Barbara West were immigrating with parents to Gainesville, FL,
where they planned to engage in fruit farming. Pregnant mother and both daugh-
ters survived and returned to England.
YEAR/AGE OF DEATH: 1963/56
CAUSE OF DEATH/BURIAL: Pneumonia/Truro, England, cremated

NAME: **Barbara West**   SEX: Female   AGE: 10m
NATIONALITY: English   LIFEBOAT NUMBER: 10
YEAR/AGE OF DEATH: 2007/96
CAUSE OF DEATH/BURIAL: Unknown/Truro, England, cremated

	Male	Female	Total
Second Class	13	15	28
Lost	2	0	2
Saved	11	15	26
Percentage saved	85%	100%	**93%**

** Many reports say no children were lost in second class, but this list includes 16-year-old Thomas Mudd and 14-year-old George Sweet.

Third Class: 114 children from 62 families

NAME: **Rossmore Abbott**   SEX: Male   AGE: 16
NATIONALITY: English-American   BODY NUMBER: Body 190
DESTINATION/TRAVELLING PARTY/REASON FOR VOYAGE:
The two Abbott teens were returning with mother to East Providence, RI, after living in England for less than a year after mother's separation from her husband. The family is rare in that the mother survived, but both sons were lost.
BURIAL: Buried at sea

NAME: **Eugene Abbott**   SEX: Male   AGE: 13
NATIONALITY: American   BODY NUMBER: Not recovered

NAME: **Kalle (Karen) Abelseth**   SEX: Female   AGE: 16
NATIONALITY: Norwegian   LIFEBOAT NUMBER: 16
DESTINATION/TRAVELLING PARTY/REASON FOR VOYAGE:
Karen was immigrating to join her sister in Los Angeles, CA; travelling with a family friend and a small group of Norwegians.
YEAR/AGE OF DEATH: 1969/73
CAUSE OF DEATH/BURIAL: Parkinson's disease/Inglewood, CA

NAME: **Philip (Frank) Aks**   SEX: Male   AGE: 10m
NATIONALITY: English   LIFEBOAT NUMBER: 11
DESTINATION/TRAVELLING PARTY/REASON FOR VOYAGE:
Frank was emigrating with mother from London to Norfolk, VA, to join his father who had secured work there.
YEAR/AGE OF DEATH: 1991/80
CAUSE OF DEATH/BURIAL: Heart failure/Norfolk, VA

NAME: **Erna Andersson**   SEX: Female   AGE: 16
NATIONALITY: Finnish   LIFEBOAT NUMBER: D
DESTINATION/TRAVELLING PARTY/REASON FOR VOYAGE:
Travelling with the Backström family to join her brother in New York.
YEAR/AGE OF DEATH: Unknown
CAUSE OF DEATH/BURIAL: Unknown

NAME: **Sigrid Andersson**   SEX: Female   AGE: 11
NATIONALITY: Swedish-American   BODY NUMBER: Not recovered
DESTINATION/TRAVELLING PARTY/REASON FOR VOYAGE:
The Andersson children were immigrating with parents to Winnipeg, MB.
Travelling with the Danbom family. All were lost.

NAME: **Ingeborg Andersson**   SEX: Female   AGE: 9
NATIONALITY: Swedish-American   BODY NUMBER: Not recovered

NAME: **Ebba Andersson**   SEX: Female   AGE: 6
NATIONALITY: Swedish-American   BODY NUMBER: Not recovered

NAME: **Sigvard Andersson**   SEX: Male   AGE: 4
NATIONALITY: Swedish-American   BODY NUMBER: Not recovered

NAME: **Ellis Andersson**   SEX: Female   AGE: 27m
NATIONALITY: Swedish-American   BODY NUMBER: Not recovered

NAME: **Filip Asplund**   SEX: Male   AGE: 13
NATIONALITY: Swedish-American   BODY NUMBER: Not recovered
DESTINATION/TRAVELLING PARTY/REASON FOR VOYAGE:
The Asplund children were re-immigrating with parents to Worcester, MA,
where the four oldest of five children had been born. Father and three children
were lost, including Lillian's twin, Carl.

NAME: **Clarence Asplund**   SEX: Male   AGE: 9
NATIONALITY: Swedish-American   BODY NUMBER: Not recovered

NAME: **Carl Asplund**   SEX: Male   AGE: 5
NATIONALITY: Swedish-American   BODY NUMBER: Not recovered

NAME: **Lillian Asplund** SEX: Female AGE: 5
NATIONALITY: Swedish-American LIFEBOAT NUMBER: 15
YEAR/AGE OF DEATH: 2006/99
CAUSE OF DEATH/BURIAL: Unknown/Worcester, MA

NAME: **Felix Asplund** SEX: Male AGE: 3
NATIONALITY: Swedish-American LIFEBOAT NUMBER: 15
YEAR/AGE OF DEATH: 1983/73
CAUSE OF DEATH/BURIAL: Pneumonia/Worcester, MA

NAME: **Maria Baclini** SEX: Female AGE: 5
NATIONALITY: Syrian-Lebanese LIFEBOAT NUMBER: C
DESTINATION/TRAVELLING PARTY/REASON FOR VOYAGE:
The Baclini sisters were emigrating with mother to join their father in Brooklyn, NY, where he had settled two years prior. All were saved.
YEAR/AGE OF DEATH: 1982/75
CAUSE OF DEATH/BURIAL: Unknown/Queens, NY

NAME: **Eugenie Baclini** SEX: Female AGE: 3
NATIONALITY: Syrian-Lebanese LIFEBOAT NUMBER: C
YEAR/AGE OF DEATH: 1912/3
CAUSE OF DEATH/BURIAL: Meningitis/Queens, NY

NAME: **Helen Baclini** SEX: Female AGE: 33m
NATIONALITY: Syrian-Lebanese LIFEBOAT NUMBER: C
YEAR/AGE OF DEATH: 1939/29
CAUSE OF DEATH/BURIAL: Breast cancer/Queens, NY

NAME: **James van Billiard** SEX: Male AGE: 10
NATIONALITY: French-American BODY NUMBER: Not recovered
DESTINATION/TRAVELLING PARTY/REASON FOR VOYAGE:
The two oldest van Billiard brothers were travelling with father, who had lived abroad for several years and was now returning to his native Pennsylvania. None survived. Walter and his father's bodies were recovered and shipped to Pennsylvania.

NAME: **Walter van Billiard** SEX: Male AGE: 9
NATIONALITY: French-American BODY NUMBER: Body 1
BURIAL: Flourtown, PA

NAME: **George Borek**　　　SEX: Male　　AGE: 7
NATIONALITY: Syrian-Lebanese　　LIFEBOAT NUMBER: C
DESTINATION/TRAVELLING PARTY/REASON FOR VOYAGE:
George, William, and their mother were being escorted by a family friend from their village to join their father in Houtzdale, PA. Mother and sons survived.
YEAR/AGE OF DEATH: 1979/74
CAUSE OF DEATH/BURIAL: Aneurysm/Hanover, PA

NAME: **William Borek**　　　SEX: Male　　AGE: 4
NATIONALITY: Syrian-Lebanese　　LIFEBOAT NUMBER: C
YEAR/AGE OF DEATH: 1975/68
CAUSE OF DEATH/BURIAL: Heart attack/Pittsburgh, PA

NAME: **Laura Boulos**　　　SEX: Female　　AGE: 10
NATIONALITY: Syrian-Lebanese　　BODY NUMBER: Not recovered
DESTINATION/TRAVELLING PARTY/REASON FOR VOYAGE:
The Boulos siblings were immigrating with mother to Chatham, ON, to join their father. Travelled with others from their region. All were lost.

NAME: **Akar Boulos**　　　SEX: Male　　AGE: 7
NATIONALITY: Syrian-Lebanese　　BODY NUMBER: Not recovered

NAME: **Mary Burns**　　　SEX: Female　　AGE: 15
NATIONALITY: Irish　　BODY NUMBER: Not recovered
DESTINATION/TRAVELLING PARTY/REASON FOR VOYAGE:
Mary, with two friends, was immigrating to New York, where her aunt lived and where she hoped to find a job as a domestic.

NAME: **Ellen (Helen) Corr**　　　SEX: Female　　AGE: 16
NATIONALITY: Irish　　LIFEBOAT NUMBER: 16
DESTINATION/TRAVELLING PARTY/REASON FOR VOYAGE:
Ellen was immigrating to New York to join two sisters and find work as a domestic. Several others from her region in County Longford were also on board.
YEAR/AGE OF DEATH: 1980/84
CAUSE OF DEATH/BURIAL: Unknown/Westchester, NY

NAME: **William (Willie) Coutts**   SEX: Male   AGE: 9
NATIONALITY: English   LIFEBOAT NUMBER: 2
DESTINATION/TRAVELLING PARTY/REASON FOR VOYAGE:
The Coutts brothers were immigrating with mother to Brooklyn, NY, where their father had moved two years before. All survived.
YEAR/AGE OF DEATH: 1957/55
CAUSE OF DEATH/BURIAL: Stroke/Pittsburgh, PA

NAME: **Neville Coutts**   SEX: Male   AGE: 3
NATIONALITY: English   LIFEBOAT NUMBER: 2
YEAR/AGE OF DEATH: 1977/68
CAUSE OF DEATH/BURIAL: Unknown/Islamorada, FL, cremated

NAME: **Laura Cribb**   SEX: Female   AGE: 16
NATIONALITY: American   LIFEBOAT NUMBER: 12
DESTINATION/TRAVELLING PARTY/REASON FOR VOYAGE:
Laura was returning to her birthplace of Newark, NJ, where her father lived while the rest of the family resided in England. Her father, who had gone to England to fetch her, was lost.
YEAR/AGE OF DEATH: 1974/78
CAUSE OF DEATH/BURIAL: Stroke/Carlsbad, NM

NAME: **Gilbert Danbom**   SEX: Male   AGE: 5m
NATIONALITY: Swedish   BODY NUMBER: Not recovered
DESTINATION/TRAVELLING PARTY/REASON FOR VOYAGE:
Infant Gilbert had been born in Sweden while parents were on a year-long honeymoon there. Now the family was returning to Stanton, IA; travelling with the Andersson family: mother's sister, her husband, and their five children. All were lost.

NAME: **Bert (Bertram) Dean**   SEX: Male   AGE: 23m
NATIONALITY: English   LIFEBOAT NUMBER: 10
DESTINATION/TRAVELLING PARTY/REASON FOR VOYAGE:
Bert and Millvina Dean were immigrating with parents to Wichita, KS. Father was lost, and the family returned to England.
YEAR/AGE OF DEATH: 1992/81
CAUSE OF DEATH/BURIAL: Pneumonia/Southampton, England, cremated

NAME: **Millvina Dean** SEX: Female AGE: 2m
NATIONALITY: English LIFEBOAT NUMBER: 10
YEAR/AGE OF DEATH: 2009/97
CAUSE OF DEATH/BURIAL: Pneumonia/Southampton, England, cremated

---

NAME: **Alfons (Alphonse) De Pelsmaeker** SEX: Male AGE: 16
NATIONALITY: Belgian BODY NUMBER: Not recovered
DESTINATION/TRAVELLING PARTY/REASON FOR VOYAGE:
Alphonse was immigrating to join his older brother in Gladstone, MI.

NAME: **Hans Eklund** SEX: Male AGE: 16
NATIONALITY: Swedish BODY NUMBER: Not recovered
DESTINATION/TRAVELLING PARTY/REASON FOR VOYAGE:
Travelling alone, Hans was immigrating to Prescott, AZ, where his uncle lived.

NAME: **Joseph Elias Jr.** SEX: Male AGE: 15
NATIONALITY: Syrian-Lebanese BODY NUMBER: Not recovered
DESTINATION/TRAVELLING PARTY/REASON FOR VOYAGE:
Joseph was immigrating to Ottawa, ON, with father and older brother. All were lost.

NAME: **Virginia Emanuel** SEX: Female AGE: 6
NATIONALITY: American LIFEBOAT NUMBER: 13
DESTINATION/TRAVELLING PARTY/REASON FOR VOYAGE:
Virginia, under the care of nursemaid Elizabeth Dowell, was being sent back to grandparents in New York by her mother who had secured a long-term position as an opera singer in England. Both survived.
YEAR/AGE OF DEATH: 1936/30
CAUSE OF DEATH/BURIAL: Unknown/Paris, France

NAME: **William Ford** SEX: Male AGE: 14
NATIONALITY: English BODY NUMBER: Not recovered
DESTINATION/TRAVELLING PARTY/REASON FOR VOYAGE:
The two youngest Ford children were immigrating with mother and two older siblings to New London, CT, where uncle lived. Their aunt and uncle, the Johnstons, were travelling with them. All were lost.

NAME: **Robina Ford** SEX: Female AGE: 7
NATIONALITY: English BODY NUMBER: Not recovered

NAME: **Amelia Garrett**   SEX: Female   AGE: 14
NATIONALITY: Syrian-Lebanese   LIFEBOAT NUMBER: C
DESTINATION/TRAVELLING PARTY/REASON FOR VOYAGE:
The young brother and sister were travelling alone to their mother and siblings in Jacksonville, FL. Both saved and spent time recuperating with a brother in Liverpool, NS.
YEAR/AGE OF DEATH: 1970/69 (or 71)
CAUSE OF DEATH/BURIAL: Unknown/Jacksonville, FL

NAME: **Louis Garrett**   SEX: Male   AGE: 12
NATIONALITY: Syrian-Lebanese   LIFEBOAT NUMBER: C
YEAR/AGE OF DEATH: 1981/79 (or 81)
CAUSE OF DEATH/BURIAL: Heart attack/Jacksonville, FL

NAME: **Frank (Frankie) Goldsmith**   SEX: Male   AGE: 9
NATIONALITY: English   LIFEBOAT NUMBER: C
DESTINATION/TRAVELLING PARTY/REASON FOR VOYAGE:
Frankie was immigrating with parents to Detroit, MI, where several members of his extended family had settled. Father was lost.
YEAR/AGE OF DEATH: 1982/79
CAUSE OF DEATH/BURIAL: Stroke/Cremated, ashes scattered over *Titanic* site

---

NAME: **Lillian Goodwin**   SEX: Female   AGE: 16
NATIONALITY: English   BODY NUMBER: Not recovered
DESTINATION/TRAVELLING PARTY/REASON FOR VOYAGE:
The Goodwin children were immigrating with parents to Niagara Falls, NY, where father's brother had secured a position for him in a power plant. All were lost. In 2008, DNA analysis revealed that the Unknown Child buried in Halifax was Sidney Goodwin.

NAME: **Charles Goodwin**   SEX: Male   AGE: 14
NATIONALITY: English   BODY NUMBER: Not recovered

NAME: **William Goodwin**   SEX: Male   AGE: 13
NATIONALITY: English   BODY NUMBER: Not recovered

NAME: **Jessie Goodwin**   SEX: Female   AGE: 12
NATIONALITY: English   BODY NUMBER: Not recovered

NAME: **Harold Goodwin**   SEX: Male   AGE: 10
NATIONALITY: English   BODY NUMBER: Not recovered

NAME: **Sidney Goodwin**   SEX: Male   AGE: 19m
NATIONALITY: English   BODY NUMBER: Body 4
BURIAL: Fairview Lawn Cemetery, Halifax, NS

NAME: **Houssein Hassan**   SEX: Male   AGE: 11
NATIONALITY: Syrian-Lebanese   BODY NUMBER: Not recovered
Houssein, accompanied by an older male relative, was joining parents in
Fredericksburg, VA.

NAME: **Hildur Hirvonen**   SEX: Female   AGE: 26m
NATIONALITY: Finnish   LIFEBOAT NUMBER: 15
DESTINATION/TRAVELLING PARTY/REASON FOR VOYAGE:
Hildur and her mother Helga were en route to Monessen, PA, where her father
had immigrated the year before. Her uncle and another Finn were travelling with
them. All survived.
YEAR/AGE OF DEATH: 1956/46
CAUSE OF DEATH/BURIAL: Cancer/Cato, NY

NAME: **Catharina Van Impe**   SEX: Female   AGE: 10
NATIONALITY:Belgian   BODY NUMBER: Not recovered
DESTINATION/TRAVELLING PARTY/REASON FOR VOYAGE:
Catharina was travelling with parents to Detroit, MI. All were lost.

NAME: **Hileni Jabbur**   SEX: Female   AGE: 16
NATIONALITY: Syrian-Lebanese   BODY NUMBER: Body 328
DESTINATION/TRAVELLING PARTY/REASON FOR VOYAGE:
Hileni and her older sister, Tamini, were emigrating. Both were lost.
BURIAL: Mount Olivet Cemetery, Halifax, NS

NAME: **Svend Jensen**   SEX: Male   AGE: 16
NATIONALITY: Danish   BODY NUMBER: Not recovered
DESTINATION/TRAVELLING PARTY/REASON FOR VOYAGE:
Svend was travelling with older sister, her fiancé, and uncle to Portland, OR,
where their uncle had lived previously. Only sister survived.

NAME: **Harold Johnson** SEX: Male AGE: 4
NATIONALITY: Swedish-American LIFEBOAT NUMBER: 15
DESTINATION/TRAVELLING PARTY/REASON FOR VOYAGE:
Harold and Eleanor were returning home to St. Charles, IL, with mother from a visit to Finland. Two young Swedish women from father's hometown were part of the group. The Johnson family and one of the young women survived.
YEAR/AGE OF DEATH: 1968/60
CAUSE OF DEATH/BURIAL: Pancreatitis/St. Charles, IL

NAME: **Eleanor Johnson** SEX: Female AGE: 20m
NATIONALITY: Swedish-American LIFEBOAT NUMBER: 15
YEAR/AGE OF DEATH: 1998/87
CAUSE OF DEATH/BURIAL: Pneumonia/Elgin, IL

NAME: **William Johnston** SEX: Male AGE: 8
NATIONALITY: English BODY NUMBER: Not recovered
DESTINATION/TRAVELLING PARTY/REASON FOR VOYAGE:
William and Catherine were immigrating to New London, CT, with Scottish-born parents and the Ford family. All were lost.

NAME: **Catherine Johnston** SEX: Female AGE: 7
NATIONALITY: English BODY NUMBER: Not recovered

NAME: **Michael Joseph** SEX: Male AGE: 4
NATIONALITY: Syrian-Lebanese-American LIFEBOAT NUMBER: D
DESTINATION/TRAVELLING PARTY/REASON FOR VOYAGE:
Michael and Mary were returning with mother to their birthplace of Detroit, MI, after an extended visit to Lebanon. All were saved.
YEAR/AGE OF DEATH: 1991/84
CAUSE OF DEATH/BURIAL: Stroke/Clinton, MI

NAME: **Mary Joseph** SEX: Female AGE: 32m
NATIONALITY: Syrian-Lebanese-American LIFEBOAT NUMBER: C
YEAR/AGE OF DEATH: 1914/4
CAUSE OF DEATH/BURIAL: Burns/Detroit, MI

Name: Manca Karun Sex: Female   Age: 4
Nationality: Slovenian-Austrian   Lifeboat number: 15
Destination/Travelling Party/Reason for Voyage:
Manca, travelling with father and father's brother-in-law, was en route to Galesburg, IL, where her father ran a boarding house. Manca and her father were saved but returned to Slovenia the next year.
Year/Age of death: 1971/64
Cause of Death/Burial: Unknown/Šenčur, Slovenia

Name: Adele Kiamie Sex: Female   Age: 15
Nationality: Syrian-Lebanese   Lifeboat number: C
Destination/Travelling Party/Reason for Voyage:
Adele was the first of her family that her father was bringing to Brooklyn, NY, where he had immigrated four years before. She was travelling with the Baclini family.
Year/Age of death: 1924/27
Cause of Death/Burial: Cancer/New York, NY

Name: Luise (Louise) Kink-Heilmann Sex: Female   Age: 4
Nationality: Swiss   Lifeboat number: 2
Destination/Travelling Party/Reason for Voyage:
Louise was immigrating with parents to Milwaukee, WI. All survived.
Year/Age of death: 1992/84
Cause of Death/Burial: Lung cancer/Milwaukee, WI

Name: Gertrud Klasén Sex: Female   Age: 16m
Nationality: Swedish   Body number: Not recovered
Destination/Travelling Party/Reason for Voyage:
Gertrud was travelling with aunt and an uncle to Los Angeles, where her mother had immigrated the previous year. All were lost.

Name: Patrick Lane Sex: Male   Age: 16
Nationality: Irish   Body number: Not recovered
Destination/Travelling Party/Reason for Voyage:
Patrick was accompanied on his journey to New York by a family friend who lived in Brooklyn.

NAME: **Mathilde Lefebvre**   SEX: Female   ·   AGE: 12
NATIONALITY: French   BODY NUMBER: Not recovered
DESTINATION/TRAVELLING PARTY/REASON FOR VOYAGE:
The four Lefebvre children were immigrating with mother to Mystic, IA, to join their father, a miner. All were lost. Mr. Lefebvre was deported soon after.

NAME: **Jeanne Lefebvre**   SEX: Female   AGE: 8
NATIONALITY: French   BODY NUMBER: Not recovered

NAME: **Henri Lefebvre**   SEX: Male   AGE: 5
NATIONALITY: French   BODY NUMBER: Not recovered

NAME: **Ida Lefebvre**   SEX: Female   AGE: 3
NATIONALITY: French   BODY NUMBER: Not recovered

NAME: **Meier Moor (Meyer Moore)**   SEX: Male   AGE: 7
NATIONALITY: Russian-Romanian   LIFEBOAT NUMBER: 14
DESTINATION/TRAVELLING PARTY/REASON FOR VOYAGE:
Meyer was immigrating with mother to join aunt and uncle in Chicago, IL. They had been turned back the previous year on their first attempt to flee Russia for Canada. Both survived.
YEAR/AGE OF DEATH: 1975/70
CAUSE OF DEATH/BURIAL: Natural causes/El Paso, TX

NAME: **Maria Nackid**   SEX: Female   AGE: 13m
NATIONALITY: Syrian-Lebanese   LIFEBOAT NUMBER: C
DESTINATION/TRAVELLING PARTY/REASON FOR VOYAGE:
Maria was immigrating with parents to join paternal grandmother in Waterbury, CT. All survived, but Maria died three months later; first child survivor to die.
YEAR/AGE OF DEATH: 1912/16m
CAUSE OF DEATH/BURIAL: Meningitis/Waterbury, CT

NAME: **Maurice O'Connor**   SEX: Male   AGE: 15
NATIONALITY: Irish   BODY NUMBER: Not recovered
DESTINATION/TRAVELLING PARTY/REASON FOR VOYAGE:
Maurice, a general labourer, was immigrating to New York, where his brother lived.

NAME: **Hanora (Nora) O'Leary**   SEX: Female   AGE: 16
NATIONALITY: Irish   LIFEBOAT NUMBER: 13
DESTINATION/TRAVELLING PARTY/REASON FOR VOYAGE:
Nora, part of a group of young people from County Cork, was joining her sister in New York.
YEAR/AGE OF DEATH: 1975/79
CAUSE OF DEATH/BURIAL: Unknown/Kingwilliamstown, Ireland

NAME: **Artur (Arthur) Olsen**   SEX: Male   AGE: 9
NATIONALITY: Norwegian- American   LIFEBOAT NUMBER: 13
DESTINATION/TRAVELLING PARTY/REASON FOR VOYAGE:
Arthur was travelling home with father to Brooklyn, NY. Father was lost; Arthur was raised by his stepmother in New York.
YEAR/AGE OF DEATH: 1975/71
CAUSE OF DEATH/BURIAL: Unknown/St. Petersburg, FL

NAME: **Olaf Osén**   SEX: Male   AGE: 16
NATIONALITY: Swedish   BODY NUMBER: Not recovered
DESTINATION/TRAVELLING PARTY/REASON FOR VOYAGE:
Olaf was on his way to Ethan, SD, where he was planning to work as a farm labourer and support his disabled father in Sweden.

NAME: **Torborg Pålsson**   SEX: Female   AGE: 8
NATIONALITY: Swedish   BODY NUMBER: Not recovered
DESTINATION/TRAVELLING PARTY/REASON FOR VOYAGE:
The four Pålsson children, with their mother, were joining Mr. Pålsson in Chicago, IL, where he had immigrated two years previously. All were lost.

NAME: **Paul Pålsson**   SEX: Male   AGE: 6
NATIONALITY: Swedish   BODY NUMBER: Not recovered

NAME: **Stina Pålsson**   SEX: Female   AGE: 3
NATIONALITY: Swedish   BODY NUMBER: Not recovered

NAME: **Gösta Pålsson**   SEX: Male   AGE: 27m
Nationality Swedish: BODY NUMBER: Not recovered

NAME: **Ernesti Panula** SEX: Male AGE: 16
NATIONALITY: Finnish-American BODY NUMBER: Not recovered
The five Panula children, with their mother, were on their way to Coal Center, PA, where Mr. Panula lived. All were lost.

NAME: **Arnold Panula** SEX: Male AGE: 15
NATIONALITY: Finnish-American BODY NUMBER: Not recovered

NAME: **Juho Panula** SEX: Male AGE: 7
NATIONALITY: Finnish-American BODY NUMBER: Not recovered

NAME: **Urho Panula** SEX: Male AGE: 35m
NATIONALITY: Finnish-American BODY NUMBER: Not recovered

NAME: **Eino Panula** SEX: Male AGE: 13m
NATIONALITY: Finnish-American BODY NUMBER: Not recovered

NAME: **Treasteall Peacock** SEX: Female AGE: 4
NATIONALITY: English BODY NUMBER: Not recovered
DESTINATION/TRAVELLING PARTY/REASON FOR VOYAGE:
The Peacock children were relocating to New Jersey with mother, where father worked in a power plant. All were lost.

NAME: **Albert Peacock** SEX: Male AGE: 7m
NATIONALITY: English BODY NUMBER: Not recovered

NAME: **Uscher Pulner** SEX: Male AGE: 16
NATIONALITY: Russian-Romanian BODY NUMBER: Not recovered
DESTINATION/TRAVELLING PARTY/REASON FOR VOYAGE:
Uscher left his job as a plumber in Paris to join his older brother in New York. He may have been travelling with a family friend.

NAME: **Albert Rice** SEX: Male AGE: 10
NATIONALITY: English BODY NUMBER: Not recovered
DESTINATION/TRAVELLING PARTY/REASON FOR VOYAGE:
The Rice children were returning with mother from their mother's native Ireland to Spokane, WA, where they had lived briefly and where their father had died. All were lost.

NAME: **George Rice**
NATIONALITY: Canadian

SEX: Male   AGE: 8
BODY NUMBER: Not recovered

NAME: **Eric Rice**
NATIONALITY: Canadian

SEX: Male   AGE: 6
BODY NUMBER: Not recovered

NAME: **Arthur Rice**
NATIONALITY: Canadian

SEX: Male   Age: 4
BODY NUMBER: Not recovered

NAME: **Francis Rice**
NATIONALITY: American

SEX: Male   AGE: 31m
BODY NUMBER: Not recovered

NAME: **Salli Rosblom**
NATIONALITY: Finnish
DESTINATION/TRAVELLING PARTY/REASON FOR VOYAGE:
Salli, along with mother and older brother, was to join father in Astoria, OR.

SEX: Female   AGE: 25m
BODY NUMBER: Not recovered

NAME: **Frederick Sage**
NATIONALITY: English
DESTINATION/TRAVELLING PARTY/REASON FOR VOYAGE:
The Sage children were immigrating with parents to Jacksonville, FL, where father had purchased a fruit farm. Parents and nine children (three older than 16) were lost.

SEX: Male   AGE: 16
BODY NUMBER: Not recovered

NAME: **Dorothy Sage**
NATIONALITY: English

SEX: Female   AGE: 14
BODY NUMBER: Not recovered

NAME: **William (Will) Sage**
NATIONALITY: English
BURIAL: Buried at sea

SEX: Male   AGE: 12
BODY NUMBER: Body 67

NAME: **Ada Sage**
NATIONALITY: English

SEX: Female   AGE: 10
BODY NUMBER: Not recovered

NAME: **Constance Sage**
NATIONALITY: English

SEX: Female   AGE: 7
BODY NUMBER: Not recovered

NAME: **Thomas Sage**
NATIONALITY: English

SEX: Male   AGE: 5
BODY NUMBER: Not recovered

NAME: **Youssef Samaan**   SEX: Male   AGE: 16
NATIONALITY: Syrian-Lebanese   BODY NUMBER: Not recovered
DESTINATION/TRAVELLING PARTY/REASON FOR VOYAGE:
Youssef was travelling with father and brother to join wife in Wilkes-Barre, PA.
All were lost.

NAME: **Marguerite Sandström**   SEX: Female   AGE: 4
NATIONALITY: Swedish-American   LIFEBOAT NUMBER: 13
DESTINATION/TRAVELLING PARTY/REASON FOR VOYAGE:
The Sandström girls were returning to San Francisco with mother from a trip to
Sweden to visit Mrs. Sandström's parents. Although all were saved, the family
moved back to Sweden.
YEAR/AGE OF DEATH: 1963/55
CAUSE OF DEATH/BURIAL: Unknown

NAME: **Beatrice Sandström**   SEX: Female   AGE: 20m
NATIONALITY: Swedish-American   LIFEBOAT NUMBER: 13
YEAR/AGE OF DEATH: 1995/85
CAUSE OF DEATH/BURIAL: Unknown/Klockrike, Sweden

NAME: **Betros Seman**   SEX: Male   AGE: 10
NATIONALITY: Syrian-Lebanese   BODY NUMBER: Not recovered
DESTINATION/TRAVELLING PARTY/REASON FOR VOYAGE:
Betros was travelling with uncle to join his widowed mother in Wilkes-Barre, PA.
Both were lost.

NAME: **Karl Skoog**   SEX: Male   AGE: 11
NATIONALITY: American   BODY NUMBER: Not recovered
DESTINATION/TRAVELLING PARTY/REASON FOR VOYAGE:
The Skoog children were returning with parents to Iron Mountain, MI, where
father had worked in mining previously. All were lost.

NAME: **Mabel Skoog**   SEX: Female   AGE: 9
NATIONALITY: American   BODY NUMBER: Not recovered

NAME: **Harald Skoog**   SEX: Male   AGE: 5
NATIONALITY: American   BODY NUMBER: Not recovered

NAME: **Margit Skoog**   SEX: Female   AGE: 24m
NATIONALITY:American   BODY NUMBER: Not recovered

NAME: **Telma Ström**   SEX: Female   AGE: 28m
NATIONALITY: American   BODY NUMBER: Not recovered
DESTINATION/TRAVELLING PARTY/REASON FOR VOYAGE:
Telma was returning to Indiana Harbor, MI, with mother after a visit to grand-parents in Sweden. Both were lost.

NAME: **Johan Svensson (John Johnson)**   SEX: Male AGE: 14
NATIONALITY: Swedish   LIFEBOAT NUMBER: 13
DESTINATION/TRAVELLING PARTY/REASON FOR VOYAGE:
Johan was the first of his siblings to cross the Atlantic to join father and sister in Beresford, SD.
YEAR/AGE OF DEATH: 1981/83
CAUSE OF DEATH/BURIAL: Unknown/Whittier, CA

NAME: **Thelma Thomas**   SEX: Female   AGE: 16
NATIONALITY: Syrian-Lebanese   LIFEBOAT NUMBER: 14
DESTINATION/TRAVELLING PARTY/REASON FOR VOYAGE:
Baby Assed and his young mother Thelma were among a large group of immigrants from the village of Hardin, Lebanon. Accompanied by the baby's uncle, they were en route to Wilkes-Barre, PA, where Mr. Thomas had immigrated. Mother and child were separated in the confusion but reunited on *Carpathia*. Uncle was lost.
YEAR/AGE OF DEATH: 1974/78
CAUSE OF DEATH/BURIAL: Unknown/Wilkes-Barre, PA

NAME: **Assed Thomas**   SEX: Male   AGE: 5m
NATIONALITY: Syrian-Lebanese   LIFEBOAT NUMBER: 16
YEAR/AGE OF DEATH: 1931/19
CAUSE OF DEATH/BURIAL: Pneumonia/Wilkes-Barre, PA

NAME: **Mary Thomas**   SEX: Female   AGE: 9
NATIONALITY: Syrian-Lebanese   LIFEBOAT NUMBER: C
DESTINATION/TRAVELLING PARTY/REASON FOR VOYAGE:
Mary and George were with mother, joining Mr. Thomas on his farm in Dowagiac, MI. All survived.
YEAR/AGE OF DEATH: 1953/50
CAUSE OF DEATH/BURIAL: Liver disease/Flint, MI

NAME: **George Thomas** SEX: Male AGE: 8
NATIONALITY: Syrian-Lebanese LIFEBOAT NUMBER: C
YEAR/AGE OF DEATH: 1991/87
CAUSE OF DEATH/BURIAL: Stroke/Grand Blanc, MI

NAME: **John Thomas** SEX: Male AGE: 16
NATIONALITY: Syrian-Lebanese BODY NUMBER: Not recovered
DESTINATION/TRAVELLING PARTY/REASON FOR VOYAGE:
John was with father and relatives en route to Columbus, OH, where his father had immigrated. He planned to continue his education there. Father and son were lost.

NAME: **Leo Vanderplancke** SEX: Male AGE: 15
NATIONALITY: Belgian BODY NUMBER: Not recovered
DESTINATION/TRAVELLING PARTY/REASON FOR VOYAGE:
Leo and his sister were travelling with brother and his wife to first visit relatives in Detroit, MI, before joining another brother in Ohio. All were lost.

NAME: **Hulda Veström** SEX: Female AGE: 14
NATIONALITY: Swedish LIFEBOAT NUMBER: Not recovered
DESTINATION/TRAVELLING PARTY/REASON FOR VOYAGE:
Hulda was travelling with her aunt to aunt's home in Los Angeles. Other Swedes in their group included the Sandströms and Klaséns.

	Male	Female	Total
Third Class	64	50	114
Lost	48	27	75
Saved	16	23	39
Percentage saved	25%	46%	**34%**

ALL CLASSES: 151 CHILDREN FROM 89 FAMILIES

	Male	Female	Total
All Classes	82	69	151
Lost	50	28	78
Saved	32	41	73
Percentage saved	39%	59%	**48%**

CREW

Name	Age	Nationality	Occupation
Arthur Barratt	15	English	Bell Boy
Paolo Crovella	16	Italian	Assistant Waiter
Clifford Harris	16	English	Bell Boy
Frederick Hopkins	14	English	Plate Steward
William Watson	14	English	Bell Boy
Saved			**0 / 0%**

CROSS-CHANNEL PASSENGERS

Name	Age	Sex	Embarked	Disembarked
Dennis Lenox-Conyngham	10	M	Southampton	Cherbourg
Eileen Lenox-Conyngham	11	F	Southampton	Cherbourg
William Noel	13	M	Southampton	Cherbourg
Jack Odell	11	M	Southampton	Queenstown
Saved				**4 / 100%**

IMAGE SOURCES

American Press Association, public domain via Wikimedia Commons: 148

APK, cc by-sa 4.0, public domain via Wikimedia Commons: 201

Author photo: 214

Bain News Service, publisher, public domain via Wikimedia Commons: 144

Charles Dixon, public domain via Wikimedia Commons: 74

Cobh Heritage Centre courtesy of Dee Ryan-Meister, Titanic Society of Atlantic
Canada: 46

Courtesy Julie Hedgepeth Williams, public domain via Wikimedia Commons: 20

Encyclopedia Titanica: 187

Ewan Munro from London, UK, cc by-sa 2.0 via Wikimedia Commons: 170

Francis Browne, public domain via Wikimedia Commons: 7, 54

Internet Archive book images, public domain via Wikimedia Commons: 102

Julie Hedgepeth Williams, University of Georgia Press: 167

J. W. Barker (Carpathia passenger) credited in *The Sphere* (London, May 4,
1912), p. 91, public domain via Wikimedia Commons: 104

Lewis Hine, public domain via Wikimedia Commons: 221

Library of Congress LC-B2-1234: 184

Library of Congress LC-DIG-GGBAIN-11212: 101

Library of Congress LC-USF33-002613-M1: 157

Library of Congress LC-USZ62-34976: 19

Library of Congress LC-USZ62-105864: 139

Library of Congress M1978.T55 K: 205

Library of Congress, Serial and Government Publications Division: 183

Maritime Museum of the Atlantic: 213

Nova Scotia Archives newspaper collection, 27 April, 1912: 60, 87

Nova Scotia Archives photo drawer—Transportation & Communication—
Ships & Shipping—RMS Titanic #1: 117

Odell family, public domain via Wikimedia Commons, 36

Public domain via Wikimedia Commons, 6, 12, 17, 50, 67, 111, 127

Robert Welch, public domain via Wikimedia Commons: x

Royal Navy Official Photographer, public domain via Wikimedia Commons: 160

The Story of the Greatest Nations, Internet Archive book images, public domain
via Wikimedia Commons: 164

Thomas Barker, public domain via Wikimedia Commons, 27, 189

Томас Баркер, public domain via Wikimedia Commons: 77

Unknown photographer, public domain via Wikimedia Commons: 30

BIBLIOGRAPHY

Barczewski, Stephanie. *Titanic: A Night Remembered*. London: Hambledon and London, 2004.

Barratt, Nick. *Lost Voices from the Titanic: The Definitive Oral History*. New York: Palgrave Macmillan, 2010.

Beavis, Debbie. *Who Sailed on Titanic? The Definitive Passenger Lists*. Hersham, England: Ian Allan, 2002.

Beed, Blair. *Titanic Victims in Halifax Graveyards*. Halifax: Nimbus, 2012.

Biel, Steven. *Down with the Old Canoe: A Cultural History of the Titanic Disaster*. New York: W. W. Norton & Company, 1996.

Boileau, John. *Halifax and Titanic*. Halifax: Nimbus, 2012.

Bouchard, Jean-François. "Une Équipe De L'UQAR S'intéresse à Une Lettre Qui Proviendrait Du Titanic." Université du Québec à Rimouski, May 6, 2021. uqar.ca/nouvelles/uqar-info/3666-une-equipe-de-l-uqar-s-interesse-a-une-lettre-qui-proviendrait-du-titanic.

Brewster, Hugh. *Gilded Lives, Fatal Voyage: The Titanic, Her Passengers and Their World*. New York: Crown, 2012.

Cimino, Eric. "Carpathia's Care for Titanic's Survivors," *Voyage: Official Journal of the Titanic International Society, Inc.*, Fall 2017. academia.edu/35011190/Carpathias_Care_for_Titanics_Survivors?email_work_card=title.

Cook, Julie. *The Titanic and the City of Widows It Left Behind*. Yorkshire: Pen and Sword Books, 2020.

Cox, Frank. *In Titanic Times*. Self-published, 2012. EPUB.

Cunningham, Anthony. *Titanic Children: Eyewitnesses to History*. Amazon Kindle Books, 2021.

Eaton, John P., and Charles A. Haas. *Titanic, Destination Disaster: The Legends and the Reality*. New York: Norton, 1996.

Elias, Leila Salloum. *The Dream and Then the Nightmare: The Syrians who Boarded the Titanic, The Story of the Arabic-Speaking Passengers*. Damascus: Atlas, 2011.

Encyclopedia Titanica. encyclopedia-titanica.org/.

Geller, Judith B. *Titanic: Women and Children First: Poignant Accounts of Those Caught up in the World's Worst Maritime Disaster*. New York: Norton, 1998.

Gracie, Archibald, and John B. Thayer. *Titanic: A Survivor's Story*. Chicago, IL: Academy Chicago Publishers, 1998.

Greenleaf, Barbara Kaye. *Children Through the Ages: A History of Childhood*. New York: McGraw-Hill, 1979.

Hart, Eva and Ronald C. Denney. *A Girl Aboard the Titanic: The Remarkable Memoir of Eva Hart, a 7-year-old Survivor of the Titanic Disaster*. Stroud, Gloucestershire: Amberley, 2014.

Hausenblas, Coraline. "Hoax Analysis." April 2022. coralinehausenblas.com/wp-content/uploads/2023/07/Titanics-letter-analysis.pdf.

Heyer, Paul. *Titanic Legacy: Disaster as Media Event and Myth*. Westport, CN: Praeger, 1995.

Howells, Richard. *The Myth of the Titanic*. Basingstoke: Palgrave Macmillan, 2012.

Hyslop, Donald, Alastair Forsyth, and Sheila Jemima. *Titanic Voices: Memories from the Fateful Voyage*. New York: St. Martin's Griffin, 1999.

Jordan, Tina. "The Titanic Sank. So Did These Commemorative Poems," *New York Times*, April 17, 2022, nytimes.com/interactive/2022/books/review/what-is-poetry.html.

Linnolahti, Jano and Elisabeth Uschanov. *Sunken Dreams: The Finns on Board the Titanic*. Turko, Finland: Presentation of the Institute of Migration, 2013.

Lord, Walter. *A Night to Remember*. New York: Henry Holt, 2005.

_____. *The Night Lives On*. New York: Morrow, 1986.

Lynch, Don and Ken Marschall. *Titanic: An Illustrated History*. New York: Hyperion, 1992.

Marten, James Alan. *The History of Childhood: A Very Short Introduction*. New York: Oxford University Press, 2018.

Maxtone-Graham, John. *Titanic Tragedy: A New Look at the Lost Liner*. New York: W. W. Norton & Company, 2011.

McMillan, Beverly, and Stanley Lehrer. *Titanic: Fortune & Fate: Catalogue from the Mariners' Museum Exhibition*. New York: Simon & Schuster, 1998.

Merideth, Lee W. *Titanic Names: A Complete List of Passengers and Crew*. Sunnyvale, CA: Rocklin Press, 2002.

Molony, Senan. *The Irish Aboard Titanic*. Cork: Mercier Press, 2012.

O'Riordan, Sean. "Titanic memorial garden to open in Cobh," *Irish Examiner*, April 7, 2014, irishexaminer.com/news/arid-20264459.html.

Pierce, Nicola. *Titanic: True Stories of her Passengers, Crew, and Legacy.* Halifax: Nimbus, 2021.

Quinn, Paul J. *Dusk to Dawn: Survivor Accounts of the Last Night on the Titanic.* Hollis, NH: Fantail, 1999.

Rogers, Jenny. "What's up with D.C.'s Titanic memorial?" *Washington City Paper*, January 24, 2014, washingtoncitypaper.com/article/205748/whats-up-with-dcs-titanic-memorial/.

Ruffman, Alan. *Titanic Remembered: The Unsinkable Ship and Halifax.* Halifax: Formac, 2001.

Setterdahl, Lilly. *Not My Time to Die — Titanic and the Swedes on Board.* New York: Nordstjernan Förlag, 2012.

Smallidge, Allan. *Musquito Harbor: A Narrative History of Winter Harbor, Maine, 1790–2005.* Winter Harbor: Ironbound Press, 2006. Smith, Mac. *Mainers on the Titanic.* Camden, ME: Down East Books, 2014.

Spedden, Daisy Corning Stone, and Laurie McGaw. *Polar: The Titanic Bear.* Boston: Little, Brown, and Company, 1994.

Stafford, Stephen. "Southampton's lost Titanic generation." *BBC News*, April 10, 2012, bbc.com/news/uk-england-hampshire-17535757. Thomas, Joseph L. *Grandma Survived the Titanic.* Bloomington, IL: Author House, 2006.

Tibballs, Geoff. *Voices from the Titanic: The Epic Story of the Tragedy from the People Who Were There.* New York: Skyhorse, 2012.

Titanic Historical Society Inc. titanichistoricalsociety.org.

Titanic. titanic-titanic.com.

"Titanic memorial garden completed," *Irish Examiner*, April 14, 2012. irishexaminer.com/news/arid-30547507.html.

Titanic. "Memorials." titanic-titanic.com/category/memorials.

Wade, Wyn Craig. *The Titanic: End of a Dream.* New York: Rawson, Wade, 1979.

Wilson, Andrew. *Shadow of the Titanic: The Extraordinary Stories of Those Who Survived.* New York: Atria Books, 2011.

Wormstedt, Bill, Tad Fitch, and George Behe. "Titanic: The Lifeboat Launching Sequence Re-Examined." February 2023. wormstedt.com/Titanic/lifeboats/lifeboats.htm.

INDEX

B

Backström, Alfhild, 181
Backström, Maria, 94
Baclini, David, 132
Baclini, Eugenie, 41, 42, 83, 93, 132, 235
Baclini, Helen, 41, 42, 83, 93, 138, 235
Baclini, Latifa, 41, 42, 83
Baclini, Maria, 41, 42, 83, 93, 156, 235
Baclini, Mr., 42
Bala Cynwyd, 225
Ballard, Dr. Robert, 179, 206, 207
Ballinloughane, Ireland, 49
Baltic, RMS, 149
Bangkok Christian College for Boys, 20
Bankeryd, Sweden, 143
Bar Harbor, ME, 182
Baron de Hirsch Cemetery, 175, 195, 202, 203
Barratt, Arthur, 5, 197, 250
Battle of the *Kearsarge* and the *Alabama*, the, 37
Bay of Fundy, 31
B Deck, 66
Becker, Marion, 20, 70, 138, 151, 227
Becker, Nellie, 20, 138
Becker, Rev., 20
Becker, Richard, 20, 70, 91, 138, 151, 162, 227
Becker, Ruth, 20, 70, 72, 92, 102, 138, 162, 163, 227
Beesley, Lawrence, 163
Belfast, ix, 2, 3, 190, 199, 200, 204, 211, 212, 217
Belfast City Cemetery, xi
Belfast Lough, 3
Belfast Titanic Society, 207
Belgians, 32
Belgrave Square, 2
Bellevue Hospital, 132
Bennington, VT, 13, 152, 230
Benton Harbor, MI, 20, 227
Beresford, 248

Bernardsville, NJ, 13, 231
Bessant, Emily, 192
Bessant, William, 192
Biggsville, IL, 21, 228
Billiard, Austin van, 22, 121
Billiard, James van, 22, 121, 235
Billiard, Walter van, 22, 120, 235
Björnström-Steffansson, Mauritz, 85, 86
Bonaparte, Napoleon, 37
Borek, Amenia, 41, 42, 84, 151
Borek, George, 41, 42, 84, 93, 151, 236
Borek, William, 41, 42, 84, 93, 151, 236
Boston Globe, 111
Boulos, Akar, 41, 43, 236
Boulos, Laura, 41, 43, 236
Boulos, Mr., 43
Boulos, Sultana, 41, 43
Bowyer, Lord Mayor Henry, 191
Boxhall, Fourth Officer, 78, 79, 107
Braf, Elin, 76
Branson, MO, 212
Bremen, SS, 114
British Empire Child Passengers, 12
British Titanic Society, 178, 188, 207
Brooklyn, NY, 16, 29, 42, 49, 73, 134, 138, 141, 156, 182, 185, 226, 235, 237, 242, 244
Brown, Edith, 15, 55, 64, 91, 99, 109, 171, 173–175, 212, 227
Browne, Fr. Francis, 47, 48, 53
Brown, Elizabeth, 15, 55, 64, 109
Brown, Thomas, 15, 171
Brussels, 137
Bryn Mawr, PA, 156
Buckley, Daniel, 49, 73, 151
Burns, Margaret ("Muddie Boons"), 39, 62
Burns, Mary, 49, 236

C

Café Parisien, 10
Caldwell, Albert, 20
Caldwell, Alden, 20, 73, 92, 167, 175, 228

Retired colonel John Boileau served in the Canadian Army for thirty-seven years, including command of Lord Strathcona's Horse (Royal Canadians), and went on to be appointed Honorary Colonel of the Halifax Rifles (RCAC) for ten years. He is an author and media commentator who specializes in military history and has written fifteen books and more that 650 magazine and newspaper articles. Two of his books, *Fastest in the World* and *Halifax and the Royal Canadian Navy*, were shortlisted for the Dartmouth Book Award for Non-Fiction. John was founding chair of the Halifax Military Heritage Preservation Society and chair of the National Council of Honorary Colonels. He is a recipient of the Order of Nova Scotia, the Queen Elizabeth Diamond Jubilee Medal, the Queen Elizabeth Platinum Jubilee Medal (NS), a Lieutenant-Governor of Nova Scotia Vice-Regal Commendation, and a Commander Canadian Army Commendation. He and his wife, Miriam, live in Bedford, Nova Scotia.

Patricia Boileau Theriault, a native of Moncton, New Brunswick, has degrees in English and education from the University of New Brunswick and the University of Maine. Retired from a career in adult education, she continues to be a lifelong learner. Her interests include exploring national parks, volunteering at an art museum, and visiting her grandchildren—each a learning experience in its own way. Pat lives in Waterville, Maine.